THE ADVENTURES OF TIGER TIM

THE ADVENTURES OF
TIGER TIM

The Authorised Biography
of Tim Stevens

BRIAN BEACOM

BLACK AND WHITE PUBLISHING

First published 2000
by Black & White Publishing Ltd
ISBN 1902927133
Copyright © Brian Beacom 2000

British Library Cataloguing-in-Publication Data:
A catalogue record for this book is available
from the British Library

Printed by Omnia Books, Bishopbriggs

Contents

	Preface	7
1.	Superman, Chin Kissing and Wobbly Legs	9
2.	Bare-knuckle Fights, Gay Proposals and Deborah Kerr	21
3.	Swedes, Sombreros and Railway Sheds	34
4.	Blackpool Rocking and Jet Mayfair	43
5.	Jet, Crabs and Geriatrics	54
6.	Railway Exits, the Funeral and Hughie Green	65
7.	Marriage, Frogs and Alice Cooper	76
8.	Mooning, David Cassidy and Life as a Pop Star	88
9.	Huge in the Hebrides	101
10.	Steely Dan and Fresh Lager	112
11.	Dunoon, Vegas and Radio One	125
12.	Captain Sensible Gets into Women's Clothing	136
13.	Naked Video, Perfect Breasts and Andy Cameron	147
14.	Frank Carson, Biggins and the Beauty Queen with the Horse	160
15.	Life's a Beach	170
16.	MS	182
17.	Humble Pie and Bad Headlines	186
18.	TV Blondes and Marti	196
19.	Cool Blondes, Crimpers and Excess Baggage	203
20.	Carol Smillie, Wedding Bells and Bluenoses	215
21.	Green Jungle Juice, Faith-healing and Noddy	226
22.	Diet Coke Cures and Married Eight-year-olds	237
23.	Blood, Sweat and Bacteria	249

Acknowledgements

Pictures of Alice Cooper and Jet Mayfair taken at
the Apollo Theatre – 'Nécol, your dad took these'.

Thanks to Fiona, for showing patience above and beyond
the call of duty, when times spent in the Tiger cage left
my brain in little pieces.

Preface

When writers agree to work on an authorised biography with a
celebrity the expectation is one of general co-operation. That was
certainly my thought when, a couple of years ago, Tim Stevens
suggested I write a book on his life. It seemed a good idea; we'd been
pals for a few years and I knew he had had a fascinating life with all the
good and bad which that entailed, so writing his story would be a
straightforward enough task.

Wrong.

It's not that he wasn't an open book. He's a man who wears his heart
on his sleeve and he told vivid accounts of the most personal aspects of
his life. And, unlike so many people in showbusiness, he was resolutely
unafraid to tell stories against himself. But ask him to recall the date he
began working at West Sound Radio or the date he was married (he
can't even recall the years) or even get close to where and when he has
gone on holiday—no chance.

This has nothing to do with his MS condition; in fact, Tim can
recall the phone number of practically every female he has ever gone
out with. His selective memory was amazing; he couldn't for the life of
him remember the name and chronology of a single panto he'd performed in but he could remember who he'd upset and the names of all
the female cast (or the good-looking ones, at least).

The more I worked with Tim the more I realised that he is brilliant

7

at coming up with excuses. He couldn't make edit notes on the manuscript because he'd lost his pencil. He couldn't post pictures off to the publisher because he didn't have a stamp. He couldn't get his hair darkened back to something like its original colour for the book cover photo because his hairdresser told him it was likely to make his hair fall out.

And, to compound the frustration, he would constantly remember a hugely relevant story when the chapter was already complete.

By the time his copy of the first draft of the book came back to me, partly unread and mostly covered in milk after an accident with his Coco Krispies, it was me tearing my hair out and counting the days till it was all over.

But now that it is all over I can take the overview. I can appreciate that this book is full of stories about the Tiger making a fool of himself—and laughing about it. It's full of tales where he opens his soul to the world, where he's been brave and frighteningly honest. And I can once again remind myself that he has more guts than most people I know.

When I call him up now he sounds like a naughty schoolboy and says, 'What is it? What have I done?', expecting a telling-off because that's been the relationship we've had for months.

All I can say now is that it's been a shoulder-broadening experience which, with hindsight, I wouldn't have missed for the world. I'd like to think we're still pals.

And that in a couple of months I'll have completely forgotten about the Coco Krispies.

BB

Superman, Chin Kissing and Wobbly Legs

The little boy with the big brown eyes and chestnut hair had a determined look on his face as he dragged the wooden stool from its resting place in the corner of the living-room. It took a few minutes, but he finally made it through the glass door that blocked his way to glory and out onto the verandah that looked out over the whole of Easterhouse. This was a five-year-old with a mission.

Outside he paused for just an instant to admire his new outfit: the bright blue T-shirt and matching trousers, the red underpants worn over the trousers and the flowing red cape his mother had made for him that week.

Satisfied he looked the part, he placed the stool against the wrought-iron railing, stood on top and then began to hoist himself up to the top of the rail. His heart leapt with excitement.

Precariously balanced, he pointed his left arm out in the direction of Wardie Road and tucked his right arm neatly into his chest. 'Up, up and away!' he yelled and prepared to fly off into the heavens above Banton Place.

But just at the point of take-off a sharp yank of the cape pulled him back down onto the verandah with a thump. The First Adventure of Tiger Tim was over.

'I must have been in the kitchen at the time, because I hadn't noticed him dragging the stool out onto the verandah,' said Dora

McGrory, mother of the daredevil boy, Jim.

'It was 1957 and it was the first time the *Superman* TV series starring George Reeves was on in the UK. Jim had begged me to make him the cape and the outfit, but it was clearly a big mistake. Honestly, I don't know what made me look in to see what he was up to—it must have been intuition—but I opened the living-room door only to see the wee legs of the bold boy climb up on top of the rails and push one arm outward, ready to fly just like Superman. But just as he flew off to certain death down below in Mrs McCormick's garden I managed to grab him by the cape around his neck. I was terrified but he looked at me as if I'd just spoiled his fun for the day. I'd have killed him if I hadn't been so upset.'

Dora Kelly and Jimmy McGrory, an engineer, met when they worked in the munitions factory in Springburn during the war. Both Catholics from Irish immigrant parents, they were married in 1947 and made their home in the East End of Glasgow. They had no idea what they had unleashed onto the world five years later on St Gerard's Day, 4 February, when they produced James Gerard Dickson McGrory. (Tim Stevens is the name he chose for himself many years later.) They had no inkling that their baby son would go on to become a trailblazing disc jockey, a wannabe pop star and one of the most popular showbiz characters Scotland has ever produced. They would have been aghast if they could have predicted the pranks their son would get up to—a man who refused to grow up and continued to see life as a series of dares. And they—and teams of behavioural psychologists—would have been stunned to discover the extent of his exhibitionism, and wonder why he felt the constant need to take his clothes off in public (Dora swears she never put his nappy on too tightly). Dora and Jimmy may not have been totally shocked to learn that their very popular son was something of a chronic attention-seeker (little signs of that manifested themselves from an early age), a curious mix of being naturally shy yet with an underlying need to be noticed. But had young Jim McGrory's dad lived long enough, he would have surely shaken his head at the discovery that his son, always different from the rest of the kids, was more than willing to wear women's clothing for shock effect. In fact, a great deal could have been learned from their Superboy's behaviour, because not only was exhibitionism evident early on, so too was the capacity for self-destruction.

Regardless, young Jim McGrory was adored from the moment he was born at Stobhill Hospital in Glasgow. 'We had been married five years at this point,' recalled Dora, now a remarkably youthful eighty-year-old. 'But I had lost a boy in between that time who didn't live very long. Jim turned out to be his double. He was a lovely wee boy whom everyone took to immediately.'

Jimmy and Dora, who had been brought up in Partick, were perfectly happy together. Dora was—and still is—a livewire and she loved Jimmy's sense of fun.

As was the case for most Glaswegians, the early 1950s was not a fun time to bring a baby into the world. King George VI had died in 1952, Elizabeth had been crowned queen and newspapers were either full of stories of the changing life in Buckingham Palace or tales of the other famous Elizabeth, Elizabeth Taylor, who had recently married Michael Wilding and now lived in Hollywood splendour. Like most people in the north-east of Glasgow, however, the McGrory family lived in a dark tenement, in a room-and-kitchen with no indoor toilet and a tin bath that was brought out to be filled in the living-room.

'We lived in Roystonhill, in a flat that belonged to my father-in-law,' said Dora. 'The rent was thirty-five shillings a quarter, which was just affordable because Jimmy's father owned the property but the flat was too small. You couldn't really bring up a family in it.'

There was barely room to swing a cat in the house in Roystonhill—and Dora, by the time young Jim was two, wished there wasn't. The family cat almost killed their son one day when he was lying in his pram. 'The cat scratched Jim on the arm. It wasn't a huge scratch but he developed blood poisoning and we rushed him to the doctor. As we made the journey, the skin began to peel off his body. It was horrific. I had to put little mitts on him to stop him scratching. His whole body looked like it had first-degree burns. We thought our baby was going to die.'

Luckily, doctors were able to treat the allergy. And it says a lot for Tim's easy-going spirit that he still has a pet cat today, Claw. Clearly, he shouldn't be exposed to them. Dora took no such chances: the cat had to go.

And so did the family. The McGrorys were offered a house in Easterhouse, one of Glasgow's new housing schemes built on a greenfield site and, like thousands of others, they were thrilled with the idea of a home where everyone could have a bedroom of their own and each house had its own indoor bathroom.

A few months before moving, however, young Jim had to start school. On that first day at St Roch's in Royston in September 1957, five-year-old Jim displayed an attachment to his mother that was never to change. He found it very difficult to leave his mum for the day. In fact, he refused point blank. 'He had had his tonsils out just a couple of months before in the Royal Infirmary,' said Dora, defending her boy's performance, 'and he broke his heart at having to stay in for a few days. Then, when it came time to start school so soon after, I think he felt he was being taken away again.

'On the first day he went down with his cousin Elizabeth and his Auntie Jean, all shiny hair and new uniform and schoolbag with the shoulder strap. Elizabeth was fine when the bell rang but Jim began yelling, "I'm not going in!" and he simply refused to walk into the corridor. The headmistress came out—she was my old geography teacher when I was at school—and stood no nonsense. She told Jean just to take him home. She wanted nothing to do with him. And so Jean brought him back. By this time his dad was home for his lunch, as he now worked just down the road at the railway.'

The first Dora and Jimmy were aware their little soldier was a conscientious objector was when they heard him calling from down in the street. 'We looked out of the window and there he was, shouting up to his dad, "I didn't go to school!" with a big grin on his wee face and oh, I could have battered him. But his father took him back to school and as they waited outside the secretary's office he noticed a box of footballs sitting there. He started kicking a ball about with Jim and before long a couple of other wee boys came by and got caught up in the action. Jimmy just left them to it then slipped off. When Jim came home from school at three that afternoon he announced it had been great fun. There were never any problems after that.'

Nor did he have any problems when he transferred to the Blessed John Ogilvie primary school in Easterhouse.

The family were all so excited about the move to their dreamworld. 'When we moved to Banton Place we all loved it at first,' said Dora. 'It was a huge change coming out of an old tenement and getting a bathroom and a bedroom for Jim. The house was expensive, though. It was £4/6s/10d a week and his dad earned just over £5. I never went out to work when he was young, though. It just didn't seem the right thing to do.'

The family lived in the next close to Jimmy McGrory's sister Jean and her husband Paddy. In the same close at no. 21 lived Jimmy's brother Jackie and his wife Betty. They had a daughter, Elizabeth, who was later to share a tragic illness with her DJ cousin, and two sons,

Johnny and Stephen. It was as cosy and mutually supportive as you could get. Young Jim and cousin Johnny would often go out and wait by the close of Stevie Chalmers, the famous Celtic player who lived behind the McGrorys, to ask for his autograph.

Life in the new world of the late 1950s was a time of optimism. Jimmy McGrory had gone on to work as an engineer at the British Rail depot in Springburn and become a foreman, which allowed the family a few luxuries. Dora was determined to make sure her son didn't suffer the same hardship she'd known as a girl growing up during the Depression. But she denies her wee boy was spoiled rotten: 'We gave him what we could,' she said smiling, 'but he wasn't spoiled. People thought he was but, no, that wasn't the case. Maybe he just looked spoiled. His hair, for example, was always perfect. He would put Loxene on it all the time and people would ask me how his hair was always so tidy.'

When Loxene-haired Jim turned seven, a change came over him. He began to realise that females of his own age were not simply people who didn't like playing football. He'd seen Cliff Richard at the pictures. Cliff was the face of Britain in 1959, a time of petticoats and teddy boys. And he was old enough to realise the power that Cliff's new film *Espresso Bongo* was having over every young boy in the land. They all imagined they could look cool like Cliff and girls would come running to hang out with them in the new coffee bars and listen to groovy tunes on the jukeboxes.

Jim's very own Una Stubbs was the most gorgeous creature in the world: a girl in his class called Annemarie McCluskey. When they made their First Communion Father Healy had Jim (dressed in a new white shirt and short grey trousers from Goldberg's) and Annemarie cut the cake together. 'I was totally in love with her,' said Tim. 'Her blond hair just left me speechless and I worshipped the ground she walked on. The tragedy was that, although she became my girlfriend, I never got to kiss her.' That sense of immediate absolute devotion to women was to stay with Tim as he got older, but it would be another two years before a woman was to capture his heart in such a way again.

Meanwhile, Dora and Jimmy had all the usual parenting problems to contend with and it was obvious their son was a fairly emotional boy. He coped well with a serious dose of chickenpox when he was eight and was forced into quarantine on the verandah, covered in spots, while he watched the other kids play down below. But he had a very difficult time dealing with being apart from those he loved. When his maternal grandfather died, the boy was devastated. 'He's always been emotional,' said Dora. 'Jim was eight years old when my father, Charles Kelly, died. My parents thought the world of their grandson and Jim felt exactly the same about them. I didn't know how I would break the news. And when I did, later that night, he took it very badly. It broke his heart and he cried for days. Then one day his father and I got the fright of our lives when Jim disappeared. I was demented with worry and the family searched the whole of Easterhouse. But it turned out he had taken a bus into Buchanan Street and then the subway up to my mother's in Partick. He felt so sorry for her that my father had died and wanted to spend some time with his granny.'

Mary Kelly's flat in Hyndland Street was something of a second home for young Jim. 'He loved going over to Partick where my parents lived. My mother would spoil him rotten and the boys—my brothers Danny and William—did as well. I remember once going to Woolworth's in Argyle Street and Jim asking me to take him to the restaurant upstairs for a fish tea. I told him we couldn't afford it and Jim couldn't understand why his granny could take him for fish teas but his mother couldn't. The Kellys were a hard act to follow.'

At the age of nine, young Jim was made a school prefect and this new-found status added to his growing confidence. He reckoned it was time he had a girlfriend.

'Ellen Hendry was dark and she was beautiful and statuesque and all the guys fancied her,' Tim recalled. 'She was a bit bigger than all the boys but I think one of my pals told her I fancied her and I got the feeling she wasn't against the idea of being my girlfriend. So we became an item and talked to each other and looked at each other longingly over the desks, although she would never agree to kiss me. Maybe it was because she was too tall. But I remember one day I thought I'd kiss her anyway. After school I walked up to her and jumped up in the air to plant one on her mouth, but I didn't quite make it past her chin.'

He would adopt that same subtle tactic in later life. But, for the moment, now that he had awakened to the attractions of the fairer sex, there was no stopping his admiration from developing. 'He had a definite fancy for Linda Thorpe who lived across the road,' said Dora. It was true: when playing Kiss, Catch, Torture, Jim would always develop running problems whenever Linda Thorpe or Linda Donelly (he was fickle at an early age) would chase him along the backyard.

There was another interest—or rather a passion—which developed in tandem with his appreciation for the opposite sex.

Dora and Jimmy had spared no expense in indulging their son's love of music. He had grown up listening to the family record collection of Sinatra and Crosby and tuned in to pop music on the Light Programme, the BBC's precursor to Radio One, and to Radio Luxembourg. Young Jim was very much aware of the pop idols of the day.

'In his bedroom he had a big table with a record-player and a microphone,' said Dora, 'and the fake earphones would go on as soon as he came home from school and he'd pretend to be a DJ. He used to write to David Symonds at the BBC and tell him all about himself and his Auntie Jean. And whenever he got a new record he'd go to Mrs

McCormick downstairs and tell her, then go up to his bedroom and play it loud enough so that she could hear it. Goodness, it blared out. One day I yelled at him to turn it down and he shouted, "I can't, Mrs McCormick wants to hear it." How could you argue against that sort of logic?'

Young Jim's interest in music swelled. Most of his boyhood recollections are tied in with the pop records of the day. In 1963 the Great Train Robbery took place as did the Profumo Affair, but Tim remembers two stand-out moments. One was the arrival of Beatlemania in October when the Fab Four were mobbed wherever they went and Pathé newsreels featured them nightly. 'The other was in the November when I was in my Auntie Jean's in the next close. I used to go up there and sing for her. I'd sing along with Beatles songs I'd put on her record-player at 78rpm and she thought it was hysterical. I'd only do it in front of her and my Uncle Paddy—I was too embarrassed to do it in front of other people. But up at her house I'd give it laldy. One day I'd finished singing and was having a glass of ginger when the news came on. I was only eleven but I remember the impact the story had on everybody. They were all very upset. President Kennedy had been killed and I realised he was a really famous man.'

Jim also listened to a pirate station, Radio Scotland, when it crashed onto the airwaves. And while the BBC in London relied on broadcasters with plummy voices, Jim loved the local accents. He was clearly music daft. His favourite TV show was STV's *Roundup*, a show which featured the new songs in the hit parade. It was presented by Paul Young, the actor who once played Wee Geordie in the film classic and went on to become hooked on fishing, and a lady who wore nice gingham dresses, Morag Hood.

But although there was a love affair with music going on, Jim McGrory managed to find time to fit in the ordinary pastimes of the housing-scheme boys. His pals were constants in his life. There was Suave John McDade, who came from Queenslie but whose Uncle Pat lived in the same close as the McGrorys. Suave John got his nickname for entirely perverse reasons: he simply wasn't suave, although he did wear a cravat. He was a heavy built boy and the sort who'd wipe his nose with his sleeve and then grin widely. And when he walked he flicked up his heels in order to kick himself on the backside. There was also Freckles Miller, whose real name was John, a slim boy with blond hair who, strangely enough, did have freckles. And Jim's cousin Johnny made up the foursome.

They had fun as kids, despite the fact that as the 1960s marched on, Easterhouse was becoming a much more abrasive place to grow up and many of those who lived there felt the tremendous sense of isolation that came from being at the failed end of a town-planning experiment. Nice houses may have been built in Glasgow's shiny new scheme but the architects had forgotten to provide any infrastructure. There were few amenities or focal points.

Understandably, a little of that fermenting aggression spilled over onto kids like Jim and his pals. 'My friends and I went through a spell of trying to prove to the world that we were hard men,' he admitted. 'One day we took to throwing empty milk bottles into closes and running away. But I was found out. One lady in Eddlewood Place called my mammy and told her what I'd been up to. My mother showed incredulity and disbelief when confronted with the news, but she later got a hold of me for interrogation. I remember her saying to me: "Now, tell me the truth, were you smashing bottles?" And I said no, for a couple of basic reasons. The first was I was scared and I didn't want to get a doin'. And the second was I didn't want to let my mammy down.'

The unlikely rebel without a clue still felt peer pressure, however.

'We played a form of chap-door-run-away except that we didn't run away,' said Tim, grinning.

'There was an arrangement between Suave John, Freckles, Johnny and me that we'd knock the door and stay there. And the first boy who ran away would get a doin' off the rest. The last one to run was the winner. I remember standing there one day there until the very last minute because I was so desperate to win this contest, and one guy actually came to the door so fast and said, "What?" And I just stood there and stared. So he got angry and said, "What do you want, ya wee bastard?" And now I couldn't run away—I was petrified with fear. It was three or four seconds before my legs would function and sprint me off into the night.'

There was other naughtiness. 'We'd get a rope and tie it to opposite door handles on a close landing then knock both doors at the same time. And when the people tried to open them from the inside they couldn't. We would all go up to the first landing so we could watch the havoc we'd created.'

Life on the streets wasn't always about fun at other people's expense. 'I had great fun with my guidey,' recalled Tim. 'It was made from old pram wheels and on top was an orange box and I used to have an incredible time going down the huge hill on Banton Place. Of course, the guidey didn't have any brakes and one Sunday afternoon I crashed right into a lamppost and I took the blow on the face. It hurt so much that my ears bled. I was so ill that night I couldn't go to Mass the next day.'

Like most boys he became a football fanatic—and of course he shared the name of Celtic's star player from the 1930s, Jimmy McGrory (no relation). 'My Uncle Danny and my Uncle William were big Celtic fans but they wouldn't take me to Celtic matches, even though that's where most of my school pals went. I'd been on occasion but my uncles reckoned it was too dangerous and rowdy for a kid.

And I think they were right—it was a bit rough at the time.'

Tim would rather play football. He had played quite a bit in Easterhouse for his school, Blessed John Ogilvie, with his pal Tommy Nevin; Tommy was a good player, although he didn't turn out as good as his younger brother Pat, who at this time was still sucking a bottle in his pram but would later go on to represent Scotland. 'My worst football nightmare took place playing for the school against St Modan's in a league decider. I missed a penalty late on in the game and I fell flat on my face. The other players had to come and pick me up because I couldn't move for crying. We lost the match 6–5.'

But he had better times over in Partick. Jim would go west at weekends to stay with his granny and his two uncles and he played in the St Peter's Guild Boys Club League for a team called the Kelly Babes.

That in itself presented a problem. Uncle William was the manager. 'For me to get a game I had to be a bit better than good, otherwise there would be accusations of nepotism.'

The little winger held his own in the West End league. But there was one question mark over his running style that not only stayed with him but came back to haunt him in later life. 'I can always remember my uncle saying to me: "Why do you run like that?" Now, I might be havering here, but Uncle William was always telling me to run with my legs straighter. My legs would just go all over the place. I still wonder if there was something wrong with me at the time.'

2

Bare-knuckle Fights, Gay Proposals and Deborah Kerr

Success came to young Jim McGrory at the age of twelve when he passed the Eleven Plus exam that took him to St Mungo's Academy in Townhead. It was a prestigious single-sex grammar school with a very good reputation. Exciting times there lay before him; in the first year he was to experience his one and only fight—and his one and only homosexual experience.

Meantime, Jim worked hard at his new school. 'I didn't let him out until he had done his homework,' said Dora. 'He didn't get out to play with John McDade and John Miller and his cousin Johnny until it was all finished. But he didn't need too much pressure. He was a good wee boy.'

There were a lot of youngsters in the neighbourhood who didn't fit that description. The dream that was Easterhouse was dissolving fast into a nightmare of ghetto housing where gangs ran wild, fighting over territory defined by street corners and lampposts. 'We lived in skinhead land,' recalled newspaper columnist Rikki Brown, Tim's pal who grew up in nearby Wardie Road.

'The guys who terrorised people were called Nervo, Virgo and Alka—it seemed you needed a vowel at the end of your nickname to be taken seriously. But, to be honest, Tim and my other pals never really had any problems. The bad boys fought with each other. It was like the line from The Beach Boys' song *I Get Around*: "The bad boys know us so they leave us alone." But whenever Tim—or Jim as he was then—got hassle he would handle it pretty well. I remember this evil thug walking up to us one day and shouting to Tim, "Hey, you— wanker!" And Tim said, "Yes, you're right, as it happens. I do in fact enjoy single-person sex. What's your point?"'

Young McGrory had already come to realise he was more of a lover than a fighter. Sure, he liked a bit of rough and tumble with the boys but his friends couldn't understand how taken he was with other more gentle facets of life. When Mary Quant came along with her new fashions in 1964 Jim took note. He would readily discuss the merits of the current blockbuster film, *Mary Poppins*. And he was more than happy to sing the praises of the females who captured his attention on screen: Diana Rigg in *The Avengers* and Cathy McGowan on *Ready Steady Go*.

There came a time, however, when Jim simply couldn't avoid a fight. The challenge came from a schoolfriend, a tough boy with a very appropriate name: 'Fred Savage was a big bloke. You know how it is at school, people grow up at different rates, and Fred seemed huge. Anyway, one day he and I were sitting at our desks punching each other's knuckles till they bled—for fun, of course. It was part of the afternoon history class ritual: we really were being neanderthal. But somehow my wee knuckles must have hurt Fred and he went into a real temper and said, "Right, outside, at the sheds,"—the sheds being the arena where the school gladiators fought. I bravely said, "Aye, I'll be there."

'And, of course, the whole school turned out to watch. I was scared stiff but, being from Easterhouse, I had to go through with it. I couldn't back down. So we got to the sheds and Fred threw the first punch and he hit me right on the head and nearly killed me. So I went down on one knee, all wobbly, and then held up my hand to indicate

I had given in. And that was acceptable. I had a very sore head for a couple of days but, because I'd agreed to fight him, I managed to depart the battleground with some dignity.'

Outside of school Jim managed to avoid the gangs but there were other dangers lurking in the streets of Easterhouse. 'We were terrified of the vigilantes who prowled the street in a white van,' recalled Rikki Brown. They had different names—the White Panthers or the Untouchables—and we don't know to this day if they were locals or cops, although they were always big fat blokes with anoraks, and their arses started at their knees and ended at their necks. So, thinking back, it's unlikely they were Strathclyde's finest. But I'm sure the police turned a blind eye to what they got up to.'

The Untouchables, facing anarchy in the township, took it upon themselves to clean up. The reputation of the area had plummeted. City council chiefs introduced new names to such areas to give them more appeal and help kids who were looking for jobs—Blair Tumnock, Easthall and so on—to try and take the stigma away. But it didn't work. And, as such, people couldn't get work. The weaponry, meantime, had changed from fists and sticks to knives and swords.

Jim saw the battle for survival as something that was part and parcel of everyday life in the scheme. 'I was threatened a few times, but usually got out of being beaten up by the main gang in our area, the Torran Toi, because I knew someone in the gang and that got me a free pass. Looking back, it wasn't unusual to see someone run along the road being chased by a guy with a sword, but we were always just observers, trying to keep our distance.'

But the Untouchables weren't always too particular about who they dragged in to the back of the van and administered their own justice to. 'They used to pull us kids into the van and slap us about for doing little other than wearing college jumpers and what they thought were

Doc Marten's,' said Rikki. 'In my case the aggro boots were actually my Uncle Joe's steel-toecap workie boots.'

At times, it was clearly hard to tell the good guys from the bad guys. One night Tim, Suave John, Freckles and cousin Johnny were out wandering aimlessly around the streets when they spotted a group of girls out in Wardie Road. The girls were all dressed up for a hen night and the bride-to-be was wearing the usual sticky-out frock, toilet seat around her neck, L-plates dangling from her arms and carrying a baby's potty as a container for the money she would collect for selling kisses. Jim and the boys shouted teasing abuse at the girls from the top of the hill, the usual rude comments that adolescent boys make, and just then the Untouchables pulled up in a big van and hauled the boys inside. They slapped them around a bit, then took Tim home and told his mother he'd been fighting with a gang. 'I got off with it as far as my mother was concerned because I think I was crying, which I seemed to do a lot in times of crises,' he said. 'I was telling the truth about having been doing nothing really and my mother believed me.'

Dora McGrory recalled this incident as being far more serious than her son remembered. 'Breach-of-the-peace charges were brought by the police because of what these vigilantes had told them. We had to hire a lawyer to sort things out, but I remember John Miller's parents were going to plead guilty in court, just to avoid the fuss. The rest of the parents got together, though, and put them straight as to what to do.'

Rikki Brown put the work of the Untouchables in perspective: 'I suppose they were doing what they thought best. It's just that they weren't that discriminating about who they got hold of and slapped about. I've yet to hear about them dragging any of the sword-wielding lunatics into the back of the van.'

Looking back, Tim refused to see Easterhouse through anything but rose-coloured glasses. 'It was a pretty hairy place but it was no worse than any other scheme in Glasgow.'

It seems the threat of violence was something that existed in people's lives and, like those who live in war zones around the world, young people in Easterhouse and the surrounding housing schemes simply had to go about the business of life.

Jim, luckily, had his own interests to take his thoughts away from the growing anarchy round about him. He became wrapped up in what had become his greatest passion, music, and formed a little band with his pals, The Trespassers. Jim played the Spanish guitar his mother had bought for him for two pounds; there was Suave John playing Jim's single Beatle drum, and Freckles and another boy, Robert Armstrong, on guitar and bass. 'We played outside in the gardens and all along the street, singing Beatles songs, of course, and we thought we were fantastic. People would come out into the verandah and throw money down to us. At the time I thought it was in appreciation of the quality of our music.'

His parents had bought him a tape-recorder and Jim began to pretend he was a disc jockey, just like David Symonds. 'I'd go into his room and listen quietly,' said Dora. 'The bold boy would be lost in his own wee world playing records and taping them on his reel-to-reel, then talking into the tape-recorder. He could be in there for hours. I didn't mind so long as he did his schoolwork. He was enjoying himself.'

Jim's life at St Mungo's was enjoyable. Even with his awkward legs he made it into the school relay team. 'I was the third runner and I recall a big race at Bishopbriggs where we had the sports day. The first two guys were losing and I came from behind to re-establish the lead for the team. We won the race and I got a medal.'

The school trip to Paris was another highlight. 'We had a great time.

Charlie Burchill, the cousin of the Simple Minds guitarist of the same name, was in my class and he was my pal. At school I think my best subject was French and I felt incredibly at home in Paris.'

Tim would later learn—via hypnotic regression—just how powerful that link with France was, but back at school he learned some of the facts of life the hard way. In fact, his first sexual experience at the age of thirteen turned out to be of the non-heterosexual type. 'I can't mention his name for obvious reasons, but it's enough to say this guy had glasses and his hair was always perfect, and he was a very odd-looking character who lived in the Gallowgate. One day we were sitting in homework class and he asked me if I had a girlfriend. I tried to act the big man so I said, "Of course, I've got plenty." Then he said, "So what do you do to them?" And since I had a captive audience I embellished a little. In fact, I made it all up. I said, "Well, I take them round the back and take their pants down and do things to them. I feel them."

'He looked fairly impressed. And he took a few moments to digest this. Then he said, "Mmm. When you say you feel them all over, do you mean there?" and as he asked the question he pointed downwards and at the same time touched me in the trouser region. I thought, "Oh, oh, that's a bit strange." But I replied that yes, that was in fact where I'd touched my (non-existent) girlfriends.

'Then he said, "Yes, but what if they have trousers on or a skirt with a zip? Do you pull it down like this?" And while he's saying this line, he's demonstrating his question and before I know what's happening he's got his hand inside my trousers. I didn't know what to do, so I said, "Aye," in a trembly voice, now more than a little uncomfortable while he was feeling all around my family business. But as he footered about, my confidence came back and I called out, "Chuck it!" and pushed him away. For some reason, no one else had witnessed any of this and we went back to straight conversation—pardon the pun—and he asked me how often my experiences with girls happened. Still lying and desperate not to lose face, I said, "Nearly every night." He then asked me, "Oh, but is it always with girls?" and I said, "Aye, how?" He said, "What about boys?" And I said, "Nut." And he marched off in a huff. It wasn't until much later on that I realised that I had been propositioned. Yes, I know: I was a pretty stupid wee boy.'

It wasn't too much later that he began to receive interest from his preferred sex. 'I was fourteen when I met Jean Bradley,' Tim recalled. 'She worked at the newsagent's at the top of our street. Jean was a couple of years older than me—the older woman, I guess—and I really, really fancied her. I used to get half a crown pocket money but I would only ever spend sixpence at a time so that I could go into the shop and see her. Eventually she noticed me and we started seeing each other. And she'd come down to my house and have a glass of ginger. It was a real romance, like Burt Lancaster and Deborah Kerr in *From Here to Eternity*. The real thing.

'The big day for me came when she invited me down to her pal's house. The girl had it to herself because her mother was at the bingo, and we went into the bedroom for a kiss and a cuddle. But, to my horror, she took the upper hand and set about the seduction process. But nothing happened. I couldn't come to terms with a woman making all the moves and I was confused. This wasn't what happened in the movies. I wasn't ready for this. I could only just get my head round the fact that England had won the World Cup. This was all too much. I think she dropped me after that day.'

The same terror scenario was repeated later that year with Tim's next girlfriend. 'I got matched up with a girl—let's call her Mary, because she has some very big brothers who still live in Easterhouse.' In the time-honoured tradition of the west of Scotland they came together when Tim's pals, Suave John and Freckles, announced to the young lady's entourage: 'My pal fancies your pal.' And with all that elaborate ceremony and courtship over, the hormone-enraged teenagers found themselves a place in which to unleash their passion.

'So we went round the back of the houses,' recalled Tim. 'She was clearly quite happy to explore the sexual side of life. She touched me and I returned the compliment. The next thing I knew was I standing there with my trousers round my ankles. To be honest, I didn't really know the geography of the female and I was scared with what I found. Sure, I'd seen pictures of naked women, but not with any real anatomical detail. I wasn't scared—I was absolutely horrified. It was a shocking experience. Things just didn't seem to be where I had imagined they would be. To put it in its basic form, I reckoned the parts should have been far more horizontal and less hidden than they in fact were. And, as a result of my inability to cope with the basic geography of the female body, the fact it was freezing (it was the middle of winter) and sheer terror, nothing happened except that it put me off the idea of sex for a very long time.'

With girls pushed aside, Jim could concentrate on his true love—music. In 1965 the pirate station Radio Scotland had begun broadcasting from off the coast of Troon and this opened up a whole new world of pop to Scots youngsters. Pirates came into being to satisfy an immense demand for pop music that the BBC wasn't supplying. These stations hired young radio hopefuls from the mobile-disco circuit. Of course, since they had no government licence, they had to broadcast from safe waters. Now, for the first time Jim had real role models. Sure, he'd been a devoted David Symonds fan on the Light Programme but now there were disc jockeys broadcasting with real Scottish accents. People like Jimmy Mack, Jack McLaughlin, Richard Park and Tony Meehan would all later work with Tim at some point in his life. And there was also Stuart Henry, a man whose illness later in life would be so poignant for Tim Stevens. But, for the moment, Jim McGrory could only listen and dream of being a radio DJ. Such was his passion for the pirates that he would ask his Uncle Danny to take him up to Radio Scotland's HQ in Cranworth Street, in the West End, in the hope of seeing one of the DJs walk through the hallowed doors. Jim wanted to gain experience any way he possibly could. That experience came via women's clothing.

Tim's dad Jimmy didn't go to the football on Saturdays like his mum's brothers. He worked instead at the Barras market where he and Tim's grandad had a little prefab booth called the Separate Centre which sold ladies' clothes. Tim can recall a particular ladies' coat he had a great fondness for, although he denies any feelings of juvenile transvestitism. 'I remember the shop had these great long corduroy coats and I was desperate to get one. It didn't matter if they buttoned to the left, I just thought they looked so cool. And remember,' he added defensively, 'this was a time when the unisex look was in.' He was right. In the summer of 1966 The Rolling Stones were at the top of the charts with *Paint It Black* and the androgynous look was in. Mick Jagger looked as feminine as his girlfriend, Marianne Faithfull.

But as well as offering the young Jim the chance to admire the latest fashions, he saw his dad's little shoplet as a career opportunity. 'My dad would go into the street with a mike to drum up business—he was actually a very good crooner, very Bing Crosby-like—and I'd walk around with him wearing pilot headphones my Auntie Maisie had given me. They didn't actually work, but they looked good. And it gave me an idea. I suggested that I bring my record-player down to the Separate Centre and play music while my dad addressed the passers-by. It all worked fine for a while, but I got frustrated and wanted to talk as well.'

Nevertheless, it was broadcasting experience for the youngster. 'I was in effect talking to myself,' laughed Tim, 'but I was on Cloud Nine.'

Dora agreed with her son's teenage experience. 'To Jim this was showbiz. And I guess for the first time I could see he had got that bug from his father. His dad had been a bit of a singer in his day and had actually entered a talent contest and won. But in those days it was all about getting a proper job.'

Jim decided to follow in his father's footsteps as a hopeful singer one day when he opened up the *Melody Maker* and spotted an interesting ad. A music publishing company, Major Minor Records, were looking for young singing talent. Jim knew he was exactly what they were looking for. All those years of singing for his Auntie Jean weren't for nothing. That night he recorded a song in his bedroom, playing the guitar his mother had bought for him in Spain. 'The song was *Hey, Hey, Bo Diddley* and I thought I improved on the original,' said Tim. Unfortunately, Major Minor Records didn't.

Still, at least he looked the part. At this time Jim was wearing the woolly hat which had become a permanent fixture on his head. 'He was a great fan of The Monkees,' said Dora. 'That's why he wore the woolly hat. Of course, he'd already changed his hairstyle. I remember one day he walked into the bathroom with his usual lovely side shed and Loxene and came out with it all dry and combed forwards like The Beatles and The Monkees. I was horrified and I told him so, but the bold boy just laughed.'

It wasn't to be long before Jim's hat, fringe and disc-jockey talents were unveiled to the world for the first time. Just as he turned fifteen, the desperately keen hopeful approached the local priest with a view to playing his first gig. Jim had gone to Father Reilly with an innovative idea: he would take over the church hall for a disco on a Saturday with a sixpence admission and the money raised would go to the church building fund. 'We had this notion that we would act like some kind of virtual UN peace-keeping force by taking the young people off the streets and into the hall,' said Tim.

The gang situation in Easterhouse was becoming horrific. Evidently, the local hard men were a million miles away from Scott McKenzie and the peace-loving kids in San Francisco with flowers in their hair. While the pop world and The Rolling Stones were up in court on drugs charges, the Glasgow courts were full of would-be conquistadors. 'It worked,' said Tim of his first gig. 'Suave John, Freckles and cousin Johnny, my fellow DJs, all sold loads of tickets. Only one gang came to the hall, the Torran Toi, and they didn't cause too many problems.'

The story of the young disco pacifists made the papers. Jim McGrory had his first taste of fame. 'The *Evening Citizen* came along and took our pictures,' he remembered. 'It was an incredibly exciting time.'

The Mike Nesmith influence didn't go unnoticed in Easterhouse. 'He looked a right tube,' said his pal, Rikki Brown. 'But at least the hat got him some attention.'

It was to be a couple of years before Tim really began to be noticed for his odd sartorial selections. But at least the church hall performance left the youngster with the confidence to push himself forward as a DJ. One night at a disco in Shettleston Town Hall the regular DJ didn't show up. Jim, who was there with his cousin Linda Brown, saw his chance and leapt from the darkness into the spotlight. 'Harry Murphy, the guy with the mobile disco, hadn't turned up. But all his gear was in place and I told the organiser I was experienced and could do the job. He said to go ahead and I did. And it was fantastic.'

Or at least it was for the first fifteen minutes. 'A local gang, the Shettleston Tigers, crashed in through the door and screamed at me, "Are you Rick Macy?" I said, "No!" worriedly, and wondered what the hell Rick Macy had ever done to upset them.' It turned out that Rick Macy and Harry Murphy were one and the same. And the reason Rick/Harry didn't show up that night was because he knew his card was well and truly marked. It was a piece of good fortune for Jim, and he capitalised on that success. Or rather his dad did.

'His father was his unpaid manager,' said Dora. 'Whenever we'd go out on a Saturday night Jimmy would go and see the manager and try and get his boy a wee job.'

His dad's efforts paid off. Jim was offered a job in the Dennistoun Roller Arena. Mecca owned this top ten spot—where the DJ played the same ten records back to back all night—which had been converted from the old Dennistoun Palais. Jim landed a Sunday afternoon roller disco and on his first shift he admits he made a complete backside of himself. 'It was a fabulous place with huge lights and rainbow-coloured decorations. Up on stage there was a wonderfully vivid psychedelic paint job, all over the back walls. Unfortunately, the exit from the stage was through a door on this same back wall.

'Things went really well until it was time for my break. I announced to the audience, "Here's a great record from The Monkees, *I'm a Believer*. I'll be back in ten minutes," and then turned to go through the stage door. But I couldn't find it. I was baffled. And meantime the crowd laughed themselves senseless as I felt my way along the psychedelic wall, feeling for a door handle, all the time looking like an Easterhouse mime artist. It took me at least five minutes to locate the knob. The crowd had already found one, though.'

The lack of any sense of direction was to result in catastrophic problems in later life but, for the moment, Jim could bask in the glory that had come his way. And apart from the sheer delight at performing before a crowd, he discovered an added benefit to being a public entertainer. 'One Sunday I went to the La Cubana disco, which was inside the Palais, with Charlie Burchill and he pulled a couple of girls. By that I mean he got a hold of couple who would agree to talk to us and have a bit of a winch. But I did nothing about it. I was far too shy to be mixed up in that sort of thing. But what I did notice during the gig that all the girls would be running up to the DJ, Dean Jeffries, to get him to sign their hand. I was young but I can remember thinking, "If that's the power DJs have, I want some of that." I wanted them eating out of my hand rather than offering me a biro to sign theirs.'

It wouldn't be too long before he had his wish. But before that time came along he reckoned the world would have to do without James Gerard Dickson Joseph McGrory.

3

Swedes, Sombreros and Railway Sheds

Jim had come to realise that showbiz people in the 1960s didn't, in general, use the name they were born with. Pop was littered with stars who had begun life with a different moniker. Cliff was Harry Webb, Adam Faith started out as Terry Nelhams and so on. Even Paul McCartney was actually a James. Jim McGrory wasn't a showbiz name. It had to go.

'The realisation that a local DJ like Harry Murphy had changed his name to Rick Macy had an effect on me,' said Tim. 'It made me realise that "Jim McGrory" wasn't trendy. But the problem was thinking up a name that sounded cool.'

One day it came to him when he was watching television. 'One of my favourite programmes was *Bewitched*, the American sitcom, and as the credits were rolling I looked hard at the male character's name— Darren Stevens. I thought, "That's it—Stevens, I'll have that." To get the "Tim" part took a bit longer, though. I wanted something not far removed from "Jim" so I played with idea of changing one letter. I went through the alphabet and stopped at "K" and thought about "Kim Stevens" but decided against it because Kim was also a girl's name and in Easterhouse you could be killed for that sort of thing. Anyway, I got to the letter "T" and I quite liked the name "Tim", and so Tim Stevens was born.'

He had no misgivings at all about choosing the surname of a TV witch's husband. 'When I introduced myself to new people I'd call myself Tim and eventually it stuck. When I did little gigs I'd put posters up advertising "The Tim Stevens Roadshow" and that sort of made it official.'

The family of course couldn't forget he was really called Jim and it was to be almost ten years before he changed his name officially. (The Tiger part would come later.) The fact he was too lazy to do it properly created problems, but for the moment all he had to contend with was a bit of teasing from pals in Easterhouse.

In the meantime, Jim—sorry, Tim—was to learn that the path to true love was laid with crazy-paving.

He fell in love again, this time far away from the backdoors of Easterhouse. The whole family, including Uncle Paddy and Auntie Jean, went to Benidorm for their summer holiday. The McGrory family were leaping on to the bandwagon of Scots heading off for exotic foreign holidays. They didn't fly, of course—they couldn't afford it—but travelled on the train thanks to Jimmy's free rail-passes. Thankfully, for Auntie Jean's sake, her nephew had now given up singing Beatles songs at 78rpm.

The train journey was long and boring and hot for a fifteen-year-old with a woollen hat stapled to his head but Jim took to Benidorm straight away. When they arrived at the Hotel Melina the family discovered the hotel had a resident band, but no disco. Tim's mum immediately offered her son's services, stating he was already an accomplished DJ. 'I loved it,' he recalled. 'I sat at the reception area playing records and talking. I even got to sing with the band one night, wearing a big sombrero. And at the hotel I met some boys my own age from Glasgow and became friendly with a wee guy from Springburn called Tommy. Life couldn't get any better, or so I thought. The next day I met this Swedish girl, Kirsten, who had long blond hair and the bluest eyes imaginable. I would meet her at lunchtimes and we'd go for walks and hold hands. At night I'd play records and chat to the audience, most of them from Glasgow, and by day I'd meet up with Kirsten and stare into her eyes. I was in raptures. My world was a gift from the gods.'

It was to end in tears. 'All I did with Kirsten was to stare longingly into her eyes. I considered her to be mine. She felt the same—or so I thought. But while I was building a relationship with my hotel audience, Tommy, my new pal, was developing a relationship with Kirsten. One morning he made an announcement as we waited in the breakfast queue. "I've done the business," he said, declaring he had in fact had a sexual relationship with the girl of my dreams. I was devastated. The words hit my ears like a huge bass drum. My whole head shook from the earthquake that was going on inside. The holiday romance was over. The romance of the holiday was over. Later I rationalised it and reckoned she got fed up waiting for me to take the relationship further. But I learned one thing from that experience: don't hang about.' It was a salutary lesson Tim was to bear in mind in future years when opportunity knocked with the opposite sex.

Meantime, back home, he focused on the more positive aspects of his holiday experience and sent off a demo tape, recorded in his bedroom, to the Light Programme. 'This was pre-Radio One, of course, and I was determined to try my hand and be up there with the Light big boys like David Symonds. However, my tape was sent back with a very snooty letter.'

He also tried sending a tape to a new pirate station called Radio Nothing. Undaunted, he despatched yet another recording to the new Radio Scotland, the official BBC station that had opened up in Glasgow. 'I sent it with a covering letter billing myself "The Youngest DJ Ever". A very nice man at BBC Scotland, producer Ben Lyons, sent me a letter back suggesting I shouldn't bill myself on the basis of my lack of years. He said I wouldn't be young forever and I'd need something else that stood the test of time. But the letter was very encouraging and it gave me the determination to keep going.' Not that Tim needed it. For some reason he was blessed (or cursed) with a need to be recognised, a longing to be famous.

It was this longing that saw his parents traumatised when, in the summer of 1967, Tim announced to Dora and Jimmy that he wasn't going back to school. It was all to do with a desperate desire to make his way in the world. It was about forging his own destiny, about living life for the moment. Che Guevara, the Argentinian revolutionary, had been killed in Bolivia and teenagers' minds were focused on rebellion. Tim's great act of rebellion was to walk out of the doors of St Mungo's and not look back.

'I was fifteen and I thought I was grown up,' said Tim. 'I was doing really well at school and I certainly wasn't stupid. But I wanted to leave. It was one of those things you did. I couldn't be bothered with O-levels or any of that, even though my English and French teachers had suggested I stay on and maybe try for Highers. I just wanted to get out into the big bad world. It wasn't easy to leave. I was both elated and deflated at the same time. I was scared of what lay ahead, and yet I was happy and excited.'

Dora and Jimmy were horrified. 'Oh, we tried to talk him out of it,' said Dora. 'We tried for hours. But he was having none of it. And even the headmaster, Mr Kelly, called to say he was very disappointed that Jim had decided to go. I was totally in agreement. We thought he should have stayed on and done his O-levels.'

Tim didn't have far to look for a job. At this time Dora had been working at Goldberg's store in Candleriggs in Glasgow for a few years. 'My mammy spoke to the personnel officer for me and before I knew it I was offered a job in the Incoming Goods Department. My job was to be in charge of sending the van to the Edinburgh branch, which was quite a bit of responsibility for a fifteen-year-old. I felt like a man. I could kid on I was grown up. This was what it was all about.'

Not entirely. Jimmy McGrory could accept the fact his son had left school—but to make his way in life without a trade was unthinkable. It was decided: Jim would join his foreman father working as an apprentice electrician at British Rail in St Rollox, the huge maintenance yard in Springburn.

Tim had mostly positive feelings about moving from Goldberg's after six months to the might of British industry. 'I wasn't convinced this was what I wanted to do, but somehow it made me feel like a man, even though I was a skinny wee teenager. This was the real world of dirty dungarees, where men carried their flasks and pieces to work and at the end of the day they looked as though they'd been hard at work. I endeavoured to make the most of it. I suppose I was a bit of a fish out of water but I took each new experience as it came, and every day my eyes were opened wider.'

Tim was to go through all the usual rites of passage apprentices would suffer. 'On my first day, Mr Woodrow the foreman, sent me for a left-handed screwdriver. And of course, I walked to the other end of the building, gave the chitty to the storeman and he smiled. Then he disappeared for about twenty minutes, came back and told me they were out of them. I just looked daft and still had no idea what was going on—until I got back to the electrical department where the men were all beating their desks and laughing like maniacs.'

There was to be greater humiliation.

'A few weeks later a bloke called Andy Lamb and three others grabbed me at the back of the train, pulled my trousers and pants down and said, "Right, ya wee bastard!" and covered my groin in the green, gungy cleaning agent, swarfiga. There was tons of it. All I could do was shout, "Chuck it!" 'cause I didn't swear at the time, but of course they didn't until there was enough swarfiga down there to clean out the nation's sewers. Then they pulled my trousers back up and left me to it. And I walked about all day squelching with green soapy slime running down my ankles. I couldn't even tell my daddy about what had happened because he would have been affronted.'

Tim adapted to his new habitat in the only way he could: by becoming the yard's unpaid entertainer. 'I used to walk about the workshop singing into a giant screwdriver and that passed the hours away. And at lunchtimes in the workshop there was a huge cupboard with a shelf that opened up and it looked like a little stage and I used to get up on top of it and perform for the men eating their dinner. I would stand there and tell jokes and sing Beatles songs like *She Loves You*. In retrospect, they must have thought I was a bit odd, like Gloria out of *It Ain't Half Hot Mum*, and destined for a career as a Dale Winton or something, but I was enjoying myself and that's all that mattered.'

It was at this point that the nickname Tiger Tim was conceived. Many years later he would tell newspaper journalists fibs about how he was given the nickname after saving a young damsel from wild animals while on safari in Africa. But the truth was far less exotic. There are two versions. Tim's version runs like this: 'A guy called Big John started calling me "The Tiger". It was after the character in the 1950s children's comics, Tiger Tim. It was a nickname that stuck.'

Dora tells the other version: 'There was a record out at the time by a Hen Broon-lookalike novelty act called Tiny Tim. I guess when the men at work saw him singing they got the idea he really was a Tiny Tim but to be kind they called him Tiger.'

Tim's other activities at work weren't always so well received. 'One day I was in the toilets with my best railway pal, Harry Anderson from

Partick, and we were kidding ourselves on about the gangs from our areas. The main Easterhouse gang was the Torran Toi and his was the Cross. Anyway, the toilets had just been painted and so we took a cubicle each and started scraping gang slogans into the wall. This in itself was crazy, since neither of us had anything to do with gang warfare, but just as we stepped out, the toilet attendant grabbed us. He began shouting, "Right, you pair of wee bastards!" and dragged us up to the training officer. I was terrified. I knew I'd be sacked. This was the ultimate disgrace. But in the end I got off with a real rollicking and I managed to keep my job, probably because my dad was a foreman. And because I'd got off with it, Harry did too.'

Tim couldn't recall actually learning anything from working at the yard. 'Nothing remotely useful,' he said, grinning. 'If someone asked me to wire their house I wouldn't know where to start. I couldn't raggle a wall or anything. I suppose if you brought me a train I'd know my way around the fuse box, though.'

It was clear young Tim's working life was not going to feature locomotives and signal boxes for ever. He was becoming more and more in demand locally as a DJ, playing the church halls and community centres of the East End. His dad acted as his publicist, telling youth clubs about his son the DJ, but it was his mum who was responsible for Tim landing his first 'away' gig. Dora was in the habit of having her hair cut in a trendy salon in Sauchiehall Street and her hairdresser, a young blonde named Sally Carr, was a singing hopeful. Sally would later gain international stardom with pop band Middle Of The Road but for now she was more than happy to listen to Tim's mum talking about her talented boy. Sally had an agent, Ivan Taylor, and she promised she'd call him to ask if he could fix up a gig for young Jim. She was true to her word.

'Sally got me a gig in Helensburgh, which to me was the other end of the world,' said Tim. 'I had no idea where it was. But I felt I'd made it. I had no disco equipment, of course, so I played a pile of records on my wee Dansette record-player at home and recorded them on to my new reel-to-reel recorder my mammy and daddy had bought for my Christmas.

'At the gig I would speak through the mike then put it down to the tape-recorder and the sound of The Rolling Stones or whatever would come through the PA system. It was primitive and the quality must have been really bad, but it was a gig. I was in business.'

The night wasn't a total success. 'I got the train there because my daddy got cheap tickets, and my mammy and daddy came along to see me. They got the train home but I was so late in finishing I had to get the bus back into town then another out to Easterhouse. It cost me more on fares than I got paid for the gig. But the crowd seemed to like the music.'

Jim was now convinced that being a DJ was the most glamorous life he could think of, perhaps next to that of a pop star. All over Britain others just like him dreamed of becoming the next Tony Blackburn. Radio One's birth had immediately elevated DJs to the same status as the stars whose records they played.

At this point Jim decided to set himself up as a mobile DJ and reckoned he would have to invest in some real disco gear if he were to build on his part-time job. 'There was a company in London called Sound Electronics who were doing a deal for twin decks with speakers and flashing lights—the works—and I asked my daddy for a loan. Without a word of complaint he handed me £285, a huge amount of money in those days. And not only did he bankroll me, he went out and got me my first gigs, the Bowler's Rest in Parkhead and La Caverna in Bath Street and a couple of pubs in Shettleston. This was it. I was officially a DJ.'

Tim already had a showbizzy name. He was good, he was keen and he was young. He could do no wrong. And, as the work built up, so too did his confidence with the opposite sex. 'One girl from Easterhouse became, I guess, what you'd call a groupie and seemed to be wherever I appeared. One Sunday afternoon I was gigging at La Caverna and she hung about afterwards and hauled me into the cloakroom. Before I realised what was happening she was having a right old fiddle about with my technical equipment. I can just remember thinking I was so glad it wasn't cold. I was still shy and naïve with girls but somehow my confidence was growing.'

Now that he had approached intimacy with the fairer sex, his mind raced forward to the time when he could go all the way. After all, he was sixteen now. And it was time for the virgin cub to become a tiger.

4

Blackpool Rocking and Jet Mayfair

The summer of '68 was to be a memorable one for Tim. Pushing aside the cynical laughter of the whole housing scheme when singer Frankie Vaughan rode into town to coax the bad boys into surrendering their knives, guns, anti-tank missiles and so on, Tim was excited at the thought of his summer holiday. With Dora, Jimmy and his best mate Suave John, he set off on the train for two weeks in Blackpool. Those free tickets were again a godsend. Sixteen-year-old Tim and the gang checked into a boarding-house the family had used many times before. Life was never to be quite the same again.

'There were two chambermaids working in the boarding-house and I fell for one of them,' recalled Tim with a sigh. 'Her name was Edwina Scott Duffy and she came from Yorkshire. She had long strawberry-blond hair and her job was to serve up the breakfasts and make the beds. She was gorgeous and I got to talking to her every day. She wouldn't go out with us at night, though. She was two years older than us and she was getting into pubs. As you can imagine, she didn't want to be seen with a wee boy like me.' Not one who was still wearing a Monkees tribute hat.

'Anyway, by the end of the first week I got to mentioning what room we were in—not that she didn't know it already—and one night about midnight Suave John and I were in the big double bed when we heard giggling at the door.

I immediately said to John, "It's the girls! You kid on you're snoring and I'll try and get Edwina into bed with me." I don't know how I even came up with the idea in the first place. As if a girl whom I'd never even kissed would get in beside me. I suppose it was a triumph of optimism over reality, and I was incredibly frustrated. The thought was running wild through my head that I might—just might—get to lose my virginity. My heart was a mix of excitement and sheer terror.

'Anyway, Suave John snored on command. But it was one of those fake snores that you hear people do on TV movies and it was all too obvious and loud. Nevertheless, Edwina came in with her pal and I asked her to lie down beside me. To my astonishment, she did. Not only that, she took off her clothes. Meanwhile, I guess, her pal sat on the chair and watched. Well, I think she watched—to be honest I wasn't paying her the least bit of attention. And such was my passion that I forgot all about Suave John who, to his eternal credit, was still performing the role of Sleeping Man.'

Tim's development from boy to man had happened in those fateful few minutes. While the world around him was debating the shocking spectacle that was the nude musical *Hair*, his own sexual revolution was taking place under the candlewick bedspread of the Easy Feelings boarding-house. 'It all took about thirty seconds,' he said, grinning. 'I didn't know any better. But it didn't matter one bit. I felt great. I had my first experience and the weight of sixteen years of confusion was lifted. And I now knew how all the bits fitted together.'

Tim's parents immediately began to notice a change in their son and the circumstances of his board. 'Every morning my breakfast plate would be heaped so high food was falling off. My mammy couldn't understand why I was getting so many extra potato scones. I just grinned because I was in heaven. Every night Edwina would come up to my room and we'd repeat the performance, which I have to say improved a little as the week went on. Suave John and Edwina's pal had conveniently developed the routine of losing themselves and so I had a week of sheer unadulterated bliss—exciting, secretive sex every night and double potato scones every morning.'

But all good things . . .

'On the train going home I was crying. I was gutted. The loss was unbearable. And so when I got back to Easterhouse I wrote to my first love and she wrote back and we kept this up for a year or so and then things faded away.'

The young lady's departure from Tim's memory wasn't the greatest loss in his life that year. He never saw his pal Suave John again. 'Suave John's Uncle Pat died,' said Tim. 'So Suave John never came back up our way. It was a tragedy. I never saw him again.'

Luckily, the loss of his first love and his best pal in the same summer was compensated for by the DJ work that came his way. 'I was doing more and more gigs and loving it. I got a gig at the Maryland in Scott Street. They had a do on a Sunday afternoon called The Miniteens. I was only a young boy so they figured I'd be fine for the thirteen-year-olds' junior disco. It all went well for a couple of months and fortunately the boss, Bob Gardiner, liked me so much he asked me to come and do the seniors on a Friday night. This was the city centre. This was the big time. God, was I excited.

'But on that first Friday night I nearly blew it. The band playing were called The Beings. Needless to say, they were quite a heavy band. And I had this naïve picture in my mind that I'd be following on from them and playing to a crowd of people who would be dancing. But it wasn't like that at all. It was sheer hedonism in nightclub form. Nobody danced. *Nobody.* There were couples lying on the floor on top of each other, faces were being sucked till there was no air left in them, and there was me with my nice smart clothes, my Monkees haircut and my wee box of records. I began by playing all the bubblegum songs like The Tremeloes and it was awful. I was booed and the crowd started shouting and bawling at me. I had nothing else to play but my usual pop records.

'But just as I was about to make headlines "Teen DJ Has Pickety-witch Album Surgically Removed From Rectum—World Exclusive", Bob Gardiner came to my rescue with a couple of Black Sabbath and Deep Purple albums. I learned a couple of things that night. I learned you had to be prepared to play music to suit the crowd and also I realised I had to do something about my appearance. This was now nearly 1969, the time of Jimi Hendrix and Yes and Emerson, Lake and Palmer and I had to appreciate The Monkees' time was over. The experience really made me think about the way I looked. I was nearly seventeen but I looked like a lost soul.'

Drastic measures were called for—although he resisted the temptation to take a walk down to the Separate Centre. 'I couldn't grow my hair that quickly but I decided to go to the City Cash Tailors at Glasgow Cross and buy a kaftan and a pair of herring-bone-style hipster trousers. The problem was that they were woolly and jaggy as hell. I spent whole nights at gigs scratching my legs. Thinking back, I must have looked a sight—this unusual mix of hippy gear and short haircut.'

Regardless, Tim was beginning to be talked about in the East End. 'He was becoming a wee bit of a local celebrity,' recalled Rikki Brown, 'so much so that in the scheme several others followed his lead as a DJ, obviously thinking along the lines of "Well, if he can do it . . ." But there's no doubt he was a bit of a trailblazer. I can remember my pal Brian Macaree buying Tim's worn disco gear and starting up his own mobile DJ business. Showing incredible imagination he picked a name that was entirely appropriate for the period: The San Fran Disco.'

The hard work paid off for Tim when he finally landed work at Glasgow's top nightclub, the Electric Gardens at 490 Sauchiehall Street. The club was not only a disco but a major showcase for bands. The Electric Gardens was owned by an entrepreneur named Frank Lynch, a man who had single-handedly transformed Glasgow's teenage social scene. Former spit-and-sawdust bars were ripped up and replaced with kaleidoscopic chrome palaces such as the Muscular Arms. Lynch combined end-of-the-decade space-age fantasy (after all, a man had now walked on the moon in 1969) with a hard-cash reality and came up with clubs like the Mayfair, the White Elephant and the Electric Gardens. The new wave of nightclubs opened up an opportunity for people like Tim, where a housing-scheme boy could become a star in his own backyard. Before this time if someone wanted to dance to records they'd go to Whitecraigs Tennis Club or whatever. Now kids from housing schemes all around the city could come into town and taste the new glamour and sophistication.

'I heard there were auditions being held up at the Electric Gardens and I decided to give it a go,' said Tim.

Eddie Tobin was the impresario and agent who booked the major acts into the main Glasgow nightclubs at the time. He was the first person at the Gardens to catch sight of the young Tiger. 'I was going down the stairs one night and Tim was coming up and he certainly caught my eye. He was wearing lederhosen at the time.'

Their conversation ran along these lines:

'What do you want?'

'I want a job as a DJ.'

'You've got *no* chance.'

But Eddie was merely testing the young man's resolve. 'He persisted,' said Eddie. 'He kept saying "Look, I can do this, I'm mad, I want the chance of an audition." And you couldn't not give the chance to a guy who'd come to the club wearing leather shorts. He was exactly the style of DJ we were looking for in the club. He fitted the bill perfectly. He was completely off his head. He had no reverence, no respect for anything or anybody.'

Tim was delirious with excitement at being given a chance. 'That was an amazing time for me. Here I was at the top club in Glasgow and I couldn't believe my luck.' Nor could he contain his excitement at his first official meeting with the Electric Gardens team.

'When I met the resident DJ, a guy called Tony Meehan (who is now a major PR boss in Glasgow), he was not only really helpful but had worked on pirate Radio Scotland, and it was as much a thrill meeting him as it was getting the job. Tony had even played my first ever radio request on his show *TM in the AM*. I can remember it. It was The Turtles' *She'd Rather Be with Me*. It came on at five past twelve at night and I ran in to tell my mammy and daddy. They were delighted to be woken up at that time.

'Anyway, before my first official night, Tony invited me along to have a look around and, amazingly, that night Edison Lighthouse were playing live. They were a big band, at no.1 in the charts with *Love Grows Where My Rosemary Goes*.

'So I got all prepared. I washed my hair and wore my new suedette jacket and sunglasses because that was the cool thing to do. Incredibly, the manager Colin Robertson told me I was to introduce them later to the audience.

'I went down to their dressing-room to meet the band and as this was my first time meeting pop stars I was completely starstruck. I led them upstairs and onto the stage and all the time my heart was going like a train and it got worse because I could hear the crowd were going crazy.

'As I hit the stage with the band the girl fans started screaming and grabbing onto my legs—even though they didn't have a clue who I was. The place was absolutely jumping and obviously they thought I was one of the band. I had to fight them off, prying slim little wrists away from my ankles and gasping for breath at the sheer effort. Gradually— thanks to one of the stewards who helped me, a heavy guy called Bobby Preston—I made my way over to the safety of the DJ box. I was thankful still to have all my limbs intact and most of my suedette jacket in one piece but I can clearly remember thinking, "This is the life for me."'

Bobby Preston had a son, also named Bobby, who became a song-writer, and was to help Tim out in later life with a spot of serious seduction. But, for the moment, Tim simply had to get used to the idea he was in disco heaven. He was taken on by Frank Lynch to do three nights a week.

Tim couldn't believe it. Neither could Dora and Jimmy. 'He was seventeen when he started with Frank Lynch,' said his mother, the pride still audible in her voice. 'He was picked out from hundreds of hopefuls and I remember his wages were £3 a night. In the railway he was making £3/17/6d a week. I think that was the turning point for me and his father, realising he could get something out of that sort of life.'

The name Tiger Tim was now to be made known to the world. Or, at least, to the readership of the *Sunday Mail*. 'Every DJ in the club at the time had a stage name, like Gorgeous Gary or Dougall DJ or Tommy Tinsel, which we listed in an advert with the *Sunday Mail*,' said Frank Lynch. 'Tim already had his name so it saved on the inven-tion process.'

Tim's first night working in the Electric Gardens proved to be strange but memorable. 'I was standing down at the snack bar with a Coke having a break during the gig when I spotted this guy staring over at me. He was wearing a long, thick overcoat and sunglasses which I thought odd because we were in a very hot nightclub. The place was roasting. He stared for the longest time and then eventually walked over. He said, "Hi" in a deep drawl that sounded American. "I'm Jet Mayfair." I said "Hello, Mr Mayfair." And he announced that he was a part-owner of the Electric Gardens, alongside Frank Lynch. He went on to tell me he liked my act but had a few pointers as to where I was going wrong. I listened intently and he went through his list. I was in awe of the man because he seemed to talk sense. But as he spoke I began to hear bits of Glasgow in his voice. I was curious, but just then he disappeared and I felt relieved.

'Later than night I was in the office with Frank Lynch and I told him I was talking to his partner. He said, "My partner? What partner?" And I told him about meeting Mr Mayfair. He burst out laughing. And then he told me the story of Jet Mayfair. Jet was—and still is—a Glasgow character who seemed to spend his life in all the clubs, yet who never paid to get into any of them. He was adopted by all the club bosses because he was such an unusual character.'

Jet Mayfair was a Zelig-like creature. Wherever you turned the spotlight, Jet would be there, either mingling with the rest of the social butterflies, looking cool or grabbing a piece of the action. And it was as if everybody in the nightclub world eagerly bought into this alter ego he had developed.

'I've known him years and never found out who he really is,' said Tim. 'But, nevertheless, he's famous—in a Glasgow sense. Although he tried to look and talk like a cool American the reality is he's a tiny bloke. Danny DeVito must be taller than Jet Mayfair. And he's not slim. People describe him as "pyramid-shaped".'

Rikki Brown had another description of Jet: 'He looked exactly like Doberman out of *Bilko*,' said Rikki.

Eddie Tobin explained Jet's rise to Glasgow fame. 'Jet was a go-go dancer,' he said, straight-faced, as if the notion of a beach-ball-shaped character up on a podium made perfect sense, because at the time it probably did. 'He used to be a podium dancer and the company bought him gold lamé suits to wear. He was completely off his head— and Tim fitted Jet into his act.'

Jet (who, incidentally, was incredibly well endowed, as Tim would later discover) was to become a great friend of the DJ. They clearly had something in common. Perhaps it was the same idiosyncratic behaviour. Both were capable of going to the edge and then leaping over.

'At this time,' recalled Tim, 'Frank Lynch used to own a pub in Glasgow in West Nile Street called the Muscular Arms. One day, Jet walked in and sacked all the bar staff. Something annoyed him and he simply told the lot of them to beat it. The staff left. They had imagined Jet had the power because he'd been around so much and been seen with Frank. Luckily, one of the customers phoned Frank Lynch and told him the place was deserted.'

Rikki Brown explained why Jet could get away with murder. 'Frank Lynch regarded Jet as a lucky mascot. Whenever he opened a new pub or club, Jet was there. When Frank later went to America in 1979 to open a nightclub he had Jet and his wife flown out.'

Tim did attempt to uncover the true identity of Jet Mayfair. But the most he learned was that his new pal worked at British Rail's Red Star department in Central Station. 'He told me the only reason he worked there was as an undercover agent. He was working on a case, he told me quietly, that involved drugs being brought into the country wrapped up in Wrigley's Doublemint.'

Nowadays, Jet Mayfair will actually admit he uses an alias. 'I got the "Mayfair" part from working at the Mayfair Club,' he said, teasingly.

'The "Jet" part came from working behind the bar and tossing glasses quickly from one hand to the other. One of the other barmen noticed how fast I was and began calling me Jet.'

He had a sense of humour that clearly matched his pal from the East End. Was that because he was an eastender as well? 'No, I'm more central, originally,' he said. 'Central Memphis.'

Among the Glasgow nightclub set, there seemed to be no problem accepting Jet's tales of fantasy. 'He made people smile,' said Tim. 'He was great. No one had a bad word to say about him. I think they loved the fact that he had the bottle to be whoever he chose to be. And in his head he wanted to be a New York high-flier. But he had such presence people instantly took to him. I remember one night when Slade were appearing and Noddy Holder brought us both on stage to sing *Roll Over Beethoven* with the band. Both Jet and I played a bit of guitar and this was a song we knew. But it wasn't even announced as "Here's Tiger Tim, with his pal Jet Mayfair." It was announced as "Here's Jet Mayfair—with Tiger Tim." Jet was The Man.'

Colin Robertson stressed Tim's—and Jet's—stage appearance with a top band was not unusual. 'You have to remember that Tim was such a personality and a draw at the time. And Jet was Jet. Here were two soul brothers together who loved the limelight. And Jet was never, ever shy.'

Tim explained how he came to know of Jet's enormous reproductive organ. 'One night a band called The Poets were playing and I decided to put on the strobe light for a bit of effect. I had a word with Jet beforehand. I said, "Jet, when the strobe light goes on I want you to get up on stage with the band and see what sort of reaction you get." I thought it would look funny. After all, Jet was wearing a Viking helmet at the time and a fur waistcoat. So I switched on the strobe and Jet made his way to the piano and the band carried on as normal. As I strained my eyes in disbelief I realised Jet was playing the piano, but not with his hands. I couldn't believe it. It was bigger than the horn on the top of his helmet.'

5

Jet, Crabs and Geriatrics

The Electric Gardens' success story continued. Frank Lynch, Eddie Tobin and Colin Robertson could do no wrong. The punters flocked to Sauchiehall Street in their thousands and bands loved to play there. 'Slade loved playing the Electric Gardens so much they promised us that when they hit the big time they would come back and do their first concert with us,' said Eddie Tobin. 'They did. And we broke the club record with 1800 people squeezed in. We also had T-Rex and Pink Floyd and Deep Purple for the Monday-night crowd. Luckily, they hit no.1 with *Black Night* just after we booked them.'

Even when the bands were less than successful there was fun to be had and the team kept the show going. 'One night we booked Thunderclap Newman,' recalled Colin Robertson, laughing at the memory. 'And in walked this old, knackered guy. Thunderclap? He didn't even look like a tiny cloudburst. But if we had a band on and the dance-floor wasn't busy—some bands simply couldn't do it and they became collectively known as Freddie and the Snack-Bar Fillers—we always knew that Tim could fill the floor.'

Eddie Tobin highlighted such a case. 'Manfred Mann was a classic example of this. We had booked Manfred, who was a big, big name, a superstar at the time, but he came up to Glasgow just as he'd turned himself into The Earth Band. His head was full of absolute shit. And, believe it or not, he opened up the set with *There'll Always Be an England*.

'You'd think some alien had fired a death-ray because suddenly everyone on the dance-floor was gone. There were no *Doowadiddy-diddies* that night. Just a diddy. So we pulled the plug on him after about ten seconds and the next thing the Tiger was up there saying, "Manfred seems to have a little problem with his equipment. Meantime, here's a great new record . . ." He handled it like a dream. You could always rely on him. He had such a feel for what the punters wanted at any given time. He played good music then and he still does nowadays. He's always had great light-music tastes.

'What we had at the club was a collection of very different characters. Tony Meehan on the one hand was intense and could make you cry. God only knows what dark secrets were in that man's mind! But he was terrific and always laidback.'

Tim was so good he became the resident DJ on Fridays, Saturdays and Sundays. 'He would wear pyjamas on stage,' said Colin Robertson. 'Tim had no problem being outrageous. Yet he didn't stand out just because of what he wore. Or rather didn't wear—I began to notice he had a propensity for dropping his trousers and revealing some really shocking underpants. He stood out for his technique. Most of the DJs doing the rounds tended to be mobile DJs who wanted to work different clubs and do the odd night. But Tim treated it like a full-time business. And as such he became very good very quickly—he couldn't get any better. He had an uncanny way of talking to the people who weren't that bright and to those who were a bit more switched on. He was a punter's DJ. The punters liked him and they could relate to him.'

Frank Lynch, now in America and running carwash businesses in the southern states, recalled what made the young DJ from Easterhouse stand out. 'He was prepared to do anything for the sake of the club. He was totally committed to getting a result. And that meant getting the punters to dance and to like him. Tim didn't care if he was cool or not. While most of the guys in Glasgow were wrapped up in image and wouldn't dress up unless it made them look like James Dean or a sex machine, Tim would send himself up mercilessly. He was prepared to sacrifice his dignity.'

The nightclub boss likened Tim's attitude to a North American ethos. 'The feeling here in America is that people will do anything so long as it works and they get paid for it. That was the way Tim thought. For a seventeen-year-old, he was ahead of his time. And he was professional. Some DJs would oversell themselves at the expense of the music. Tim played the records, got people to dance, *then* bothered about being noticed.'

Eddie Tobin disagreed about Tim being prepared to sacrifice his dignity and later club and theatre experiences would prove him right. Tim was prepared to send himself up to the point where he would get laughs, but not to the point where he'd be laughed at. While Tim's stint at the Electric Gardens was crazed at times it was all on his terms—and he was comfortable with that. And none of it did anything but improve his reputation as an entertainer. 'He was a local superstar,' said Eddie Tobin. 'There's no doubt. There were other DJs in the Gardens but to them it was just a job. Not with Tim. Tim wasn't playing or practising or working at it: all that madness *was* him. You can't sustain it unless you are that mad. And a lot of what Tim did was spontaneous. He was the first DJ to run competitions such as the first girl who brings a pair of white knickers up to the stage gets an LP. It was mad, risqué and a little bit dangerous. Nowadays, DJs will do this and it seems a bit tacky. No one took offence at Tim because, as he still does now, he put people at ease. He was the best of that genre of DJs. This was the time when you really had to have a personality to be a jock.'

That's not to say life in the Gardens was always rosy for the young jock. Eddie picked up on other unusual personality traits. 'He has the highs and lows of a comedian. The performance could leave him seriously upset if he felt he hadn't done his best. Today's DJs don't care, emotionally; whether the hall or the promoter is satisfied is absolutely irrelevant. No matter if you pay five grand for club DJs, you still get acts who fundamentally don't care that much. Tim would care every time.'

Colin Robertson agreed about Tim's devotion to work. 'Eddie had an agency at the time and Tim did gigs everywhere. He was very successful. But sometimes he'd be offered gigs and he'd turn them down. The money was good but he reckoned the show wouldn't be what he wanted it to be, whether it was something to do with the hall or the crowd, and he'd complain on that basis to the agents. A lot of DJs would have said, "I'll take the twenty quid, thanks very much," and run—but Tim would say, "I'm not going back there."'

Like his pal Jet, Tim was still working for British Rail during the day. He was DJing at the Electric Gardens three nights a week and, as his fame grew, he was offered more and more outside gigs. But he needed transport. He could no longer rely on his dad's train pass. As luck would have it, he passed his driving test at the first attempt. 'I'd only had twelve lessons,' he said, proudly.

Having passed his test, Tim planned to buy a car, but coincidentally his Auntie Joy, who lived in Mount Vernon, offered him her old Ford Popular. 'I think I ended up giving her a tenner for it, just so that it wouldn't look like charity,' he said, 'and it was a great car except that it wouldn't start in the mornings.'

Without any degree of shame whatsoever, Tim revealed how he managed to get his car running. And if any of the women who were to play a part in his future saw how he operated, they'd have been given an indication as to their future role in the relationship. 'What I would do is get Mrs Thorpe, who lived at number 7 across the road, to come out and push the car till I bump-started it.' It didn't once occur to Tim to let Mrs Thorpe put the car into gear while he pushed from behind. 'Mrs Thorpe was a big woman,' he said without a trace of conscience. 'She was a very strong lady and she could handle the hill no bother.'

The little Ford gave Dora sleepless nights. Her boy, she learned via the grapevine, was using it to ferry young ladies home from the clubs. 'I worried when he was out in it,' she said. 'I would be awake till he came in at two in the morning but pretend I was asleep.'

Perhaps Dora should have been worried about what her son was up to during daylight hours. On his way into town Tim made a habit of popping into R.S. McColl's to pick up a Mars Bar and an *Evening Times*. The young woman behind the counter was a fan from the Electric Gardens. And, more often than not, just as it was near to closing time, the cute blonde would take Tim into the stock room and show him the full range of confectionery. Then, of course, he'd go to work at the disco and find himself running yet another young lady home. Life was an endless cycle of Mars Bars, playing music, psychedelic lighting and long detours home.

At this point Tim, now eighteen, was introduced to the world of drugs for the first time. He was feeling very grown up. He even felt bold enough to dabble. 'I tried cannabis one night at the Electric Gardens,' he said, shaking his head as a reminder of his regret. 'One of the girls there had some, but I nearly choked on the stuff and felt violently sick. I vowed never to take it again. And since I hate people smoking it's not really surprising I felt so awful having taken it.'

Back in the real world, the railway world, Tim made it into work each day on time but his heart wasn't in it. It never had been, really, but he knew he had to go through the process that led to future security. After a night at the Electric Gardens he'd haul himself into the yard where he'd do the odd bit of wiring while still singing the hits of the day.

Hashish experiences apart, life was great. He had a trade, a car and he also had the most glamorous night job in the city. But although he figured he was now an adult (the days of the Monkees hat were now long gone), Tim wasn't as worldly wise as he would have liked to think. The female fashion at the time was hot pants. It also turned out to be a medical condition contracted by unfortunate Tigers. One morning at the yard Tim spent his break-time scratching frantically around his underpants. His journeyman, John Sweeney, noticed the teenager had a problem and offered to make a clinical diagnosis. 'He told me to go into the toilet and have a good hard look and see if I could see things crawling around. And then he told me to pull out one of my pubic hairs,' said Tim. 'At first I refused but then bowed to his apparent knowledge of such subjects. I did what he asked. I had a right good look and was horrified to discover things were moving around. So I did as John Sweeney suggested, I pulled a hair out and took it back to him.'

John had a microscope in the office and with the precision and skill of a research scientist, he put this single Tiger hair under the microscope and confirmed his initial suspicions. 'You've got crabs, Tim, son.'

'Crabs? Crabs are what you get at Saltcoats when you go digging under rocks with your daddy!'

But no. John filled Tim in on the reality of the infestation—and he was horrified. 'I would have cried if I hadn't been so grown up. Luckily, he assured me he had a solution to the problem. He told me to go home and shave off all my pubic hair, and then to go into the medicine cabinet and get my dad's Old Spice aftershave and splash it on. He assured me that would kill off the beasties. I did this. And everybody in Easterhouse heard me scream. The next day I went into work and there was John Sweeney and his mates laughing like lunatics. And I still had crabs.

'I had no option but to go to the doctor and confess my condition. The first thing he said to me, amazingly, was: "Have you been sleeping out?" I mumbled something about not really knowing. Then he took a look for himself and was amazed when he discovered that my groin looked like a coconut. He told me I was an idiot for shaving myself.

'I asked him if he could cure me. He said, "Don't be stupid, you silly boy, of course I can cure you." And he gave me the ointment that sorted me in a day.'

Tim was never sure who had been the donor. Still, he was cured and he could go about the business of life with a light heart and lice-free loins.

His next sexual encounter occurred not long after he'd been to the doctor in Easterhouse. 'I took this girl home one night in the Ford and her hands began to wander. At first I was delighted but then I realised I was still in Yul Bryner condition. To her credit, she didn't bat an eyelid. Maybe she thought I was really kinky.'

Jet Mayfair reckoned it wouldn't have mattered at the time if Tim had shaved his head. 'There were women all over the Tiger,' he said. 'Tim was a disco superstar. That might sound like an exaggeration but for these teenage girls he was the real thing. He would get up on stage with pop stars like David Bowie—this was his *Space Oddity* time—and the girls all screamed for him. What was even better was they could get Tim, whereas David Bowie was a bit more difficult.'

Jet was right. The dawning of the new decade meant the breaking-down of a lot of barriers to sex. Women were becoming more sexually aggressive and they would now set the agenda. They'd all seen Woodstock in the movies. They'd seen Jane Fonda in *Barbarella*. 'It was just so easy for him. As time went on he dressed more and more outrageously in his tiger outfits and catsuits and the girls loved all of this. He was something different. 'I can remember one night a bouncer grabbed Tim and me as we were about to leave the club. He said, "Don't go out there. There are dozens of girls and they're after your bodies." Now, I know you think I'm making this up but remember we were up on stage every night and we were the closest these girls were ever likely to come to stars. That night we left by the back door. It wasn't that we were shy. It was more to do with the fact that we wanted to have had some say in the matter.'

Tim and Jet, the fast-growing double act, were often paired outside the Electric Gardens.

The gigs, as you would imagine, came with a warning of unpredictability. One night Tim turned up to play at the White Elephant in Sauchiehall Street, which also belonged to Frank Lynch, on the night the club was booked by the Young Christian Mothers Association. There were priests, nuns, ministers—some very spiritual people there. And while Tim was playing easy-listening chart music, in strode Jet. 'You couldn't miss him,' said Tim. 'He was wearing a full archbishop's outfit. Frank Lynch had clearly had the idea of dressing Jet up to suit the occasion. The crowd turned to look at him as he walked in and were totally convinced by it all. After all, he had the mitre, the staff with the crooked handle, the lot—and, most of all, he had a particularly pious look on his face.

'Anyway, I figured it would be a good idea to get him up on stage. I called out and asked if he wanted to come up and he replied, "Yeah, man," in his customary manner. Luckily no one heard the Archbishop speaking in a New York accent and up he came.

'Frank had also given Jet a new name for the evening. He was to be Archbishop White. The big mistake I made was in introducing him. I should have let it be. I announced, "Ladies and gentlemen, I'd like you to meet Archbishop White—and he'd like to say a few words to you this evening." And there was huge, deafening applause from all the happy-clappy youngsters. Jet, of course, wallowed in all this and played the part perfectly, even giving little dignified waves of acknowledgement. And then he spoke to the crowd saying, "Bless you, my children," maintaining a serene voice. But just as I faded in a record, Jet's voice suddenly boomed out over the PA system: "Okay, now kick out the jams, you motherfuckers!"'

Frank Lynch had turned up right at that moment. 'I can remember sinking to the floor laughing,' said the club boss. 'None of us, especially Jet, had any idea he would come out with that. You could have heard a pin drop.'

Tim didn't know whether to laugh or cry that night. But the following night when he played a gig at the Brunswick Club in Balornock, he was to walk away with a smile the size of the housing scheme. The gig had gone well, but afterwards, when Tim popped into the toilet, he found himself encountering a face from the past. 'I found myself looking at this guy next to me at the urinals because for some reason he looked familiar. It took a little while because it had been a couple of years but eventually it dawned on me. I said to him, "Are you Andy Lamb?" And he looked at me for a few seconds before muttering, "I don't believe it! It's you!" With this realisation, all sorts of memories came flooding back. I could almost feel the swarfiga in my pants as I stood next to him. I could almost feel the embarrassment I'd suffered at his hands that day at the railway shed when he'd held me down. So I got angry and I began to swear—by this time I did swear—so I said to him, "You'd better fucking believe it!" But I didn't hit him or anything. I honestly figured it wasn't worth it—especially when he didn't seem as big or as tough as he had appeared back then. And he certainly didn't act it.'

Tim was now officially a grown-up although he often did his best to convince others that this was not the case. His gigs were still a creative mix of good music and madness that fitted in perfectly at the Electric Gardens, but Tim's style wasn't perfect for every music medium.

John MacAlman is now a production boss at Radio Clyde. Thirty years ago he was one of the founders of hospital radio in Glasgow. 'We advertised for people to come and work on Hospital Radio Phoenix, which was based in an attic in West Campbell Street and used to broadcast to geriatric hospitals in the area,' recalled John. 'One day Tiger Tim Stevens came in to see us and he was as keen as mustard, although he looked very young. We asked if he had DJ experience and he said yes, and I remember the little test we gave him. It was a Mama Cass record *It's Getting Better* and the task was to introduce the record by talking over the instrumental without crashing into the vocal. This may sound straightforward, but it was a very difficult song to talk into. It was difficult to predict when the singing kicked in. But of course Tim got it spot on. He was a natural.'

But the Tiger never made it onto the air at any of the hospitals the station served. 'We let him do production work and I think eventually he may have been allowed on air at something like five in the morning. But we felt he was too wild, too dangerous, with little control over what would come out of his mouth. We thought there was a real chance he might send the patients over the edge.'

The radio dream still occupied Tim's thoughts for most of the time. And when one day he heard that BBC legend David Symonds was coming to Glasgow—he of the Light Programme and now with Radio One—this was a chance to meet a superstar, to worship at the feet of a radio god. David Symonds was to appear at the Electric Gardens and Tim decided he had to make an impression on the man he'd admired for so many years. So he turned up at the gig and presented the man from Auntie with an engraved haggis. David Symonds was touched by the gesture and had positive words of encouragement for his young fan with the haggis and the pyjama-striped trousers. 'You've got to believe in what you're doing and believe in yourself,' he enthused. 'And, more importantly, you've got to *be* yourself.'

The words were instantly etched in Tim's brain. He had to follow his own path. He had to follow his own instincts. For the moment it was difficult when most of his daily life was taken up fitting coloured wires into junction boxes. But that was to change.

6

Railway Exits, the Funeral and Hughie Green

Tim's success in clubland saw his confidence soar. Each night he'd give a performance that only enhanced his reputation as the most colourful and successful DJ in the area. As the demand for his talents grew, he reckoned he'd had enough of life as an apprentice. At nineteen, Tim hadn't finished his trade—he had another year to go—but it all seemed so unimportant. He was working as a DJ, something he'd dreamt about and, from his point of view, the choice was fairly straightforward. Not once had he ever imagined himself as a locomotive electrician. 'It was supposed to be a five-year apprenticeship but at this time I thought, "What am I doing here?" All I knew was that I wanted to be in showbiz, as an actor or a singer or a disc jockey. I wanted to do anything but wire up locomotives.

'There was one big problem, however. My dad was desperate for me to stay on at the railway and to finish my time and of course he tried to talk me out of leaving. But I knew I wasn't learning anything. Although I had passed my City and Guilds certificates, I wasn't achieving anything. In retrospect, I wish I'd finished my apprenticeship, if only to give my dad the peace of mind that went with knowing his son had a trade. My dad, after all, had got the job for me and I know how much he wanted me to have security. But in the end he was great about it and said I should lead my own life.'

Dora found the news hard to take. 'I was breaking my heart when he told me he was leaving,' she recalled. 'It meant he wouldn't finish his trade and I really went to town about it. I thought the DJ thing was a lot of nonsense. But, surprisingly, his father took a different view. When we talked it over Jimmy said he should get the chance to do what he really wanted in life. I'm sure that had a lot to do with Jimmy being a bit of a performer.'

Dora revealed there was more to it. 'I learned later on that Jim's father had once did a gig as a singer, playing at some town hall, and he actually won a talent contest. But his own father wouldn't let him take it any further. I'm fairly sure that's why Jimmy was more understanding than I was when our son wanted to give up the railway.'

The Electric Gardens was to offer Tim far more than Glasgow star status and the financial rewards that allowed him to buy a nice grey Morris Oxford. It was there he met the girl who was to become his wife. 'Love is never less than complicated,' he recalled. 'I had a regular girlfriend, her name was Cathy Rae—well, we weren't that serious, there were a lot of distractions around at that time—and she came from Easterhouse. She worked at the disco in the cloakroom. But while I was seeing Cathy I became friendly with a girl called Clare who worked in the snack bar. And every night at the end of the gig I'd play *You've Got a Friend* by James Taylor and I'd dedicate it to Clare. We became good pals. No romance developed, though, because she knew I was seeing Cathy. However, one night Cathy suggested we give Clare a lift home because she lived in Cranhill which is just along the road. And this sort of developed into a regular thing with me and Cathy in the front and Clare in the back. I used to look at Clare in the rearview mirror and she'd smile really sweetly. I was a bit more than intrigued, I have to admit.

'One night when Cathy wasn't working I ran Clare home. We just sat outside her house for ages, talking about anything and everything and eventually I worked up the courage to kiss her. Of course, Cathy heard about it. I guess Clare must have told a pal who then told someone else—it was pretty hard to keep secrets in Glasgow clubland—and one night as I came off stage Cathy came storming towards me and yelled, "You, you're a bastard!" And with those words she cracked me right on the jaw. It was a helluva thump.'

Cathy's public retribution sealed the fate of the relationship and that released Tim and Clare to carry on seeing each other. 'From that point on I saw Clare,' said Tim. 'I had my first official girlfriend.'

Tim, still mammy and daddy's little boy, found telling his parents he had a steady girlfriend quite a daunting prospect. 'I told them I was bringing Clare home to meet them, but I was really awkward about the situation. I was worried about getting their approval, I guess, so I made light of the whole thing. I told them she had a hump and she was tiny, almost a dwarf, in fact, but that she was a really nice girl. It was a bit of reverse psychology, I suppose, to detract from the usual questioning a boy would get when he brought a girl home for the first time.'

Dora and Jimmy were pleasantly surprised to discover Clare's growth wasn't restricted after all and that in fact she was pretty with long curly brown hair. 'He came in one night and asked if he could bring his girlfriend up for tea,' said Dora. 'He had said she had skelly eyes and bowley legs. And I remember his father at the time saying, "You know, Dora, it might be true. You know how he always goes for the underdog." But luckily it wasn't at all. I nearly died when I saw this dolly-bird with the mini-skirt coming out of the car. She was a beautiful-looking girl.'

Dora wasn't convinced that Tim and Clare were a match made in heaven, however. 'I think she was a lot older in the head than he was.'

Tim, naturally enough, developed a strong relationship with Clare's brothers Kevin and Jim. The McGinlay brothers played in local bands with their singer friend, Midge Ure. Midge was clearly intent on forging ahead in the pop business. 'One day Midge bought this second-hand piano and asked us all for help to take it to his house in Cambuslang,' recalled Tim. 'The three of us were humphing this piano up the stairs to Midge's bedroom while down below he was calling out instructions: "A wee bit to the right . . . Don't bump it!" while the other guys and I were breaking our backs lugging this great upright. I looked down and shouted, "Ure, you bastard, it's your bloody piano!" And to give him credit he had the cheek to laugh. It was clear from that time on that he was going to be the leader of the band. But he was a lovely guy.'

Midge wasn't the only one who was aiming high. Tim, too, was determined to make the big time. The reputation of the Tiger Tim Roadshow was developing but he desperately wanted more. He wanted to be a real radio star. He wanted to be David Symonds with a Scots accent. But there weren't many options in Scotland. He had been rejected (nicely) by the BBC, and hospital radio deemed him too dangerous to be let loose on their airwaves. Tim reckoned he had to try the big one, Radio One, and go for broke. One night he and Clare, to whom he had at some point in the past few weeks become unofficially engaged, hatched a plan. They would make a cracking demo tape, take a day off work and both physically take it down to Broadcasting House in London. Tim was sure that his efforts would not go unnoticed and, accordingly, not be in vain.

Since Tim was not a natural traveller, however, the journey didn't go quite to plan. 'We set off in my newish little red Fiat van and things went well until we got to the outskirts of Coventry. We were running out of petrol and I pulled into a garage. It wasn't self-service, it was the old-fashioned sort where somone fills it up for you. Anyway, after a few minutes this rather odd-looking petrol-pump bloke came out.

I said, "Can you fill it up, please?" And he replied something that sounded like "Duh?". I repeated the request and got the same answer from him. At the third time of trying and him saying "Duh?" I just said, "Yeah, yeah, that's right." And he filled up the car okay and we drove off and when we got about a couple of miles down the road the engine conked out. It was dead. It wouldn't start. Instead it made choking noises like a dying elephant. There was no choice but to call in the RAC, who towed us to another garage in the centre of Coventry.'

The garage mechanic announced he would have to clean out the entire engine. He said the tank was full of diesel. 'Instead of putting petrol in the car that pump attendant had put in diesel. He hadn't been saying "Duh?" to me. He'd been saying "Derv?". To be honest, even if I'd heard him say "Derv?", I'd have said, "Yeah, sure." I didn't even know the difference.'

The plan had been to drive through the night and reach London by the crack of dawn. At nine o'clock the next morning they eventually made it, tired and weary but excited at the notion of being close to the steps of the biggest radio station in the world.

At the backstreets of the West End, Tim crawled into the back of the van to get changed, to make an impression at the BBC. The outfit he had brought with him certainly had that effect. 'I got changed into a woman's dress, a black-and-orange frock,' he recalled, without sounding in the least bit embarrassed. But, then again, Tim had been wearing women's clothing on a regular basis since the first Electric Gardens days. 'And for some reason I can remember the label read "36-24-36", and I wore it with an African hunter's hat with a squirrel tail on top, a huge broad thing.' To top off the ensemble, Tim wore a pair of wellies. And under his arm he carried the perfect accessory—a cuddly tiger.

Leaving Clare in the car, he strolled off towards the marble-walled home of the centre of world broadcasting, wearing an outfit you wouldn't be seen dead in at Hallowe'en. Even for a bet.

'At the reception desk I asked for Johnny Beerling whom I knew was the production boss at Radio One. The woman told me he wasn't in yet but to take a seat. So I did. Literally. I walked over, picked up a chair and headed for the door, thinking this was quite funny. I guess I had been watching too many Cliff Richard movies in the 1960s. Anyway, as I got to the door the commissionaire stopped me, a big bloke in a big uniform who stuck his arm out and said, "Where do you think you're going, son? Sit on your backside."'

As people made their way into the building to go to work they all looked very strangely at this Scot with the hideous dress and probably reckoned they were seeing their first public display of transvestitism. Tim got many strange looks, most of them pitying.

'I waited there for two hours but there was no sign of Johnny Beerling,' said Tim, recalling the sense of frustration. 'Mind you, he could have walked by and I wouldn't have known.'

Seven years later Tim would meet Johnny Beerling. But, for the moment, he reckoned the Radio One adventure was at an end. After driving five hundred miles through the night, having to pay for garage bills for an complete engine overhaul and going to the bother of dressing up like Margaret Rutherford's Scots cousin, he simply handed in the tape and headed for home—and waited for the letter telling him how Radio One had loved his demo. 'About a week later I got a letter from the BBC,' he said. 'It was a polite note which basically said "Get lost".'

Tim was devastated. His gigs were going well but he needed that break into the big time. Never one to surrender to pessimism, he sat down and wrote to every television company in Britain, asking if they had any shows which were crying out for an appearance by a young

Glaswegian extrovert. He heard nothing. But that week all thoughts of ambition were to be banished from his head as he coped with family tragedy.

On St Valentine's Day Tim's dad, Jimmy, set off for work as usual at the British Rail shed at Springburn. Tim was still in bed when he heard someone banging the door repeatedly. It was their neighbour, Mrs Bambrick, and she was clearly distraught. 'She shouted out to my mammy, "Jimmy's collapsed at the bus stop!" And my mother panicked. She was in a real state. I said something about staying calm and jumped in my car and headed for the bus-stop.

'There he was lying on the grass verge and I ran over to him. I knelt down beside him and began shouting to him, "Daddy, Daddy, are you all right?" I began to panic. I didn't know what to do. I think I might have tried to open his shirt or something, I'm not really sure—it was just so confusing.

'But he didn't speak. I think he was still breathing, though. I wanted to believe that, anyway. I just wanted someone to come and help him, to make him better. Shortly after that, the ambulance arrived and the drivers jumped out and one of them began to push his chest to try and resuscitate him. I was sure that would work. But as one guy was pushing his chest I became aware the other guy was walking towards me and my daddy with a big sheet. And the next thing he did was to put it over my daddy's head. I was stunned, but I knew what it meant. They both picked him up and put him in the back of the ambulance and I followed my dad into the back. But the driver stopped me and said, "Where are you going, son?" as if I were a two-year-old. And I yelled, "That's my daddy!" The driver looked very apologetic and said he was sorry.'

Tim then knew the task he had facing him. He had to tell his mother that her husband, at the age of fifty-one, was dead. 'I left the car at the bus-stop and walked the long way back to my house. I had to try and clear my head. And I was terrified of having to tell my mother. Eventually, I walked up the stairs at 19 Banton Place and it was the longest climb of my life. Inside the house, way at the end of the lobby, was my mother. She immediately called out: "Is he all right, then, Jim?"

'My voice broke and I said, "My daddy's dead." And my mother began to scream. It was devastating. We spent the rest of the day in tears.'

The impact on Tim was far worse than he could have imagined. 'It had a profound effect on me. It made me grow up—well, initially. He had been the guy who had played football with me. He'd taken me into British Rail. He had been the one who'd instilled in me a work ethic and given me the belief that anything was possible.'

It was obvious that Tim was still saddened by the memory of that awful Valentine's Day. 'He was the one who made it all happen for me. He gave me the money to buy my record-player, my first record decks. And, suddenly, he was gone. If I could have had one wish it would have been that he lived to see me make it at Radio Clyde. It would have been a great thank-you for what he did for me.

'There's another reason why I miss him. If he'd lived longer I'm sure he'd have been my manager and I'm sure things would have been very different.'

Dora recalled how badly her son was affected by the tragic death of Jimmy, who'd suffered a fatal heart attack. 'Jimmy was never off work and that made it all the more shocking. Jim took it very badly. The stress of it all was awful for him. I remember thinking he was taking it so badly it would affect him in later life. He still can't talk about him,' she said. 'He still misses his daddy.'

A week after the death, Tim received a letter in the mail that was to induce bittersweet feelings. It was a letter from the producers of *The Sky's the Limit*, a post-*Opportunity Knocks* vehicle for the cheesy Hughie Green and his long-time TV sidekick stray, Monica Rose. The show was made by Yorkshire Television for ITV and was a popular quiz at the time. The circular Tim had sent to every TV company in the land had paid off. But the excitement was tinged with deep regret. 'I wanted my daddy to see me on national television,' said Tim. 'Somehow it all felt a bit hollow with him gone. But I decided to go nonetheless. My daddy knew what this sort of opportunity meant for me and I know he'd have wanted me to see it through.'

Tim decided to milk his moment of fame for all it was worth. 'I travelled down to Leeds on the train, eager and prepared to make the most of it.'

For his television début he decided, not surprisingly, that he would dress for the occasion. He wore a top-hat, a tiger waistcoat, a kilt and a frock-coat with huge white bobbles. To complete the outfit he pulled on a pair of dirty black wellies. Just to add to the awfulness of the picture, perhaps the worst part of the way he looked was that he had grown a Jason King moustache at the time . . .

Tim's appearance was to cause problems—not with the studio bosses who reckoned he was just the thing to brighten up an otherwise dull show, but with a studio electrician as Tim had a cup of tea prior to the start of the programme. 'I got into an argument with one of the studio hands in the canteen,' said Tim. 'He marched up to me and said very aggressively, "Where did you get that kilt? That's a Black Watch tartan." It could have been a Brigadoon tartan for all I knew, but I said, "Yes, so what? Someone loaned it to me." And I thought that was the end of the matter but this guy got really upset and very angry. He yelled at me that his uncle had fought with the Black Watch regiment and maintained that only those chosen few could wear the tartan. He yelled about dishonour and death or something like that and then started to shove me about. And of course I shoved him back and before you knew it, it was a handbags-at-dawn situation in a TV station canteen. I thought to myself, "I never got this much aggro in Easterhouse and now some looney Englishman is looking to remember his roots via my face." Luckily, others came to separate us and it all cooled down. But a stooshie about a kilt is the last thing you need before you're about to go on television.'

In front of the cameras, things went more smoothly. 'Hughie introduced me: "Here he is, Tiger Tim from Glasgow. And what do you do, Tim?" And I told him I worked for the Electric Gardens, which later proved to be a very good thing to say because I had got in a little plug for the club without realising it. Then I had to go about answering questions on pop music from listening to tunes played by a surreal little three-piece band, banging out disco songs from the charts. Meantime, Monica was dancing around like a little pixie. It was madness and I was in my element.

'I seem to remember I was doing pretty well in the competition but it's hard to be sure because Hughie began showing me the cards with the answers on them. I don't know if it was deliberate because he liked me or not, but as he read out the questions he held the big cards at just the right angle. I'd like to be able to say I ignored this tainted golden opportunity and gave the answer in my head but that wouldn't be true. I had a couple of squints and gave him the answer on the card.'

Remarkably, in spite of having a helping hand, Tim didn't win the coveted prize of a washing-machine or whatever. He came second. But on his return to the Electric Gardens Frank Lynch had a consolation prize waiting for him. 'He was delighted I had got in a plug for the club,' said Tim. 'He stuck an extra fiver in my wage packet.'

Rikki Brown remembered Tim's TV appearance as a defining

moment for many people in Easterhouse. 'One minute the artist formerly known as Jim McGrory was doing mobile discos about the scheme and the next here he was reincarnated on television as Tiger Tim. Tiger Tim? I had to look hard to see if it was the same person.

'Now, I'm not saying he was a quietly spoken character before this moment, but he had up to this point dressed fairly normally—in the scheme at least. Now he looked nuts. And people in Easterhouse thought so as well. In fact, after this they refused to call him Tiger Tim Stevens. They called him Cat Stevens because the feeling was that he was getting far too full of himself and this was their way of reminding him he was too timid to be anything other than a pussycat.'

Luckily, not everyone derided Tim at this time.

7

Marriage, Frogs and Alice Cooper

Clare thought Tim was a real pussycat. She was counting the days till the wedding. The couple had talked about cancelling their Easter nuptials after the death of Tim's dad but it was Dora who insisted they go ahead as planned. 'I wasn't happy about him getting married so young,' she said. 'I didn't think it was the right thing to do and I always felt Clare wasn't exactly right for him. But I didn't have a problem with Jim marrying so soon after the death. I said to him: "Go ahead. Not getting married won't bring your father back."'

Tim and Clare married in Cranhill where Clare had been brought up. He was just twenty and she was twenty-one. He wore a Tommy Nutter-style suit with the fashionable wide lapels and flared trousers. 'You don't know any better when you're that age,' he said. 'At that time everybody married fairly young and getting married was what you did. It felt right.'

The wedding in Cranhill was attended by vast legions of friends and family. There was one difficult moment however during the ceremony. 'The priest kept getting my name wrong—or right, as it happened. He would say, "Do you, Jim—I mean, Tim, no, Jim—take this woman . . ."' At that time I hadn't officially changed it. The whole process of deed poll seemed like too much hassle so I never bothered.' At this time Clare was working as a beauty consultant at McDonald's-Fraser's. Tim's best man was his brother-in-law, Jim, which no doubt added to the confusion.

The groom admitted he was pleased to see one ex-girlfriend make an appearance. 'Cathy Rae showed up,' recalled Tim. 'It was a nice gesture on her part.'

The honeymoon was his old favourite holiday resort, Blackpool, and the couple stayed at the Mayfair boarding-house. Thoughts of wild nights with Edwina and Suave John McDade were well in the past.

Back home, the couple moved in with Dora at Banton Place. 'We stayed in Easterhouse with my mammy because my father had died and it was hard to leave her on her own. Eventually, we got a flat in Partick and I have to admit it was a very difficult time for me, putting all my stuff in the van and waving goodbye.'

Tim and Clare weren't exactly moving into uncharted territory. Their new flat was in Gardner Street in Partick. After all, he used to go there every weekend to stay with his granny in Hyndland Street. And having played football in Partick with the Kelly Babes, he knew a lot of people in the area.

The flat had two rooms, a kitchen and a bathroom and Tim set about decorating it as tastefully as possible. 'I decided to paint the kitchen, making three walls white and the fourth an attractive shade of what I thought was peach,' he remembered, shaking his head in disbelief. 'I hadn't a clue. The paint dried in a shiny orange, because I had used gloss instead of emulsion. I can tell you, nobody felt like eating much in that kitchen!'

An unusual feature was the door of the flat. Tim had a twelve-inch-wide letterbox fitted so the postman could deliver LPs.

The couple settled down to married life. It was an unusual situation because Tim would work at night and Clare would work during the day at McDonald's. They decided they'd do something about that so both took jobs at a record shop in Bath Street called Hades. It made sense. Tim was gigging a lot but the fiver a night he earned wasn't fantastic money—certainly not when you compare it to what DJs earn today. To put Tim's fee in perspective, the average weekly wage at the time was fifteen pounds. 'I was working downstairs in the Heavy Metal section while Clare was upstairs in Pop,' said Tim. 'It worked out okay and we didn't see too much of each other during the day. And it was a means of making a bit more money to go towards kitting out the flat.

'I was a pretty rotten manager,' he admitted. 'I was bored. I really used to look forward to my lunch, which was a sausage roll and a snowball from the City Bakeries next door.'

The record-shop money came in handy although Tim didn't enjoy the job. He wasn't a natural organiser or a manager and the idea of having any sort of responsibility filled him with dread. Worst of all, the nine-to-five containment left him all too subdued. Luckily, his gigs in the following year saw his popularity in the area soar.

Another drastic change was to come about in Tim's life. Frank Lynch had given up the Electric Gardens and set up a new disco in the city. The team moved up into Clouds, a state-of-the-art disco six floors above the Apollo Theatre, which had previously been Green's Play-house.

'Clouds was a unique disco,' said Colin Robertson. 'We had the best of everything, including the best DJ talent. In the early weeks, Eddie Tobin came up with the idea of using a resident band. They were called Salvation, and Eddie brought in a young man called Midge Ure to front them. The whole thing worked incredibly well. The place was packed out.'

Tim took up the story. 'It was up in the clouds and I think that's where my head was at the time,' he recalled. 'Coming from the Electric Gardens with Frank, Eddie and Colin, I was looking forward to being the main DJ at this new venue. But the reality was a little different. The first thing that Frank Lynch did was to change my name. He reckoned the public had had enough of the Tiger. He decided I'd be known as the Frog. He even had a giant frog outfit made with a green nylon all-in-one suit with flippers at the bottom. I had to climb up into the DJ turret and speak only in frog speak. My voice is normally a bit croaky but not *that* croaky. And of course this suit with the giant frog's head weighed a ton. To make it worse, nobody ever saw my face. In fairness to Frank Lynch, though, he was very inventive and you had to laugh at his imagination.'

Colin Robertson painted a very different picture to Tim's pragmatic recollections of life as a record-playing amphibian. 'For some reason Frank decided that the DJ couldn't be known. There was no real logic to it, but he wanted total anonymity. So Tim had to get changed in the manager's office and make his way along the hall to the DJ turret. He hated it with a vengeance. Physically, the head was huge and to put on his croak every night was soul-destroying, especially when you consider the rapport Tim had had with the punters at the Electric Gardens. All of this was negated for the sake of a wacky idea. But, then, Frank Lynch was the man for wacky ideas.'

Eddie Tobin agreed: 'I'm not sure why the DJ had to be in a frog's suit. I was running the place and I never got any explanation. And, thinking back, perhaps it was more to do with Frank's cockney partner, Max Langdon. Mind you, it could have been any of us having to wear the frog outfit. You see, it was a fun organisation—we could be asked to do anything, like fixing it for Slade to drive a hearse through the centre of Glasgow as a promotion for the band's appearance downstairs at the Apollo. But I don't think we had a lot of time to indulge individuals. The preparation involved in entertaining 2,500 dancers at the weekends was quite incredible. Wear a frog suit? You do it.'

After a year or so, Frank Lynch allowed Tim to come out of the frog suit. The unmasking of the Frog in itself made for a great club night and attracted huge publicity. Tim, allowed to become human again, was fast becoming a local superstar.

Helen Chilton was one who recalled going to Clouds discotheque with her best friend, Angela Thompson.

'Both of us loved Tim. We would go there and stare at him. I remember one of his little contests involved taking thirty teenage girls up on stage for a "Kiss The Tiger" competition. The idea was that the girl who could kiss Tim for the longest time would win an LP. Angela and I, sadly, didn't have the bottle to get up there and kiss him. We were too in awe of the Tiger.'

It's clear the Tiger was having the time of his life running wild. 'Frank Lynch had me doing other stunts,' said Tim. 'I remember wearing ladies' nightdresses a lot in those days. And one day he had me dressed up as George Best. But of course I forgot George was Irish. As soon as I opened the mike and said, "How are you doin', Glasgow?" the game was up.'

Frank Lynch's imagination knew fewer limits than even that of Tim. 'One night Alice Cooper was playing downstairs at the Apollo and Frank came up with this wild idea to dress me up as Alice Cooper, with the black tights, the white mask, top-hat—the works. But this was where the madness came in. He even had me go and buy a chicken. Alice was very big on the ritual sacrifice (faked) of poultry at this time so I followed Frank's instructions to the letter. I went round to a wee shop in West Nile Street and bought a chicken with the neck still dangling on it. It was a dead one, of course. And I remember Frank getting me a sword—goodness knows which hat he pulled that one from—and I was all set.

'Halfway through the night Frank introduced me as Alice Cooper, and of course the crowd bought it completely. And as I ran about the stage miming to one of his records, I suddenly pulled out the chicken and began to stab it. People down below me were screaming. At first I think this had to do with the excitement of seeing Alice Cooper but then the screams turned to horror when parts of the chicken began to explode all over the punters down on the dance-floor below. Frank thought all of this was just hilarious.'

He and the rest of the team also had regular laughs with Jet Mayfair, who was now on the way to becoming a mini-legend, at least in his own mind. He would often join Tim in the DJ turret dressed as a fairy princess. 'God knows why,' said Tim.

Colin Robertson recalled a particular night when Jet once again provided the cabaret. 'One Saturday Chris McClure (who later changed his name to Christian) was playing and before the gig Chris was in the band's dressing-room watching some American soap opera on television. I walked in, saw Chris and said hello and then looked over to the corner and there was Jet, doing the business with a girl whose arse was perched on the end of a Marshall bass cabinet. It was hilarious, but even funnier was turning back to look at the reaction on Chris's face. He was totally immersed in the TV soap.'

Tim—without the frog outfit—made as much a success of Clouds as he had done at the Electric Gardens. That's why Colin Robertson, Eddie Tobin and Frank Lynch were stunned when the boy from Easterhouse told them he was leaving to go it alone. Eddie was saddened. He and Tim had had a very good relationship. 'Tim would go the extra mile for you and we didn't want him to leave because he was a real asset. He had more to do there. And the fact was he was playing in front of huge crowds every Friday, Saturday and Sunday. He could have made the place his own. But I don't think he ever forgave Frank for the frog suit.'

It seemed as though the damage had been done. Frank Lynch had got it wrong a couple of years back when he figured Tim would sacrifice his dignity for the club. The DJ would dress up in ridiculous outfits such as baby-doll nighties—women's clothing was never a problem—but a frog suit was crossing the line of acceptability.

'There were long conversations but he had made up his mind, which was a shame,' said Eddie.

Colin Robertson also tried to talk Tim into staying. 'He would make these unilateral decisions sometimes about the gigs he would do or not do and sometimes they'd backfire. I think leaving Clouds was a big mistake.'

Tim's mum wasn't at all surprised when her one and only announced he was leaving Clouds. 'He never liked it the way he had the Electric Gardens,' she maintained. 'I don't think he liked being a frog at all. And I don't think he liked playing at being Alice Cooper, especially when someone sent for the police claiming he'd killed the chicken while up there on stage.'

Dora shook her head at the memory. 'The things that this boy has done!'

Colin knew how difficult it would be to replace an act like the Tiger's. 'We brought in a guy, Dougall DJ, who would always speak about himself in the third person. He did okay, but he wasn't at all like Tim. I remember one day he walked into my office and said, "Dougall is not very happy with you today, Colin. He thinks he could have been presented a little better on stage." I wasn't impressed. I said, "Well, if you happen to see Dougall, tell him to keep clear of my fucking office." Tim never gave me those sort of problems. He would mope sometimes but he was never moody on stage.'

A big part of Tim was sad about leaving Clouds. 'I remember thinking Eddie Tobin was the funniest guy I'd ever met. I just used to go up to his office and hang about for hours listening to his stories. To leave that world—and all the madness that went with it—was very difficult.' Nevertheless, he was convinced he'd made the right move in going it alone. He decided to take the Tiger Tim Roadshow on the road full time. Eddie Tobin booked some gigs for him.

To be accurate, Tim wasn't totally alone. He had two dancing girls on tour with him, the Wild Tiger Women, two 'voluptuous females', one of whom was his wife's sister Margie, who was just sixteen, and the other his little cousin from Mount Vernon, Linda Brown. At times, Linda was substituted by a pal, Helen Dunion. The girls wore tigerskin outfits and they had much the same effect on teenage boys as Raquel Welch had when she appeared in a fur bikini in *One Million Years BC*.

Eddie Tobin was impressed with the result. 'This was a guy who, a year before, had been behind the decks; now he had a show that was in every sense a real performance. Tim went to a level where he could make the girls scream, a level of total adulation. He was a young, good-looking guy and as a DJ he was the best.'

The timing was perfect for the likes of Tim: 1971 was the era of pop superstars, people like Bowie, Bolan and Elton who had talent and created a larger-than-life image. It was a time of absolute excess and the Tiger was Glasgow's representative in the nation's neon showmanship contest.

Eddie, boosted by Tim's ever-improving act, lined up a whole series of gigs for him. 'At this time,' recalled Tim, 'I had a wee Ford van with "THE TIGER TIM ROADSHOW" printed on the side. And I'd go off to do the gigs with the go-go dancers. We did the likes of the Corran Halls in Oban with The Bay City Rollers and sometimes when we couldn't afford to stay in a hotel we'd sleep in the van. I guess we did this for about a year, going up and down the country.'

Margie proved to be a great travelling companion for Tim and sometimes they'd team up with her brothers, Kevin and Jim and his pal Midge who were on the circuit with Salvation.

Acting against advice, Tim continued with his Alice Cooper routine which had caused such mayhem in Glasgow. The Alice gag, he was to discover, didn't travel well, however. One night he played in Cumnock Town Hall in Ayrshire. 'This was an under-eighteens night,' he recalled, 'and often there would be fights. I remember Jock McCurdie was the big guy who ran it. Anyway, I went out and did the usual routine of giving the dead chicken a real hard time of it with the sword and all that. But this time the whole stunt backfired. People were actually trying to climb on stage to get to me. I later learned there was a Marshall's Chunky Chicken factory near by and this company was a major source of employment for the local area. The Cumnock people thought I was taking the mickey and attacked me.

'So I threw the knife down and ran off stage and headed straight for the dressing-room. I was shaking. My breathing was really hard and just then the door was barged opened and four blokes stood there. They were older, but hard-looking. One of them approached me— remember, I was terrified at this point—and said, "Are you the guy who was doing that thing with the chicken out there?" I mumbled something like "I guess" and he said, "What the hell was that all about, sonny?" And I said, "Well, it's just a joke, really. It's my Alice Cooper act." And the leader of the group, a big guy, came close up to my face, bent over and said, "Oh. Is that right? And who's she, then?" I was too scared to laugh—luckily, 'cause they'd have beaten me stupid. Just then he gave me an ultimatum. He said, "Look, we don't want to see you wearing ladies' nightdresses any more, son. And we don't want to see you leading the kids astray." At this point I had to laugh. The notion that this was all about some perverse behaviour, a hidden transvestitism on my part, was tearing up my head. But I nodded politely and accordingly they didn't beat me up.'

What they did do was call the police. 'Tim was arrested the night he decapitated the chicken in Cumnock,' said a grinning Eddie Tobin, who was now Tim's unofficial manager and was called to help out. 'He was taken away for having an offensive weapon. They said, "You are charged with cutting the head off a chicken. Whether it's an offence or not, we don't really care. It's oor offence."'

Under the Special Powers Act (Cumnock) Tim could no doubt still be rotting in jail for his offensive behaviour towards dead poultry. But after a night in the cooler he was freed to prepare for the next gig.

Meanwhile, he was fast becoming a major celebrity and it wasn't too long before he came to embrace the notion that night-time DJ superstars didn't flog vinyl during the day. He left Hades to concentrate on gigging, and his focused professionalism paid off. Unknown to Tim his talent was spotted early in 1973 by agent/manager Henry Spurway who had been in the business since the 1960s. Henry was responsible for pulling in new talent for a new radio station that was being planned for the west of Scotland. His task was to line up potential jocks who could fit into the required slots. 'I took a special interest in each individual area of broadcasting,' said Henry. 'Richard Park, I reckoned, would be great on sport, and Tim, the most exciting unspoiled product I have ever seen, was getting a great following from young girls. Tim was in the same vein as David Cassidy and David Essex. He was a good-looking boy and I knew from watching his club performances that the girls loved him, so I recommended him to the station boss, Andy Park.'

Meantime, Tim had a phone call from his pal Tom Ferrie, another DJ on the mobile-disco circuit. Tom told Tim about a new radio station that was starting up in Glasgow and said he'd been signed up for it. Tim's heart leapt at the news. This was the chance to be a real disc jockey—like David Symonds. Of course, he didn't know he had the advantage of having been recommended by Henry. 'My first thought was I had to make up an audition tape. And I had to make it sound different from everyone else's. I got my brother-in-law Kevin to help me because he was in a band, of course, and as well as knowing what he was talking about he had a super tape-recorder. We worked hard at it, coming up with ideas that were pretty wacky and it took a long time—I remember it took an hour for every minute we ended up recording, but in the end we had a pretty good demo tape.'

Choosing to forget his previous failed experience at trying to get himself noticed at a major radio station, Tim decided to tackle landing work at Radio Clyde with the same degree of subtlety. He set off for Clyde's new offices in Anderston Shopping Centre wearing a tiger skin and a large sombrero he had brought back from a holiday in Spain. That wasn't all. His face was painted all the colours of the rainbow in homage to Wizzard's Roy Wood. Under one arm he carried an air-rifle and under the other was a stuffed tiger. But Tim being Tim, the outfit was never perfect unless he was wearing the right footwear, in this case a pair of bright blue-and-yellow boots. They had in a previous life been ice-skating boots, with the blade removed, and they'd had been given to Tim by Midge Ure.

True to form, Tiger Tim's Clyde adventure got off to the worst possible start. 'I got lost, completely lost trying to find the place and for half an hour I wandered around Anderston, creating fits of laughter amongst the afternoon shoppers. Eventually, a wee man in the street, with a look of absolute incredulity on his face, put me right. As I walked up to the correct building, the workmen outside looked at me as if I were an alien.

'I soldiered on regardless and took the lift up to the radio station. A young lady at the reception desk very bravely showed me along to a room where the Clyde people sat. But instead of knocking politely on the door I kicked it open, ran in and stuck the air-gun up a lady's nose—I learned later she was presenter Sheila Duffy—and demanded to see Andy Park. Sheila looked at me as if I were mad and said he wasn't in the office at the moment. And I can remember I was very glad my face was covered in bright paint to hide the riddy I now had. In an attempt to save face, as it were, I handed Sheila my audition tape and said, "Right then, you'd better give him this."'

The deflated Tiger had to slope off back to his lair. He returned the following day dressed in more conventional attire—well, a purple three-piece suit was fairly conventional for the early 1970s and he wore a shirt and tie and carried a briefcase and an umbrella. With his trendy moustache and blow-dried dark hair Tim now looked the spitting image of '70s heart-throb Jason King.

Andy Park had heard, obviously, of Tim's previous appearance and of course he had already been primed by Henry Spurway to expect the unexpected. Nevertheless, he called the madman with the rifle to account for himself. 'The first thing Andy said was, "Where's the gear, then?" And I said, "Well, this is me," and we sat and talked and I could tell he had a great sense of humour. He must have had—he gave me a job.'

There would be times ahead, however, when Andy Park would come to question his decision.

8

Mooning, David Cassidy and Life as a Pop Star

Within a few days of landing this fantastic new job at Radio Clyde, Tim made a discovery that was to leave him feeling both nervous and thankful. 'I learned Andy Park had stuck his neck out for me. Nobody else at Clyde wanted me. This was a new station and a new radio licence and the rest of the Clyde chiefs had reckoned they couldn't put a lunatic like me on the air. But Andy made a case for me and I was offered a Tuesday-night show, from eight till ten.'

Tim had arrived. This was Radioland, the place he had dreamed of since he was a kid. And he was confident he could broadcast—after all, he'd been doing it for ten years. All he had to do was get it right on air.

Luckily, on his first ever show he had a guardian angel in the form of fellow DJ Norman Ross. 'Norman stood behind me and said things like, "What are you going to do next?" And I'd say, "I'll talk for a bit and then I'll play this record." And Norman would say, "Well, you'd better line the record up on the turntable because it won't start to play on its own." I was just so nervous. But after the first show Andy Park came up to me and shook my hand and said, "Well done." I felt so incredible.

He wasn't the only one. 'I remember his first show,' said Dora. 'I was so proud of him. And he got telegrams from everybody he knew. But it was the end of the show that had me in tears. He played a record, *Thanks for the Memory*, and he said, "This is for someone, who, if it hadn't been for him, I wouldn't be here." I think that tells you a lot about him. He's always been a very emotional person.'

Although Tim would never get over the regret that his dad didn't see him make it into radio, he was happy he had found his spiritual home at Radio Clyde.

Clyde was different in one respect from STV in its early days: Radio Clyde didn't hire actors or presenters with RP accents. Clyde offered a broadcasting opportunity, for the very first time in Scotland, for a boy from a housing scheme to become a presenter. Not only did the Clyde bosses accept a regional accent, they welcomed it. And, as a result, the west of Scotland immediately threw its arms open to the new radio station that had immense empathy with its listeners.

They could delight in hearing voices such as those of Tom Ferrie and Richard Park, voices that bore no resemblance to those at the BBC. Sure, there had been dial options available in the past such as pirate Radio Scotland and Radio Luxembourg, but these stations were always crackly and broadcasting time limited. Clyde and Tim Stevens were the real thing.

This period of sheer joy was blighted by a death in the family at Easter. This time it was his grandmother Mary Kelly, with whom Tim had stayed at weekends at her flat in Partick. She'd died, aged eighty-one. 'He took it very badly,' said Dora. 'Although he was a married man you wouldn't have thought it. He broke his heart the same way he did when his grandad died when he was a wee boy.'

News that Radio Clyde were to use him as a front man for a massive pop concert that summer lifted his spirits. The David Cassidy concert at Shawfield was Tim's first outside gig for the radio station. It was to give him an insight into the life of the pop star he would later try and grab a piece of. But, for the moment, it was pieces of Tim that were being grabbed.

David Cassidy was an immense, worldwide star. Tony Blackburn, the top Radio One jock, was to be the main presenter but Tim got to introduce the support act, Showaddywaddy. 'I was nervous being on the same stage as David Cassidy,' he recalled. 'I remember there were thousands of screaming girls and being sort of glad that Bobby Preston, who now ran a security firm, was keeping things under control. But when David Cassidy appeared on stage it all went mental. Suddenly there was a huge rush at the front of the stage towards him and Bobby Preston came up with this idea to stop the surges. He suggested that I go up to the middle of the park where there was a mini-stage and a section of the crowd would then rush up to see me. I thought this was a daft idea. After all, hardly anyone knew me. But I agreed and ran up there wearing my canary-yellow catsuit.'

Tim couldn't have been more wrong. 'Someone announced to the world: "I'd like you all to know that Tiger Tim is now in the middle of the park." And there wasn't a rush, there was a John Wayne-sized cavalry charge. Suddenly, I was surrounded by thousands of screaming girls desperate to get at me. The next thing I knew, Bobby was running towards me and yelling to hold on. As he reached me he picked me up under his arm like a roll of carpet and ran towards the main stage. But we never made it. The girls got to us and my new yellow catsuit was ripped to shreds. Wow! It was exciting and terrifying at the same time.'

Tim wanted more of that sort adulation, but for the moment he had to content himself with the smaller fan base Clyde had to offer. And it was work he loved, every minute of it.

Colin Robertson recalls how Tim's star status swelled after those first few months at Clyde. 'By this time I had left Clouds and I became manger of Shuffles, a big new disco in Sauchiehall Street. Tim actually arrived to do one gig there in a limo. Henry was now officially managing Tim and had spent a load of dosh on his client and this was evident. Tim appeared for the first time wearing the real Tiger-type clothes, beautifully tailored outfits that really stood out. His image had taken a huge step up. He was a bit older now, twenty-two, and I'm telling you, the fan adulation was immense. We had The Bay City Rollers around at that time and I'm not exaggerating when I say it was every bit as difficult getting Tim Stevens into that club past the fans as it was The Rollers.

'Fans saw him in a different light. For example, instead of doing a whole night he would only do an hour, making it in effect a special-guest act. We would use Tim as a personality DJ—he had his own stage show at this time—and I can't exaggerate the following he had. We even had to use security to get him in and out of the place. Girls were tearing him to pieces. They loved him to death.'

Helen Chilton who used to go and see him at Clouds now made a weekly pilgrimage from her home in Drumchapel up to Anderston just on the off-chance she would see the Tiger. 'There was a block of multistorey flats that overlooked Anderston,' she said, 'and I was barred from entering them by the tenants. This was because there were always dozens of girls in there looking out to see if we could see Tim. Eventually, I got to meet him and he'd let me take his dog, Jasper, for a walk.'

The other jocks at Clyde certainly took to the young pretender. His contemporaries at the station included Steve Jones, who called Tim 'the Martini Kid' in recognition of the fact the Tim had just begun to drink alcohol. Not being a beer man, he started with dry martini and lemonade.

And all the jocks loved Jasper. 'Jasper was the most beautiful golden labrador you'd ever seen,' said Tim. 'I used to take him to Clyde with me and he'd sit under the desk while I did my show. Sydney Devine would always remark on what a fantastic dog he was. Sometimes Jasper would bark while I was on air but it didn't matter. It made for a talking point with the listeners.'

Elton John didn't share Sydney's views on Jasper. The Rocket Man came into Clyde one day on a promotion tour and popped into Tim's studio to say hello. As usual, Jasper was guarding the fort and for some reason he didn't take to the man in the bright yellow suit. 'He went for Elton,' said Tim. 'I think he gave him a wee bite on the bum. But Elton took it pretty well.'

As the Martini Kid rapidly became the station's teen idol, the fans turned up at the station daily for autographs. Tim was fast becoming a cult figure, so much so that local firms recognised this. Levi's even agreed to make all his costumes. 'A local rep, Jim Hunter, arranged for me to have about seven costumes, catsuits and that sort of thing, made free. It made me look like a pop star. It was all very showbiz.' At least it was an improvement on women's dresses.

But as his popularity rose like a hot-air balloon, Tim, unconsciously, did his very best to bring his career back to earth with a crash. In a mad moment of both exhibitionism and self-destruction, the rising star faced the sack.

It came about one afternoon in the music library when a slightly bored and rather agitated Tiger happened to notice that through the window he could see right into the Glasgow traffic wardens offices and canteen.

'It was a wee bit immature but I thought, "Bastards! I'll show them!" and I pulled my trousers down and stuck my arse out of the window. I had a right chuckle at the thought of showing them up. But about half an hour later I was called in to see one of Clyde's bosses who informed me the police had been up at the station. I asked why, all innocently, and he told me I'd been reported for flashing my backside at the traffic wardens. They had "complained bitterly" at me showing them my best side. Thankfully, Clyde had managed to convince the police I wasn't an inveterate flasher and my actions were socially and politically motivated. The boss argued the case I was simply acting on behalf of the poor man in the street with a car. I was given a final warning.'

Tim's moments of mischief and madness had always been part of his character. But apart from the time on the verandah when he'd try to fly, they weren't as potentially destructive as that day at Clyde.

It would be nice to say that from that moment on Tim became sensible and never again bared his bum to the watching world but that would be false. Dropping his trousers was to be a regular part of the act that was his regular—or, rather, irregular—life. Just about any new jock who arrived at the station had to go through this initiation. The nonsense that Clyde listeners were coming to love was never a performance. It was simply Tim as he was, being broadcast live to two million people.

Meanwhile, Henry Spurway was monitoring Tim's progress behind the microphone every step of the way. 'When Clyde went on air it was mega,' said Henry. 'It was as exciting as when Scottish Television first appeared. The following grew and grew. But what Tim had was charisma. He had it all. He was an extrovert and he had a great live DJ show. He was perfect for a manager in that you didn't have to mould him. I figured it made sense to back him.'

The plan, conceived by Henry and Tim, was to turn the boy from Easterhouse into a pop star. 'When you had a whole new crop of stars it made perfect sense to take the most popular DJ and do a cross-over, turn a jock into a pop star,' said Henry.

While at Clyde Tim had already made a couple of attempts at recording songs. 'Things had progressed at Clyde at an incredible rate and I was always being sent songs by people suggesting I should have a go at making a record,' said Tim. 'Through a guy called Jim Cowden who worked in our advertising department I was put in touch with Pat Fairlie who was once in The Marmalade who then rang the Robert Stigwood Organization. They were massive and looked after people like The Bee Gees. Anyway, RSO sent up a backing track written by Lulu's brother, Billy Lawrie. One night at midnight I took the backing track into Clyde and dubbed on the vocal. The song was called *Have You Seen My Angelina*. It seemed to go fine but the problem was what to do next.'

Henry, who had originally began his career in the casino business, decided to put his money where Tim's mouth was. 'Henry got in touch with GTO records and GTO sent up a bloke called Biddhu from London who'd once had a hit with *Summer of '42* just to work out the keys for a couple of songs he suggested. Then it was down to London to record the songs *If Saturday Night Could Last Forever* and *Hey Girl*.'

But nothing could be that straightforward where Tim is concerned. 'We went out for a Japanese meal the night prior to recording and because I was so nervous I had a couple of drinks. I don't drink much —even now—so by the time I got to the recording studio I was knackered. I found a couch and fell asleep while things were being arranged. Two hours later the producer woke me up. The studio cost sixty quid an hour so it was probably the most expensive sleep I'd had in my life. Apparently, they didn't want to wake me up too early in case I wasn't ready to sing.

'Nothing came of the records but Henry was even more convinced success was just around the corner and went into overdrive. He got in touch with Pete Shipton, a recording engineer, and Harry Barry, a Glasgow songwriter. Harry wrote *Star Girl* and I did a demo at Clyde.'

Henry reckoned this was the record with which to launch the Tiger. 'He had huge potential,' said Henry, 'and I spoke to Andy Park at

Clyde about Tim leaving the station but with goodwill and the total understanding that if things didn't work out he could go back.'

Tim wasn't aware of this safety-net that Henry had rigged up. But he didn't need it, either. He could become a pop star. After all, he had spent years singing in some form or another, whether into a screwdriver or to his Auntie Jean or into an unplugged microphone. He knew he could project himself to an audience. 'I'd always fancied the idea, seeing myself, stupidly, as the Scots Paul McCartney. And now Henry Spurway told me I should become a pop star. He reckoned that because I had such a big fan following at Clyde I should be in London making records. He also backed me financially, giving me a hundred quid a week as a retainer.

'I spoke to Andy Park about it and he was gutted. I guess I was his protégé, but he could see I was really into the singing thing. Reluctantly, he agreed I would leave Clyde but he continued to keep an eye on me and became part of the team that would try for the pop career.

'So I gave up Clyde. I left Clyde to walk the yellow brick road to pop success. Sure, I was taking a chance but I had to do it.'

It wasn't easy to walk away from the success. 'I had announced on my show that I would be leaving Clyde and on the final day about a hundred girls turned up outside the studio. I was really quite overwhelmed as I went out to sign autographs. I remember one of the girls was Violet Sweeney and she went on to become a Tennent's Lager girl. Like the rest of them she was sad to see me go. She said radio would never be the same again and I was really touched.'

To say Dora wasn't happy would be like saying David Cassidy was fairly popular with a few girls. If she had been horrified when her son left the railway, the news that he was abandoning Clyde to become a pop star filled her with dread. 'This was a real nightmare,' she said. 'I told him he was chucking in a good job, with good money, and for what? Henry Spurway paid him money but it needed more than that. I felt from the start he was being let down.'

Henry was determined Tim would be given every opportunity to make it. To test the water in Glasgow it was arranged via Henry and Frank Lynch that Tim would play on the bill at the Apollo. Frank Lynch at that time was managing an unknown pop band called Slik, fronted by Tim's pal Midge Ure. Frank reckoned Tim could join the bill as a pop talent and help fill the three-thousand-seater hall. And that's exactly what happened.

Tim had been playing his own Glasgow-recorded tracks on Clyde for several months before leaving the station and had built up a huge local fan base. By the time the concert came around the girls were desperate to see the Tiger in the flesh.

There was just one little problem: Tim had never sung before in public in his life, apart from the half a dozen electricians in a works canteen and the neighbours in Banton Place when he performed in their gardens with The Trespassers. Regardless, he was elated at the news. 'Henry did the deal and there I was, getting £350 for playing the Apollo, and I thought, "Wow!" The problem was I didn't have a band. So I got a few mates together like George Miller, who was Billy Connolly's roadie, Bill Smith, the DJ from Radio Clyde, my hairdresser Davie from Falkirk and the drummer whose name escapes me but I recall he was a plumber.'

The big night arrived and Tim was deliciously terrified. 'They all dressed up in crazy outfits. I think Bill Smith wore deep-sea diving gear, someone else had a glitter outfit and one had on a leotard. They all looked outrageous but none of them could play an instrument. We used backing tracks and all they had to do was pretend to play. But as I stood at the side of the stage waiting for the intro to end I could see they were all hopelessly out of time. Arms were all over the place and what they were doing didn't match up to the music at all. I got a message to the lighting guy to flash the lights faster, basically so the band would be harder to see. And thankfully, that had the effect.

'Meanwhile, the most important man in the hall, the bloke who was playing the backing-tape down in the orchestra pit, was surrounded by three thousand screaming teenage girls. At this point I became terrified he'd be bumped and the tape would break or something and we'd all be found out and murdered. I got word to him desperately and he stood with his shoulders over the tape-machine protecting it with his life.'

Tim took to the stage, wearing the tigerskin outfit, to the backing of an invisible forty-piece orchestra. Luckily, the teenage girls in the audience were screaming so loudly they couldn't tell the band were completely bogus and that Tim was miming. His three songs went down a storm. Then Midge Ure and Slik came on. And Midge had Tim sing with his band. 'The only song—apart from my own—I knew all the words to was *Roll Over Beethoven*. And luckily I knew the key I could sing it in, D, and Midge and the boys got me through it. We got away with sheer murder.'

Tim milked his pop star moment for all it was worth. At the end of the gig he made his way backstage and was met by his personal manager, Alex Robertson. Alex had been hired by Henry to look after his protégé and make sure Tim looked like he was being constantly looked after. 'Alex shouted he had a car waiting outside in Renfield Street to whisk me away but I was having none of that. I screamed back that I wanted the girls in the audience to have time to come running round the side of the street and catch me at the stage door. Alex was going nuts. He yelled out, "You'll be mobbed!" And I said, "Oh, so what. Let's give the groupies the chance to catch me!" And they did. There were hundreds of girls outside all climbing over the car. There was Alex, sitting in this shiny red Daimler, and he was going crazy. But there was another nightmare. Once Alex got me inside the car we realised it was blocked in by another car and the driver, we later learned, was in a bar across the road having a drink. Alex had to run into all the local pubs screaming for the bloke with the Ford Cortina to shift it pronto.

'By the time we got him to move his car we couldn't see out the windscreen for arms and legs. It was fantastic.'

Safely back in the Albany Hotel for the post-concert party, Tim continued to play the role of pop star. Hundreds of teenage girls had followed the entourage back to the hotel and were standing outside screaming their lungs out. Tim knew he had to do something pop star-like but he wasn't sure what. 'I know it sounds really wimpish but I wasn't a mad enough pop star to throw televisions out of windows or take a half a dozen girls back to my room for sordid sex sessions—and in any case Clare would have killed me.'

Clare was with Tim a great deal when they first became a couple but by the time he was making his bid for pop stardom she had had enough and didn't go to the Apollo gig. 'She would help me humph my gear around the discos but after a while I think she got fed up with it all,' said Tim. 'The whole scene wasn't really her.'

Eddie Tobin offered a perspective: 'I didn't see a change in Tim when he got married. But I can't think of any act where the wives actually like the adulation. He would be less than human if he didn't try to play it down a little for the benefit of his wife. But it was not noticeable.'

Tim isn't sure where Clare was that night at the Albany. 'She was at home, I think. By this time I think she'd become fed up with the showbiz thing and preferred to stay in the background. Anyway, it's probably just as well 'cause she'd have seen me throw cream cakes out of the bedroom windows at the girls below. They loved it, I have to add.'

Tim may have kept the teen fans at bay with the help of chocolate éclairs but when he popped into his hotel room to change he realised he had a more delicate problem on his hands. There, lying on his bed, was a stunning auburn-haired girl. Naked. 'To this day I don't know who put her up to it, but I instantly got the feeling she wasn't there because she had loved me from afar and was now prepared to sacrifice herself to me. I'm sure money had changed hands. And, to be honest, I felt very uncomfortable. For one thing I was curious as to how she'd got into my room. And then there was the fact she was setting the agenda. Nice girls didn't do that sort of thing.

'So I just said hello and smiled and suggested nicely to her that she'd better put some clothes on or she'd catch her death. Something witty and original like that.'

That night Tim did find himself naked on a bed—but not with a female. In a truly bizarre incident, the likes of which Tim was to find himself in many times over the years, he and a nightclub manager pal Davy Walters ended up stark naked. Together. 'After the incident with the girl, Davy and I had a bit of a laugh, wondering who had set it up. But then the conversation wandered naturally enough to the subject of sex and somewhere along the line he introduced a useless piece of information into the conversation. He told me that men's testicles are in a state of perpetual motion. He said if you look at them carefully you will see they never stop moving. I didn't believe this at all so off we went to my room so that he could prove it to me. Now I can only be thankful that no one walked in at that point as Davy and I were lying on the bed looking at each other's Henry Halls, with him pointing and saying, "See, it did move!"' It was one of those male bonding moments, before male bonding had been invented. But it served to illustrate Tim's propensity for taking his trousers down in the most inappropriate situations.

The night had been a huge success, nevertheless. And the following day, plans were hatched to take Tim's pop career to the next level. Henry believed the success of the Apollo show had proved that his boy had what it took. 'I got a group together and we rehearsed out at my pub, the Elm Tree Inn near Livingston,' said Henry. 'I had got Tim onto the GTO label alongside Donna Summer, so this really was big time.' The team headed to London to record *Star Girl* and hoped for the best.

Eddie Tobin, meanwhile, was not convinced Tim had made the right move. 'The next logical step, had he been manageable enough, would have been to take him forward. There's no doubt Tim could have been a contender. But he's always been emotional, and he has his own mind. If he could have been manipulated he could have been taken to a higher level. But he simply wouldn't allow that to happen. Tim always figured he knew what was best for Tim.'

Eddie Tobin's words were to be echoed many times later by others who tried to guide Tim in what they felt was the right direction. But, for the moment, at least, this individuality and single-mindedness was a strength.

9

Huge in the Hebrides

To his credit, literally, Henry spared no expense in launching the Tiger onto the watching world. He even made Alex Robertson into a full-time minder and personal manager with a remit to chauffeur Tim around Britain in the huge wine-coloured Daimler. Henry wanted to make sure that Tim always looked the part.

Alex was a big burly guy from the south side of Glasgow, a few years older than Tim. He travelled everywhere with him making sure Tim turned up at the right place for appointments. And if Tim got any hassle, Alex would step eagerly into the breech. He had a great sense of humour, although one day it was tested to the limit. Not, on this occasion, by Tim.

'Alex, in his wisdom, grew cannabis behind a shed in his garden in Thornliebank—not the perfect locale or climate for cannabis, but never mind. But the year he came to work for Henry he had a short holiday and came back only to discover his next-door neighbour, a nice old fellow, leaning over the hedge and looking entirely pleased with himself. He informed Alex that he had done him a favour by tidying up his messy garden. Alex was curious and asked what he had meant by "tidy up". The old neighbour looked more pleased with himself: "Well, I've got rid of all that really long grass behind your hut," he said. "It was about four foot high so I just cut it all down, bagged it and threw it in the coup." We couldn't get Alex to smile for a week after that.'

Alex had to smile the night he went out with Tim and a relief driver, Harry Wilson, in Glasgow. It was Friday night and Harry was driving the trio up Sauchiehall Street in the Daimler and Tim asked him to stop at a chip shop. He asked Harry to get the chips in and off the driver went and ordered them. Tim then walked in behind him, wearing the tiger suit and looking like he'd stepped out of a spaceship or a travelling circus. Then Harry turned to Tim and said, 'Would sir be requiring onions with his chips?'

'We were sending ourselves up,' said Tim. 'Alex had a great laugh because it all seemed so unreal—the flash car, the minder and the driver. I would have liked to have been more comfortable with the whole thing but it just didn't seem to be me.'

Tim wasn't entirely happy with the pop star pretensions; the boy from Easterhouse didn't sit comfortably in the sort of car, for example, that was used by civic dignitaries and those with serious cash. Nevertheless, he claimed he wanted success and that meant going back to London again to record a studio-produced version of *Star Girl*.

There were high hopes for the song. But Tim, once again, was overcome by the occasion. 'I remember laughing all the way through recording *Star Girl* and I was told to go for a walk. I walked to the East End, got lost and thought, "Where the hell am I?" '

Eddie Tobin, and several others, felt Tim's nerves reflected a deeper problem. He wasn't comfortable with the notion of UK-wide fame. Sure, he would have liked it, but it's possible he was frightened of it at the same time. Getting drunk and falling asleep the first time in London, then laughing while singing *Star Girl*; he wasn't a man who was at ease with himself. It was as if he was shooting himself in the foot. 'I think Tim wasn't comfortable outside of Glasgow,' said Eddie. 'He knew exactly where he stood at Clyde and with his gigs. But this was a very different situation.'

Eventually the song was finished. Now the video was to be recorded, back in Glasgow. 'We shot the video—the first major pop video in Scotland—at the Mayfair in Sauchiehall Street,' said Henry. 'It was a fantastic night. There were thousands of screaming girls all desperate to get hold of him. He looked set to hit the big time.'

Henry Spurway knew that Tim had to prove himself to have a chance of pop success. The Tiger was certainly working hard at improving his stage performance and singing, constantly rehearsing with the band at Henry's pub. 'What I loved about Tim was that he used to come out to the village and go out to the shop for snacks,' said Henry, smiling. 'Then he'd come back and tell me the shop had no Mars Bars or bananas. It gave him such a kick to have eaten the entire stock of the wee shop. It's this boyishness about him that makes him so endearing.'

Henry arranged a tour of independent radio stations throughout Britain for the endearing Tiger. Alex would drive Tim around the country, from Ayr to Plymouth to promote *Star Girl*. (Coincidentally, when Tim stopped off at BBC Radio Manchester, the man who interviewed him was Mike Riddoch, who is now Radio Clyde Two's drivetime jock.)

His pal from Radio Clyde, Steve Jones, also had a TV show at the time with London Weekend. It was a programme reviewing new releases, a *Juke Box Jury* copycat, and Tim was on the panel. 'I had to pass judgement on a record by The Stranglers, a band I quite liked, but this record wasn't very good and I said so. What I didn't know was that Jean-Jacques Burnel, the band's bass player, had been waiting backstage. After I'd slagged off the record he walked on the stage, marched right up to me and growled in my face. Steve smoothed things over a bit but as Alex and I left the studio later I saw this bloke dressed all in black, on a huge Harley Davidson motorbike, come roaring towards us. He mounted the pavement, hit the brakes with a loud screech and I realised it was Burnel. He stared at me again—Alex was too shocked to do anything—and he said angrily, "You didn't like my record, did you?" I was terrified. I thought he was going to run over my feet or something. But then he laughed out loud and drove off. He'd been taking the mickey.'

Later that afternoon Alex Robertson suggested a novel way for Tim to relax. He had a tin full of relaxant. It was pure cannabis. 'I don't know where he got it but I'm sure he wasn't growing it again. Anyway, he suggested I try it—and I did—but I hated it.' Many years later people in the medical profession would be suggesting Tim should try cannabis. But at that time, as now, he was not interested in the effects of drugs. Perhaps, however, hashish would have numbed the sense of failure he felt when he learned *Star Girl* had bombed, failing to make the charts. 'It was no.330 in the Hebrides,' Tim joked.

His friend, the newspaper columnist Rikki Brown, offered his thoughts on why the single failed to make an impact.

'It was minging,' said Rikki. 'It was too dated and had bits of everything you'd heard already. I can recall meeting Tim in Easterhouse a few days after the record came about. He and I walked past a bloke we both knew called Big Danny. And Big Danny summed up the mood in the camp with "I bet Jethro Tull are shitting themselves now" and Tim could only grin and bear it.'

Eddie Tobin reflected on Tim's pop career. 'I remembered talking to him when he had the record out and I thought it was all so sad. It was not him.'

Colin Robertson concurred. 'If he could have been able to sing then he would have had an amazing launch-pad, being so popular. But he couldn't sing. And Tim insisted on on doing the vocals himself without backing singers and his voice wouldn't stand up.'

Eddie Tobin argues Tim simply wasn't star material. 'I believe that an act has to have the X-factor in order to succeed, and although he was a fabulous DJ, he didn't have it. It was the same with Christian— a fantastic singer—but I thought from the beginning he didn't have it. On the other hand, Alex Harvey had it and so did Billy Connolly. Of course, this theory doesn't apply today. All you need nowadays is a body and the manager can do the rest. You can be picked up off the street and made into Kylie Minogue. But not back then in the 1970s.'

Eddie stressed that Tim couldn't be guided. He believed someone else should have supplied the vocals for Tim in the way that many of the acts of the era like Edison Lighthouse used supplied voices. 'I wouldn't have wanted to manage him, especially after the first few years. Tim had something of the Ben Gunn about him, a tragic comedian who was a nightmare. Those sorts of act are always emotional, they always have a problem—and it's always a major problem which requires instant access to you and your attention, regardless of what you're doing. Ben Gunn used to come in crying to me. As the manager you have to give them the time.

'I don't think there's a problem if the act is Celine Dion and you are making two million a year— then they can cry all night in your face. You can pander to them. But when the act is emotional and you're not making a great deal of money, it can get to you and it can drain away your time.

'The problem with Tim was in him listening to advice. You couldn't tell Tim he was a crap singer. If he's not a singer, you're an arse. He thought if someone couldn't make him a star then they were the one at fault. It was all a bit tiresome. Don't get me wrong, I think he's a fantastic talent and the very fact he's been at Clyde all this time confirms that. But Tim should have realised he was out of his league. And deep down perhaps it was a league he didn't really want to be in.'

Henry Spurway didn't see the pop failure through the same dark glasses. 'We had a lot of success,' he said. 'We did a few support shows with Tim's own band but the whole thing was probably a year too late. The likes of David Cassidy had come and gone. I'm sure if I'd got him a couple of years before Clyde we'd have had major success. He was, in a word, idolised. At every hotel, every gig, the girls went crazy. He was the bride amongst the bridesmaids at Clyde. He had the potential. But the timing was wrong. You could already see that market disappearing.

'There was another problem. If you had worked for a commercial station, the BBC wouldn't exactly bend over backwards for you. In those days, even if you did leave the commercial sector, it was very hard to get exposure. They were very nervous at Radio One in those days. Nowadays, of course, you can work for anyone.'

Henry believed Tim had the raw talent. 'He could sing, he had a great character voice. And he did want it badly enough. Tim had this feeling that the pop star's life was for him.'

Henry conceded that Tim was difficult to manage: 'Well, we fought every day in life. Tim did not like to be managed. And therefore discipline was not top of his priorities. 'But he was always appreciative of what I tried to do for him. I kitted him out with the best limousines and the best clothes, took him to the best places and I spent £20,000 on him—which in the 1970s was a fair bit of money. He did acknowledge that.'

The pair decided to call a halt to the working relationship. It all came to a head with Henry one night in Edinburgh. 'We were sitting in the car outside the Royal Scot Hotel,' remembered Tim, 'and I was complaining to Henry that things just weren't going right. He told me to get out the car and that would be the end of the relationship. And after things calmed down a little he asked me what I really wanted to do. I didn't even think for a second. I said I wanted to go back to Clyde.'

Henry had no regrets about the time—and money—spent on Tim. 'I loved every minute of it. I'd do it all again. And I'm sure Tim gained a lot from the experience. We'd done three singles by this time and I said his first career should be back on the turntables. I had to say to him: "We bought a ticket, but we didn't win." That's the way it goes.'

Tim was now a failed pop star and the weight of defeat left him severely depressed. He found he had a lot of days with nothing to do. And for someone who'd worked non-stop since the age of fifteen, there was a great vacuum in his life.

'When I left Clyde at first the phone was going all the time with people asking what was I up to. But after a few months the phone stopped ringing. I thought, "What am I doing here?"'

Tim was still living with Clare in the one-bedroom flat in Partick and thanks to Henry Spurway's retainer he wasn't starving. But it was only enough to survive on. Thankfully, he hadn't burned his bridges at Radio Clyde. Relations with Andy Park were still good. Andy had reluctanly given his approval to Tim having a go at a pop career and was pleased to have him back—although he never gave the DJ the satisfaction of knowing that. After a meeting with Henry Spurway it was agreed Tim would return for a limited period.

'He took me back to do a thirteen-week run,' said Tim. 'On the twelfth week I met him in the corridor at Clyde and he said, "Last show tonight, then, eh?" And I muttered, "Yeah." And he said, "Do you want to do some more?" My face lit up. I didn't have to be asked twice.'

Back at Clyde Tim recovered the lost ground of his confidence. He was doing what he did best. Except that one day his best wasn't quite good enough. Tom Ferrie was presenting his afternoon show and his special guest that day was Billy Connolly. Tom reckoned that Tim should come on the show, too—he figured the DJ and the comedian would play off each other well. It didn't work out that way.

'Billy came on and he was Tom's pal,' said Tim, 'so they were very relaxed together, but even at this stage, well before he became mega famous, I reckoned Billy was God. As a result, I sat there and listened to him tell stories without joining in. It's not that I didn't think I could be funny, it's just that I figured there was nothing I could say that could come close to the level Billy was operating at. As a result, I was reduced to single words and it was so obvious that during the commercial break Billy turned to me and said, "What's up with you? Come on, Tiger, give us some of your patter." And that just made me worse. Now that he expected something from me, I was totally silenced. Billy was his normal genius self.'

Now that Tim was back at Clyde his fans could once again adore their idol and that adoration continued to swell. His roadshows were revived and again hugely popular. In fact, Tim would often only perform at the end of the night after another DJ had warmed up the audience. One night Tim's support act was a young DJ determined to make his name in radio. The name was Paul Cooney. Many years later Paul would smile about how that support position was to be reversed.

Apart from the continuous stream of fan mail, there were always crowds of girls turning up outside the radio station hoping to catch a glimpse of the boy from Easterhouse. It was all aided of course by his non-stop on-air flirting. Tim spoke to every female of every age as if he were deeply interested in them. And, not surprisingly, susceptible teenage girls fell for his charm.

But the constant pursuit of the DJ was to prove to be problematic. Tim didn't mind signing autographs until his wrist was sore—in fact, he loved the attention—but the following he had became more of a full-time occupation for some rather than a part-time fixation. One day, late in 1975, he was walking across the hall at home, almost naked, when he saw three pairs of eyes following him. There were three teenage girls lurking in the close outside and they could see clearly through the specially enlarged letterbox slit.

On another occasion he was relaxing in the bath one Saturday morning after a late night when he looked up to see a pair of teenage eyes staring at him through the window. What made it all the more shocking was that the flat was on the third floor. The Tiger's fans could climb drainpipes. And these immensely enthusiastic fans caused more problems. The close was eventually covered in slogans and messages pledging undying Tiger love.

Tim came to realise that living in Partick made him entirely accessible. Reluctantly, he decided to move. He and Clare bought a house in Bishopton, just over the Erskine Bridge from the Radio Clyde studios. It was a neat, semi-detached house that the couple both liked. Village life was quiet, but for Tim it was a welcome break from the madness of live gigs and screaming girls.

But the DJ couldn't let any respectable period of time go by without a trauma in his life. This time it was down to his forgetfulness. One day he parked his car in the driveway which was on a little slope and forgot to put the handbrake on. He was on his way into the house when he realised the car was moving. Like Superman he immediately ran behind the car and held it back with his two arms outstretched and both legs digging hard into the tarmac in order to get a solid grip. Except that he didn't. Tim's arms couldn't hold the weight. The car, a shiny new silver Toyota Celica, pushed him back. And further back. He called out for help, but there was no one around in the quiet cul-de-sac. The car kept on coming at him, pushing him back even further, all the way down the driveway right onto the road and across, into the neighbours' driveway which unfortunately sloped downwards and backed up onto a brick wall. Of course, Tim could have run out from behind the car—perhaps—but at the time the raging conflict seized all his mental faculties; should he sacrifice his lovely new car to serious damage or should he risk being damaged by his lovely, gleaming hunk of metal? In the end it all happened so fast, he didn't really have time to decide. The result was Tim was pinned back against the neighbours' wall and thankfully his thigh managed to prevent the car from being badly scraped. A few minutes later neighbours arrived to rescue him. Only his pride was badly damaged.

His ego, as it turns out, which had been battered during his bid for pop stardom, was now healed. In fact Tim had recovered to the point where he felt he should have another go at singing. He couldn't shift the notion of appearing on *Top of the Pops* or on TV in any form, for that matter, from his head. 'I decided to give it another go but this time to do it my way. I thought it would be more credible—I'd write my own songs and do it at my own pace.'

The self-belief and indomitable spirit of the man had to be acknowledged. 'Davy Swan, Harry Denmark and Kenny McDonald were the boys in the band called The Dolphins. We wrote songs together and made demos. We even recorded songs for Celtic and Rangers. This time round it was fun. We could have a laugh and be more relaxed. And we did a lot of gigs. It was all a bit of laugh and even though nothing really came of it, it didn't matter.'

Meantime, one of the major successes to emerge from Frank Lynch's management stable was on his way to becoming a superstar. Billy Connolly was packing out the King's Theatre for a gala concert at the end of 1975. He got a fantastic reception from the crowd and at the end of the show, in a neat gesture of appreciation, Billy called all the supporting acts up on stage to take a bow. And there in the middle of the row, holding hands with Billy, was a face familiar to Glasgow's nightclubbers. He wasn't a performer, however. The producer of the show, Frank Lynch's partner Max Langdon, realised this immediately and became apoplectic with rage at the idea of an 'ordinary punter' being allowed on stage. Of course he had no idea this was no ordinary being. It was Jet Mayfair.

10

Steely Dan and Fresh Lager

Towards the end of the 1970s Tim found there was a growing price to pay for his popularity.

He could cope with the girls who turned up at his home looking for autographs and he always got a buzz from the 'Haw, Tiger!' yells he attracted in the Glasgow streets. But recognition didn't always come wrapped up in a pretty bow of adoration, or even respect. In fact, sometimes even just toleration would have been welcome. Tim became a magnet for Scotland's hard men who just didn't like the fact that their girlfriends thought he was cute. Or perhaps they didn't like him, full stop. After a few serious threats, Tim was told it was time to think about using security.

He had a new manager now, David Meehan, a management agent who was hired early in 1976 to promote Radio Clyde. David took Tim under his wing as well as finding bookings for all the Clyde presenters. 'It was important to have someone looking out for you,' said Tim. 'There were always lots of wee girls who were out to grab a piece of clothing, and they were hard to negotiate.'

Tim faced a terrifying moment one night at a school in Saltcoats. 'A girl jumped on stage and tried to have it away with me,' he said. 'She was wild for action and began ripping my clothes off and, as a result, I was banned from appearing in Saltcoats ever again.'

And there were always lots of wee hard men out to make a name for themselves. 'David Meehan suggested I should be protected from the nutters and, in retrospect, probably from myself.' Meehan was right on both counts.

'Locally, Tim was a megastar,' recalled David. 'He was in The Bay City Rollers' league as a DJ. Wherever you'd turn up there would be screaming girls and autograph-hunters. He needed bouncers. If not, his boots, his shoelaces, his jacket—in fact, any article of clothing he wore—would have been ripped from his body.'

The bouncers employed to look after the record-playing local hero were Tim's Uncle Danny, aka Steely Dan, and Eddie MacDonald, an old Scotstoun pal from the Electric Gardens.

Steely Dan and Eddie took their job very seriously. Steely Dan even built a massive record box for Tim, the size and shape of a coffin. And he and Eddie had jackets made with 'Tiger Tim Security' emblazoned on the back.

'For the first few months I was the guy who ran the Clyde Disco Roadshow,' said David. 'Clyde was by now a well-established outfit but it lacked a public front so it was decided to take the DJs on the road and put them into clubs all around the area—Falkirk, Kilmarnock, Hamilton—everywhere. Invariably, they sold out. And we also recorded the highlights and then broadcast the gigs on Clyde on a Saturday night. It was a great idea and all the guys did the roadshow although there's no doubt Tim was the biggest draw. At the likes of Tiffany's in Sauchiehall Street, Tim was always the last DJ on, the top name.'

Tim recalled one gig at that particular disco, which more than illustrates the entertainment phenomenon he had become. 'One night in August with the Clyde Disco Roadshow and all the jocks—Richard Park, Dougie Donnelly, Steve Jones—the joint was really jumping. It was packed full and the people who owned the club were appreciative and very kind. In fact, they were so appreciative they provided a free bar for the jocks.'

And of course this was a big mistake. 'Unfortunately, given the circumstances, I was the last name on the bill. Now, normally it's great to have the final billing, but during the time the other presenters were doing their ten- or fifteen-minute slots—and there were about ten of them—I spent the time relaxing in the free bar. By the time it was my turn to go on I was very, very relaxed—so relaxed I was almost carried downstairs to the main disco. It wasn't that I'd had a lot to drink. I probably had about three or four Martinis, but that was more than enough for me.

'Now, when I got to the bottom of the stairs the management had lined up two rows of couches, and the pathway down the middle was where the DJs approached the disco box. But on either side of the couches it was a Red Sea of screaming girls held back by red leather. It all looked precarious, as if the tide of teen adulation would come pouring over the leather at any moment. Since I was drunk out of my brain I don't recall panicking, just grinning stupidly while Steely Dan and Eddie got hold of me to make the bid for the stage at the end of the hall.

'Because I was a little unsteady on my feet the security guys had me by the arms and they ran me down the gauntlet as fast as they could. But as we got to about halfway—about twenty yards—the couch barrier collapsed and hundreds of girls came leaping over like demented salmon with mini-skirts. These girls were intent on getting to me. There was screaming, there was mayhem. Eddie and Steely Dan immediately reckoned it was far too dangerous to try and get through the girls so they spun around and ran back the way we'd come, back up the same flight of steps. But I was so drunk that when we got to the top of the stairs and they let go of my arms I thought I was up on the stage. Not realising I was facing a brick wall, I threw my arms up in the air and shouted, "Hello, Glasgow!" Eddie grabbed me and shouted, "We're only at the back stairs, you tube. Chuck it!"'

Tim took a break, stuck his head in an ice bucket and fifteen minutes later made it back on stage. His performance was as precise as ever.

Steely Dan and Eddie were often called upon to become the praetorian guard of the Tiger. One night at a gig in Ayrshire, in Kilmarnock Town Hall, Tim left by the escape route at the back to avoid the crowds outside. However, three young neds were there to make life as difficult as possible for Tim. They spotted the DJ and began yelling, 'Tiger Tim, you're a fucking poof!' But Eddie was quick to react. 'Before I knew what was happening he grabbed two of them by the throat and held them two feet up against a wall until they apologised. They did, of course, and, frozen with fear, they slid down the wall like rainwater from the overflow.'

Tim was gigging in Kilbirnie one night. David Meehan was there as usual to make sure things ran smoothly. It was his job to make sure Tim knew where he was going, the time he had to be there and so on and generally make things as uncomplicated as possible. Unfortunately, the security team, thinking all was going well inside at the gig, had adjourned to the pub for a drink. 'A fight broke out and David Meehan jumped down onto the dance-floor and tried to break it up,' said Tim. 'I remember he got a bottle in the mouth and he had his teeth knocked out. He put a lot into managing me, I have to admit that.'

Unfortunately, David Meehan had no control over what came out of Tim's mouth. And his performance one night at the County Inn in Cambuslang, where the Clyde jocks took it in turn to appear, saw Tim facing the sack—again—from Radio Clyde. 'Tim's general performance had developed,' said David. 'He introduced more and more wacky competitions and he called for girls to come up onstage to sing with him. And he had a great rapport with the crowd. But sometimes he had no control over what he said or what he did.'

Tim tells the story against himself. 'The County Inn was a real poseurs' place and rather than play a few records like the rest of the guys I decided to liven things up with a little competition. I decided to stop the music and announce that I'd give away an LP to the first person who could offer me a tampon. Yes, I know this is a bit shocking, but that was the idea. I wanted to create a little bit of consternation in this snotty wee place. Remarkably, three young ladies responded to my challenge almost immediately. So I took the Tampax, put one in each ear and one up my nose and felt very pleased with myself. The crowd thought it was hilarious and I'd managed to get up the noses of a couple of people who were a bit sniffy about the whole thing.'

The Radio Clyde management were more than sniffy. The next day Andy Park called Tim into his office. 'He yelled at me, "You daft bastard! You've done it now!" And of course I had an idea what he was talking about. He said one of the punters at the County Inn had rang the *Evening Times* to complain about the behaviour of this "disgusting" Radio Clyde jock and insisted I be sacked. Andy was furious. He said, "The managing director will probably fire you for this." Of course, I felt awful, like a kid in a headmaster's office about to be expelled for something stupid. And the worst thing was that I was told to go away without knowing my fate. I had a few days' wait before I learned Andy Park had smoothed it over with the MD and with the *Evening Times*. I don't know how he did it but I've got that to thank him for.'

Perhaps it was something to do with the trauma induced by his previous performance at the County Inn that Tim, on his return, made a special effort to appear sainted.

The gig had gone well, nothing too risqué, and Tim, wearing a new T-shirt—'Sex Appeal: Give Generously'—had been a hit with a huge crowd of girls. After the gig Tim returned to the bedroom that was set aside for the DJs to use. He had just sat back on the bed to enjoy a bottle of Coke and a Mars Bar when he heard a knock at the door. He opened it and a young woman walked in, said hello and walked over to the bed. The tiny dress she was wearing was pulled over her head before you could say 'women's liberation'.

'She was gorgeous,' said Tim. 'And suddenly she was naked. The only thing I could think to do was ask her how she felt, standing there in the buff. She told me she felt embarrassed and I said, "In that case don't you think you should put your clothes back on again?"'

Given that Tim was on his Second Final Warning it was something of a surprise to his colleagues when he became involved in bringing one of Glasgow's working girls into the hallowed corridors of Radio Clyde.

'The occasion was reporter Mike Higgins' last sports broadcast before he left the station. I'd always had this thing about trying to put Mike off his stride as he read the dog-racing results, like making barking noises into his headphones from the safety of another studio. But he usually remembered to take his headphones off so that he wouldn't be distracted.

'There was only one way to put him off his stride, we reckoned. So we had this well-endowed young lady come into the studio next to the one Mike was using and stand up against the glass wall where Mike could see her. Now, as he ploughed through the results ever so professionally, this girl suddenly took off her top and Mike couldn't fail to see this young lady's full figure pressed up against the glass.' Mike Higgins, to his credit, never dropped a vowel.

It may have seemed that Tim led a charmed life but the Clyde management were always aware of his popularity and his willingness to put something back into the job—and into life in general. The Marie Queen story was one example. Marie Queen was a young blind girl who attended the school for the deaf and blind in the East End of Glasgow and she had been a huge Tiger fan since the start of Clyde. Tim had gone to visit Marie at the school in 1976 and she'd made him shortcake. In the summer of 1979 Tim received wonderful news. It was a letter from Marie, telling him that her sight had been restored thanks to a miraculous operation. Now, she desperately wanted to see the Tiger for the first time.

'She arrived at the studio and I was overcome,' said Tim. I said, "Hiya, darlin'," and joked about her shortcake being rotten, and she just said, "Oh, Tiger," and that was it, both of us were left in floods of tears.' All of this was in front of the TV cameras, as BBC Scotland were making a film about Marie's amazing recovery. 'It was such a glorious moment though, to realise she could see.'

Meanwhile, back out on the road, each gig was crazier than the last. 'We were in Troon that winter when one guy in the audience jumped up on his mate's back and shouted, "Tiger Tim, get to fuck, you're a fucking wanker!" And for some reason on this occasion it really annoyed me. So I stopped the record—skited the needle right off the side—and shouted through the microphone, "Who do you think you're talking to?" which, in retrospect, wasn't the cleverest thing to do. This guy then challenged me to make him shut up and of course I told him to meet me at the back after the gig.

'Stupidly, I kept my side of the deal. I went out to the back door but the bouncers were there, asking where the hell I was going. I told them I was going out to see this loudmouth and sort him out—I'd probably had three Martinis and reckoned I could fight the world—but the stewards wouldn't have any of it. They said there was a crowd out there and it would be dangerous. But I persisted and so they told me to have a look and see for myself.

'No sooner had they opened the door than suddenly this barrage of bricks and bottles came flying against it. It was like a scene from Pearl Harbor. We were being bombed senseless and it was raining Irn Bru bottles and screwtops. As the bouncers yanked the door closed they had that look of "We told you so" all over their faces. Luckily, Eddie and Steely Dan had the night off and I was relying on these local guys for back-up. If not, they'd have been out there doing battle. As it was, the local bouncers called the police who turned up and escorted us out of the building.'

Tim and Steely Dan more often than not got one over on the hard men who turned up with the intention of spoiling the gig. One night the pair arrived at Kirkintilloch Town Hall to do a gig that was unusually boisterous. The place was full of noisy morons who were more intent on giving the DJ a hard time than enjoying the occasion. As soon as Tim took to the stage the abuse began, in particular from one ginger-headed boy at the front, who shouted a constant stream of obscenities, questioning Tim's sexuality and making rude hand gestures every time the Tiger started to speak. None of this went unnoticed by Steely Dan.

'We came to the part of the night where we had a competition and I made sure that this guy got to enter,' said Tim. 'The idea was that three blokes would come up on stage, dress up in a baby's nappy and drink lager from a baby's bottle. But the bottle the ginger guy drank from didn't just contain beer. Because of all the nonsense we'd had to put up with, Steely Dan had earlier taken one bottle aside and one of the roadies had a wee pee into it. This guy drank the lot. And he did it so fast there was no way he would have tasted the added mineral water. He won the prize—I think something completely useless like a Paper

Lace album—and I reckon that, along with a few squirts of someone's kidney discharge, was a fair trade for the performance he'd given earlier.'

The gigs weren't all about local hard men trying to score a point. Sometimes it was all about Tim doing what he did best—react to the moment and entertain. In January 1977 he was losing his clothes again, this time while appearing at Casanova's nightclub in Coatbridge.

True to form, the DJ decided to liven up the event with a little risqué contest. The idea was that he would invite three local lovelies up on stage to take turns at ravishing him for one minute. The thought and commitment the man put into his work had to be commended. The prize was a selection of hit singles.

'What usually happened was that the girls would kiss and cuddle me. And if they were really daring they'd run their hands up and down my bum. But even I wasn't ready for what happened next that particular night.'

As expected, the first couple of Coatbridge crackers went through the usual routine. When it came to the third young lady's turn, though, she stopped the show. 'She began loosening my trousers,' said Tim. 'But she couldn't get them off because I was sitting down. And I panicked. I know I don't usually mind having my trousers off in public, but this was different. I was thinking I'd be left wearing my socks and the girl was the one making me look daft. But the stunt was too far on for me to back out. I began to sweat. Believe me, you do when you're about to be naked in front of three hundred people.'

In an effort to save face, Tim agreed to shed his trousers—but only if the young lady agreed to do the same. Her reply brought the house down. 'I can't take my trousers off,' she said.

'Why not?' Tim countered.

'Because I've got my husband's underpants on underneath.'

The place was in an uproar, and Tim, now feeling more a little more in charge, set the audience their easiest pop poser of the night. 'Do you want to see her man's underpants?' he yelled down the microphone.

The answer was deafening and unanimous. And off they came and there she stood, clad in nothing but white tights and pair of her husband's faded mustard-coloured Y-fronts with white beading.

The place exploded in laughter and the girl was given a bunch of hit singles for her bravery. In all the excitement the crowd forgot all about Tim's own promise to take his kit off. His blushes were saved that night.

He was not so lucky the following month at Castlemilk Community Centre. That was another memorable night for all the wrong reasons.

'I was on stage, giving it yahoo and the girls were going crazy,' remembered Tim. 'They didn't wait to see if I would shake hands with them from the stage—oh no, as I walked past about ten of them grabbed my legs and I went down. They also got hold of my hair and were determined to get a piece of me. I spotted Eddie rushing across at this point and I thanked God he was coming to my rescue. Except he got it all wrong. He grabbed my legs while the girls held on to my hair. That's the last I remember because I blacked out. I was in so much pain I fainted. Eddie told me later that when the girls realised I was unconscious they let me go. I suppose they were suddenly frightened by what was happening to me.

'Eddie threw me up over his shoulder and hauled me to the dressing-room. Eventually I came round and realised what had hap-pened. 'You stupid bastard!' I screamed at him, telling him he was an idiot to pull me in the opposite direction. 'I fucking know!' he yelled back, and was so angry at himself he put his fist through the dressing-room door.'

David Meehan began to see cause for concern the longer he worked with Tim. He started to form the notion in his mind that Tim's methods of working owed more to the ebbs and flow of his emotional tides than any thought-out structured programme in life.

Tim acknowledged that as the decade came to an end, the sheer silliness that went on at gigs seemed to increase. 'I went over to Arran with Steely Dan and my pal Donnie Cowden from Drumchapel, to do a gig at the Lamlash Halls. And so as to be professional, we got there early in the afternoon. But with nothing to do till the evening, we sat on the sea wall drinking Martini. And we drank and we drank. And then we made our way to the gig.

'Apparently, the gig organiser Charlie Currie, son of the Revd James Currie, announced me over the PA with the usual big build-up: "And now, here, from Radio Clyde is . . .Tiger Tim!" And the huge crowd applauded. But there was no Tiger Tim. Charlie Currie tried again. "He's on his way up the stairs as we speak, here he is . . . Tiger Tim!" And he wasn't.'

Charlie ran downstairs to the dressing-room and found Tim still there, lying under the table, fast asleep. Steely Dan was sound asleep in the toilet and Donnie Cowden was wandering around in the hall checking out the crowd. Eventually, Charlie sobered Tim up enough to take the stage. Luckily, he had slept off the worst effects of the dry Martini and lemonade.

But the gig in the packed hall proved to be a troubled affair. One of the hall's organisers came rushing into the dressing-room after the gig to tell Tim his security man Donnie had been fighting. 'I got hold of Donnie and asked what he'd been up to. He told me one of the guys in the hall had been shouting abuse at me all through the gig. I'd been oblivious to it but Donnie, thanks to the Martini, explained to me he had decided to point out the young man's behavioural failings. "He had a right big mouth on him so I just gubbed him," he told me. I gave him hell for hitting the guy and told him not to be so bloody stupid in future. Donnie stormed off and didn't come back. He didn't return to the hotel that night and so Steely Dan—who'd finally emerged from the toilet—and I drove all around the island looking for him. Nothing.

'The next morning we set about looking for him on foot. Finally, we found him on the beach. It seemed he'd got so drunk he'd fallen over the wall and landed on a sand dune. But I couldn't really lecture Donnie too much. I'd hardly set a great example.'

Fortunately, media bosses in Glasgow saw (mostly) the positive side of Tim's work. He enjoyed ever-growing fame at Clyde with his *The Aff Its Heid Show* on weekdays and *The Tiger Trial*, which went out at midnight on Saturdays, playing new releases. The success in increased listening figures was noted, not surprisingly, by Scottish Television. In October '78 he was asked to front a new show, *The Best Disco in Town*, where the television company held a junior disco for four hundred teenagers in the studios at Cowcaddens. The show was a huge success. 'I remember it got the Roses in the *Sunday Mail*,' said Tim. 'But STV couldn't cope with the hundreds of kids running about all over the place. It was pandemonium.'

At the time he admitted he still had ambitions to be a singer. 'I've got offers from three record companies.' he told one newspaper, 'but this time it has got to be right.' There was no containing the boy's self-belief, regardless of how misguided it may have been. And there was no stopping the tales he would tell to newspapers either. He revealed his 'real' name in an interview to the *Daily Record*. 'Timothy Gerard Stevens,' he said, and the accompanying picture revealed a man who looked like butter wouldn't melt in his mouth.

That wasn't the newspaper item which captured the public imagination that week, however. The *Sunday Mail* ran a picture special featuring American superstar Diana Ross who had performed the previous night at the Apollo Theatre. Glasgow's nightclubbers were amused, but not at all surprised, to recognise the man standing next to Ms Ross in the photograph. It was Jet Mayfair.

11

Dunoon, Vegas and Radio One

Whom the gods would destroy they first make famous. Well, Tim had achieved the fame and now it was time to pay the price. The closer he soared to the huge success his talent and personality merited, the more he did to bring about his own downfall.

In 1979 he was every inch the celebrity and star—and unfortunately he began to believe it. 'Something happened to Tim,' said David Meehan. 'He lost it. He lost the plot. The first three or four years I looked after him were fine but then it became very difficult. Even getting him to turn up at gigs was so hard. I used to write letters, leave notes in his pigeonhole at Clyde telling him where and when to appear and then phone him on the day of the gig. We had a system in our office whereby one of us would always call him to make sure he knew where he was to be that night. We didn't care where he'd been the night before, so long as he turned up.

'You have to remember that his popularity was such that sometimes he'd be doing two or three gigs on the one night, turning up for an hour at a time, and that was demanding. But Tim never made it easy. With most people of quality you work with over the years you know that once you got them a booking then your job is done. With Tim, you never had that confidence. You were always scared to make that phone call the next day and say, "How's things? Everything okay?" because he could have been doing *anything.*'

Tim would sometimes lose himself in other things—high jinks, watching TV, being forgetful. 'All of those, and more,' said David.

Tim was developing more of a propensity for self-destruction. As his career progressed he became all the more likely to blow it. In September he set off to do a Clyde Disco Roadshow, which was being staged in Rothesay. Except that Tim never got on the boat at Wemyss Bay. He got on the first ferry he came to outside Gourock—one that just happened to be heading for Dunoon. To make matters worse, Tim had no idea he was fifteen miles away from his true destination. As he disembarked he asked for directions to the Royal Hotel. Unfortunately, Dunoon, like Rothesay, also has a Royal Hotel. So he trudged in search of the hotel after a local told him it was a three-mile walk up the road. David Meehan had told him the hotel was just three hundred yards from the end of the pier, but the DJ had pushed this information to the back of his mind. After a mile and half, the Tiger began to pick up the scent of misfortune and called the Royal Hotel in Rothesay. And fortunately for the thousands of fans waiting there, another ferry was despatched to pick up Tim from Dunoon. It took him a while to live that one down.

David Meehan understandably was livid. 'The first I knew about it was when I got the phone call from him from Dunoon. He said he was late—but then he was always late—and he had driven up to Gourock and told me he said to someone, "Is that the ferry to Rothesay?—or maybe I said Dunoon by mistake." He would do that sort of thing all the time.'

Meehan figured there was a reason for Tim's failure to give the job at hand his absolute commitment: he still wanted to be more than a local DJ. 'Tim did try to revive his career as a pop star and I think that was half the problem, to be honest. He was great as a DJ but he wanted to be a pop star. There's a pattern with Tim. When he was something, he wanted to be something else. He wanted to be a pop star or on TV and as soon as he got what he wanted, he did something to endanger that success. He wasn't prepared to graft and learn and then move on. He wanted the success without doing all the hard work. He felt that simply being Tim was enough.'

In February 1980 Tim decided he wanted to try being a pop star again. He made another bid for the charts, although this time he kept his name secret. Whether it was a stunt to hype up interest or whether he was terrified of yet more *Star Girl*-like criticism, he refused to say. Whatever the reason, *My Only Friend Is My Radio* by the TTS Band came out. Given the voice, it didn't take a genius to work out who the man behind the vinyl was. The song was written by Peter Nardini who wrote Andy Cameron's hit *Ally's Tartan Army.*

Not surprisingly, it wasn't too long before he revealed his secret in a newspaper interview. 'I recorded the song to see if people would like it without knowing it was me who was singing,' he said. 'It certainly wasn't a publicity stunt.'

The record was played extensively on Clyde. And Bill Smith even claimed he didn't know it was Tiger's song. But Tim stressed he was never going to give up the day job. Again. 'I learned a lot of lessons from what happened five years ago,' he pronounced to the world.

The record proved to be a turkey. But at least this time Tim still had his job with Clyde to fall back on. Nevertheless, he wasn't unaffected by the failure. What he really needed was a holiday to cheer himself up. He and Clare jetted off to the States on a trip that took in New York, Los Angeles, Las Vegas and Hawaii.

As always with Tim, nothing was ever straightforward. 'In New York we stayed in the Statler Hotel in Manhattan. The city was all I imagined it to be and although there were some scare stories about people being robbed, none of that happened to us. The problems I had were a little more basic. The first morning there was a tour bus going around Manhattan and we wanted an early-morning call. I phoned reception to book the call and I'm still laughing today at the way I asked because the girl had no idea what I was saying. I began with "Listen, see in the morning, can you give me an alarm call . . ." and she cut in and said, "See what?" I repeated what I'd said but had the same problem; "I'm sorry, sir, could you slow down, I don't understand what you're saying." So I began again: "See in the morning . . ." And she cut in again. And I had no idea which part of "See in the morning" she didn't understand. Clearly, she didn't speak Easterhouse.'

Eventually though, communication was established. 'I broke it down. "See in the morning," and she said, "In the morning?" and I said, "Yes."

'"Half past seven . . ." and she said, "Seven thirty?" and I said, "Yes."

'"Can I have an alarm call?" She said, "You wish me to give you a phone call?" and I said, "Got it in one," which was a complete lie.'

From New York, Tim and Clare flew to Los Angeles, stayed at the Ambassador Hotel and took a tour. 'The first place had me stopped in my tracks. The tour guide announced: "If you could just look out to your left you will see the spot where Robert Kennedy was assassinated." I thought, "Jesus! How tacky can you get?" I looked to see if they regularly touched up the chalk lines on the pavement but it wasn't obvious.'

Tim wasn't content simply to go on holiday and relax. After all, the pursuit of fame was a constant in his life. Before departing he had written to every radio station in each city he planned to visit. He didn't want to miss out on any opportunity to be heard across the Atlantic. One station had replied, Radio K-DWN in Nevada. And that was how the bold boy found himself broadcasting live from downtown Las Vegas. But it wasn't an experience he'd ever care to repeat.

Young James McGrory aged nine proudly displays his class prefect badge and Loxene-slicked hair to the world.

Above: James and Dora, Tim's parents on their wedding day in 1947.

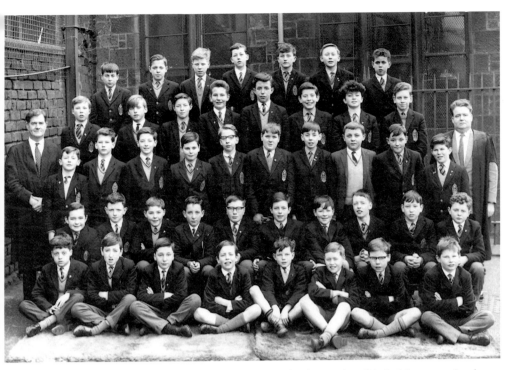

Above: It's Tim's first year at St Mungo's as he looks forward to life in his new school. Tim is seated on the second row, far left.

Right: No one could say that young James McGrory was in any way sectarian as he turns out with two older pals for a game – in his new Rangers strip.

Opposite left: The exasperated Tiger cub was a cute three-year-old as he goes digging for buried treasure in a neighbour's backyard in Roystonhill.

Opposite right: The bold boy, aged seven, makes his first communion, beaming in his new outfit from Goldberg's.

Four boys who help to make Saturdays swing

FOUR Easterhouse boys have opened their own discotheque club and are running Saturday afternoon dancing in aid of charity. The club — in the Blessed John Ogilvie R.C. Church in Wellhouse Crescent — provides a three-hour record session each week.

The boys are John McDade (15) of 5 Langbar Place, Jim McGrory (15) of 19 Banton Place, John Miller (14) of No. 17, and John McGrory of No. 21. John McDade is the only one who has left school. He is an apprentice metal fitter.

The boys held their first session last Saturday and attracted more than 70 to their club.

Says Jim McGrory: "We are charging 2s. 6d. membership fee plus 1s. 6d. entrance charge.

"We plan to spend part of the money on new records and divide the remainder among city charities."

Four boys and a discotheque—left to right John McGrory, cousin Jim McGrory, John McDade, and John Miller.

he planned to look in on

Above: A press cutting from the *Evening Times* in 1967 reveals a Mike Nesmith lookalike as Tim performs his first official gig.

Below: A year later in 1968 and by now the precocious performer has changed his name to Tim Stevens and started on the mobile disc jockey circuit. The Loxene look is long gone.

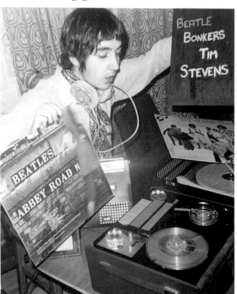

Right: By 1969 Tim was a headline act at the Electric Gardens and the fans were already lining up to have their pictures taken with the celebrity Tiger.

Below left: Tim wore dresses at nighttimes and dungarees during the day, yet by 1975 he was already recognised as a cult at Radio Clyde.

Below right: There's something of a fashion catalogue look about this Clyde publicity picture taken at the end of the seventies. But at least Jasper looks natural.

Tiger Tim Stevens

TIM 'Tiger' STEVENS

The Alice Cooper impersonation has crowds at Clouds enthralled, poultry lovers disgusted and police enraged. Dora was horrified to hear what her son had been up to.

The famous Jet Mayfair was talked into wearing a fairy outfit by nightclub boss Frank Lynch. Jet, however, didn't need too much persuasion.

It's hard to tell whether the pose is worse than the outfit, but at least it's better than women's frocks as Tim attempts to look the part of a pop star.

Outside the Apollo, Steely Dan does his best to hold back the teenage crowds desperate to squeeze the cuddly Tiger.

When the circus came to town in the early nineties they wanted
a real Tiger. Tim stopped just short of entering the cage when he saw the
size of the teeth. Nevertheless, he proved to be even more popular
with the fans than the big cats.

Above: Celtic FC asked Tim to promote Jungle Juice, a new soft drink brought out to commemorate the closure of the famous Celtic terracing. It was to leave a bad taste in his mouth.

Right: DJ's have little to do all day but think up practical jokes to play. Here, surprisingly, poor Tim was the victim during a Fire Prevention PR stunt, and had a fire hose tuned on him by Gary Marshall.

Above: Pop band Mero turn up in the studio for words with Tiger the talent-spotter.

Left: Former Ginger Spice Geri Halliwell was keen to promote her first solo single and a short time later Tim took to dying his hair a light ginger colour. Could the two events have been connected?

Opposite above: The picture on the giant crane seems to suggest Tim was being transferred to Clyde Two for a fee of £49. But in truth it was far less than that. Shortly afterwards he had another free transfer back to his spiritual home on Clyde One.

Opposite below: The Tiger visited Calderpark Zoo in 1995 and visitors discovered all the animals were securely caged, if a little frustrated at times.

Left: Paul Cooney was appointed M.D. of Radio Clyde earlier this year and one of his first acts was to transfer Tim back to his nighttime slot on Clyde One. Tim is clearly happy at the decision.

Below left: Just before Carol hit the big time she opened a fashion boutique with the Tiger. Luckily, Moira wasn't around to see her husband worship at Ms Smillie's feet.

Below right: It's not a Top Gun photo shoot. Far more seriously, Tim tries one of the first attempts at a 'cure' for MS with a visit to a hyperbaric chamber.

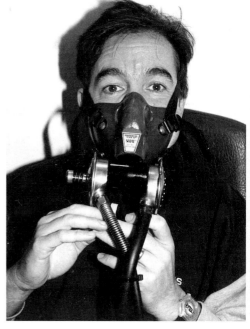

Left: It's the early eighties – which explains the awful shirt – and the Tiger is dressed up to take his mum, Dora, out for the day to visit their old home in Easterhouse which has just been renovated.

Below: The three kids in the Tiger's life; Carissa, Darren and Melanie.

Tim and Moira. They still fight like cat and dog,
according to Tim's mum, but they make a great couple.

'Well, first of all I had a problem finding the place, which wasn't unusual for me, but it was even more confusing because the station was actually on the second floor of a hotel. It was a huge operation. Eventually, I found the right studio, and Jack English, the presenter, who greeted me warmly. I remember the studio looked down onto the pool and there were dozens of gorgeous girls in bikinis at the poolside. I thought, "This is my idea of radio heaven!"'

But it wasn't. It was radio hell. 'Jack was nice and introduced me with "Well, sitting beside me this morning is my special guest, Timmy the Tiger all the way from Radio Clyde, Scotland—hi, Timmy." And I said "Hi," thinking I sounded so naff. And then Jack asked me what I thought of Vegas. I told him I thought everything was buzzing, just like my heid, and after he not surprisingly dismissed this, he said, "Tell me, Timmy, what do you think of the Iranian situation?" Well, I think my face fell about two floors to the basement. It turned out the SAS had just stormed the Iranian Embassy, where the Americans had failed to release the hostages, so I mumbled something about "you have to do what you have to do in the face of adversity". But all the time I'm thinking, "Iran? Hostages? This is America. I could walk out of this studio and some loony will blow me away with a bazooka."

'By this time I had realised this was a current-affairs radio station. And I was so out of my depth Mark Spitz couldn't have saved me. Jack, God bless him, tried to warm up the situation by taking calls but unfortunately one old lady phoned in saying she was originally from Cowdenbeath and then asked me what Cowdenbeath was like these days. As it happened, I'd never been there before in my life. In fact, I knew more about the Iran hostage situation than I did about Cowdenbeath. There was only one thing to do: I lied. I had to lie and tell her it was even more beautiful than she remembered it.'

Tim's Vegas nightmare continued. Again, it was down to sheer stubbornness on his part. 'We went to a Tony Bennett concert and I wore a jacket and collar and tie. Clare told me it was too hot to wear it but I ignored her. I had to look right. But I learned that no one wears a collar and tie in Las Vegas. It was so hot I collapsed at the back of the room at Caesar's Palace. Thankfully, I was so far away, Tony's performance wasn't affected.'

The final part of the trip took Tim and Clare to Hawaii. They had a fabulous time. 'In the hotel was a band called The Beamer Brothers and this was a huge coincidence because their song, *Honolulu City Lights*, had recently been my Record of the Week at Clyde.' Of course, Tim wasn't content simply to enjoy the show and the coincidence. 'I wrote them a note saying I was staying at the hotel but I never heard anything back. They probably thought I was some bam from Glasgow.'

In spite of the language problems, his limited political background, his lack of knowledge of Cowdenbeath and the beamer he picked up in Hawaii, it had been a great trip. But on the flight home Tim and Clare had a huge shock when the plane touched down in Glasgow. Or, rather, it didn't. 'I got lost again,' said Tim. 'I had got on the wrong flight and we ended up in Manchester. I don't know yet how I managed to pull that off. It meant I had to hire a car and drive the five hours back up to Glasgow. Clare wasn't too chuffed.'

They had got on well during the holiday—so well, in fact, that Clare was now pregnant. 'I was probably keener than Clare to have kids at that point,' said Tim. 'I was pushing for kids more than she was. I guess I thought it was time. Clare wasn't totally against it but she wasn't as excited at the notion as me.'

That month Tim had another surprise. He was to find himself in jail. He was asked to go along to Barlinnie Prison as part of a PR exercise. 'The inmates in Barlinnie used to listen to my *The Aff Its Heid Show* and it was felt that I could communicate with them. Before I went into the prison I was told there were some real lunatics behind the huge walls, but I didn't feel that at all. They weren't any different from the blokes I'd grown up with in Easterhouse. In fact, a great many of them came from Easterhouse.'

The Bar-L boys weren't the only people listening in to Radio Clyde with a close ear. At the beginning of the New Year a call came through from Radio One. A top producer revealed he'd been taping Tim's shows on Radio Clyde and wondered if he was interested in working for Radio One. Would Tim like to come down to London to discuss it?

Would he? Of course he would! It was a dream come true. All those years of listening to the Light Programme, and here was the BBC calling the Tiger and asking him to come in for a chat, to fly to London and stay overnight in a hotel at the BBC's expense. Radio One! This was the home of the top jocks on the planet such as Noel Edmonds, Mike Read and Simon Bates. Tim, after all, should be up there. He was the biggest name in Scotland.

Radio One, it transpired, were looking for a replacement for Noel Edmonds' *Sunday Show* and it seemed Tim could fit the bill. After all these years playing records, at the age of twenty-seven Tim was set to play in the premier league. And then he blew it.

'My appointment with Johnny Beerling of Radio One was for eleven o'clock,' recalled Tim, 'and so I set off on the 9 a.m. flight from Glasgow. That in itself was a mistake because I forgot about the hour it takes to get from Heathrow up to the West End. And, as you would imagine, the flight from Glasgow was delayed. I ran into the BBC, headed up the steps and looked at my watch and it was 12.30 p.m. The first face I saw was that of Simon Bates and I was enthralled. But he looked at me curiously. And I suppose there was no surprise in that because of the way I looked.'

Tim, on this occasion, wasn't wearing a dress. But he may as well have been. 'I'd got up that morning, put on a smart suit, looked in the mirror and thought, "Nah." I felt extremely uncomfortable. So, instead, I put on a tatty old jacket and a pair of jeans I'd had forever that were all frayed. I put on a pair of shoes that I remember cost me £6.99. This wasn't any homage to the punk look of the period. This was me being typically daft. Anyway, Simon Bates gave me that withering look, I guess, because I looked a tramp.

'As I was shown into Johnny Beerling's office he scarcely glanced at me. He said, "Look, you're an hour and a half late and I'm just going to lunch. Why don't you go for a walk and come back in a couple of hours." I thought that was fine, because I'd have done anything to keep him happy. So I strolled around, seeing some people I knew who worked in record companies, and then made my way back up to Broadcasting House. When I got back to his office Beerling had clearly lost interest. He just went through the motions and I reckoned, rightly, that I was getting nowhere. One of the producers, a woman called Doreen Davis, came down and was really nice to me and said Radio One had liked the tapes they'd heard of me. But the defining moment was when Derek Chinnery, who was head of Radio One at the time, came in and Dorothy introduced me. Derek was very pleasant and began to say, "I hope you enjoy your stay at Radio One . . ." and before he could get the line out Johnny Beerling jumped in and said, "Of course, Derek, I've told Tim that there is still a long way to go yet and we may not be employing him." I knew then that was it. Nice Dorothy showed me out and pointed me in the direction of the tube and wished me well and said she'd see me again. But in my heart I knew that wouldn't be the case.'

David Meehan's version of events is a little more pointed. 'He completely blew the audition,' said David. 'He was booked on a flight that gave him about five hours to get to the centre of London from the airport. He had time. From his own mouth, here's the story he told me at the time about the reason for his lateness. Apparently, he was on his way to the airport and someone, a taxi-driver, I think, told him he looked too smart. So Tim took the cab back home and changed into something much more casual and missed the plane. And when he eventually got to Radio One they said he looked too scruffy and that he had a couldn't-care-less attitude. There he was, going for the best radio job in the land, and he hadn't even bothered shaving.

'I was really disappointed. It was a very big show that could have led to anything. I felt total despair. Radio One had approached Tim and all he could do was blow it. The only thing I could have done was take him by the hand to London.'

This was a classic case of self-destruction. Tim's former manager Eddie Tobin reckoned it's quite likely that the DJ was just too frightened of taking on a Radio One job. 'Tim liked his comfort zone, which was Glasgow. That sums it up. Here he was on the brink of signing the biggest deal of his career but it was as if he had reached his limit: "Stop me from going any further. That's enough." I can relate to that.

'Some may say Tim was naïve and gullible but he always had his own mind. But an act who wants to be big cannot have his own mind in terms of his own career. In terms of his performance, perhaps. But you have to employ a manager and let him manage. Tim was a west-of-Scotland phenomenon that didn't travel.

'Tim is very comfortable within his character but he was never the type to be changed. Moving to another territory would have insisted upon that change.'

Henry Spurway was disappointed to hear of the Radio One fiasco. 'I think he could have made it at Radio One, if he'd had the right management,' said Henry. 'But then again Tim was sometimes of the opinion that all he had to do was be Tim. Once you get a job and you're in the door, that's fine, but to get in you have to be a bit more diplomatic.'

Did Tim subconsciously not want the job, not really want to leave Glasgow and his mammy behind for that great Venus fly-trap that is London? 'That's a hard question to answer,' said the man himself. 'I don't know. I would have seriously considered moving to London but then again my roots were in Glasgow. Maybe what I wanted was to be offered the chance to go. Whether I took it up or not is another thing. I'll never know.'

It seemed he didn't want it. Tim hadn't offered himself unconditionally to Radio One. He'd told them he'd like to continue at Radio Clyde two days a week. Yes, he was showing loyalty to Clyde but did that suggest to the Radio One bosses that Tim wasn't brave enough to make the leap into national radio? 'Yes, it does,' said Eddie Tobin. 'Perhaps he knew it wasn't for him. I later managed Mark Goodier who went from Clyde to Radio One but although Tim had far more personality he couldn't have done what Mark did, namely to change. The Glasgow in Tim's voice would never have been acceptable. They would have wanted to change Tim and that wouldn't have happened. Stuart Henry got away with the accent because he sounded like someone playing at being a Scotsman, like Scotty from *Star Trek*. But Tim couldn't have occupied that kind of head space.'

It turned out the BBC replaced Noel Edmonds with the former Blue Mink singer, Madeline Bell. It wasn't a successful appointment and that only made Tim feel worse with the way he'd slammed the door in his own face. He didn't take defeat lying down, though. He wanted to try and find out if Beerling's objection was down to his poor timekeeping. After all, Tim had worked at Clyde for seven years and was never late for a show. Well, except the Saturday breakfast show and that was only once. So he decided to write Johnny Beerling a letter. Or rather, a poem. 'It was a funny sort of rhyme basically asking what the hell was going on,' he recalled. 'He wrote back in rhyme also, which was quite funny, but basically his little ditty said "Beat it".'

Back at Clyde it took Tim time to get over the Radio One disaster. He felt bad and stupid but then he turned the problem on its head. It wasn't really his fault after all, he told a newspaper: 'I guess from Johnny Beerling's point of view I hadn't tried hard enough and that's probably right. But I think I never cared enough because I was really happy at Clyde.'

Clare took a pragmatic approach to the Radio One trip, just as she had all those years earlier when she travelled with Tim down to London in the red Fiat. 'She just said, "Wait and see what's offered. Let's think about it if it happens." And it didn't. She said to me one day, "You don't travel well." And she was right. Take me out of Easter-house and I'm lost.'

David Meehan agreed that Tim didn't really want to leave his comfort zone, that the tatty gear and the indolent attitude were all part of him pressing the self-destruct button. 'That's probably the case,' said David. 'I didn't really look into why he was pressing that button but I can see with hindsight that every time something good happened he would blow it.'

According to David, there was little Clare could have done to stabilise him: 'Clare was a lovely girl, but Tim was such a personality I think she was in his shadow at the time. I don't think I can recall her ever coming to any of the gigs. She would stay at home and look after things and I hardly ever saw her out socially. She really wasn't part of his professional life. What Tim did wrong was his own decision.'

But the Tiger did do one thing right.

12

Captain Sensible Gets into Women's Clothing

In June 1981 Clare presented Tim with a baby daughter, Melanie. The baby, like Tim, was born in Stobhill Hospital. 'I said to the doctor, "I'd like to thank you for all your help," which was a completely stupid thing to say, but I think he realised I was caught up with the excitement of it all.'

With a new baby it made sense to move from the detached house they had since bought in Bearsden's Gray Drive. But Tim's knack of creating problems wherever he went carried over into home-building. He and Clare moved up in the world—literally. The couple had a house worth £90,000—an enormous amount of money at the time—built high up on the hill of the Bearsden district of North Baljaffray. 'I can remember sitting on the steps outside just after it was built and looking out over the whole of Glasgow,' said Tim. 'It was a fantastic feeling. It felt like the boy from Easterhouse had finally arrived.'

The construction work had been a six-month nightmare. At one stage Clare even had to go home and live at her parents' home in Renfrew while work was going on. 'I was working all the hours imaginable to pay for it,' said Tim. 'I was doing gigs with Steely Dan just about every night of the week. I had a mate, Frank Smith, help build it but there were problems from the start. They began when he came up with his pal, dug out the foundations for the house and poured in the concrete. So far so good. But then we had a visit from the Planning Department who said they had to see the state of the foundations before the concrete could be poured. It meant digging the whole thing up again. It cost a fortune.'

The house was to be a splendid affair with pillars like a Greek temple outside the front door and a canopy. But Tim's temple had another fault: when the canopy was laid across the top of the pillars, it obliterated the view from the front windows. 'The builders tried to argue that it was supposed to be like that, but I protested and the pillars were cut down to size. There were other problems, too. When the toilet light switch was flicked the lights came on in the garage. And one day the back wall of the garage was demolished. A workman had gone into it with a JCB and couldn't reverse back out again. So he went right through the back wall.'

It seemed Tim and Clare were destined not to enjoy life in their Greek temple, although once work was completed life returned to what passed for normal. Yet, once the dust had settled, Tim was to create a mini-sandstorm in their lives once again. To be fair, this time Clare and her sister Anne were partly responsible.

They all reckoned it would be a good idea to open a shop in Renfrew selling designer clothes. Tim's old pal Dougie Donnelly backed him in the publicity drive through the town. But opening the shop was one of the worst decisions Tim would ever make.

'We decided to open a clothes shop in the main street and we called it Melanie's,' he said in a newspaper interview at the time. 'I've got a restless nature and I always like to keep doing new things. But I wouldn't say I'm a businessman. I certainly don't look like one,' he joked, indicating the tracksuit he was wearing at the time.

His words would come back to haunt him. But for the moment he was full of the joys of life. He was clearly delighted with his family. 'We've been married ten years now,' he said. 'And when we got married

I was earning just twelve pounds a week in a Glasgow disco, so we've come through the tough times together. Being married to Clare has helped me calm down a lot. Before I got married I used to do outrageous things for a laugh, like lying down in the street in front of cars, and I'd walk around with a toy tiger on a lead. I was a pretty crazy youngster.'

Clare hadn't been able to stop Tim from wearing the dress at the BBC's headquarters. Nor had she managed to get him to London on time for the Radio One interview. Nevertheless, Tim maintained his wife had had a calming influence on him. 'If I hadn't married her I'd probably have killed myself doing one of those crazy stunts.'

That was not to say that Tim was announcing complete maturity in life. 'Although I'm thirty I don't feel as old as that. I feel I'm still as young as I was when I started out being a DJ. I'll probably still be doing daft things when I'm sixty. Whatever happens, I'd still like to be playing records at that age.'

David Meehan played down the DJ's early-1980s comments that Clare had changed Tiger Tim into Captain Sensible: 'You had to remember that Tim always had the ability to embarrass someone,' said David. 'When he was out for a meal he'd invariably sit at the table with his trousers round his ankles. And presumably he still sticks his tongue out with the food still on it—and still thinks it's funny.

'If you were out with a couple of mates Tim would arrive and give you a kiss, just to make you feel awkward, and he'd have that cheeky smirk on his face. It was all about seeking attention.

'You're not going to change someone like that. No one is. And that sort of behaviour wasn't Clare's cup of tea at all. It's not even enough to suggest that Tim needed a really strong character to push him in the right direction because I think he would have rebelled against that. He needed a yes-person, which is what he got all the time. I'm sure he got that with

Clare up until the point when she reckoned she'd had enough.'

As was so often the case with Tim, joyful musings about the present were often a precursor to that gloom that lay ahead. An indication of the dark clouds came when he took a trip to London. The day before he had been playing squash for a newspaper photo with a former Miss Scotland, Linda Gallagher, and raising money for the charity Cash for Kids, then playing in the garden with his dog, Jasper. 'I went down to London to buy clothes for the shop and when I got there I heard that Jasper had died. I was distraught. I can remember crying all the way back to Glasgow.'

There was more bad news in the following months. Marie Queen, the blind girl who'd regained her sight, lost it again. No one could explain why. Tim was devastated. Then he learned the shop was a disaster. 'We thought we'd sell designer wear but it just didn't work. It nearly made me bankrupt.'

David Meehan wasn't at all surprised that the shop proved to be a bottomless money pit. 'Tim never listened to advice at all. I'm pretty sure we sent monthly statements to his accountant as well as to him because we were certain they wouldn't get there otherwise. I doubt if he ever took advice from anyone about anything.'

The shop's failure meant more hard graft and, luckily, he was still in demand for gigs. He had to make money: Clare was pregnant again. Despite the financial pressures he faced, the thought of another baby filled Tim with delight.

His other great delight that month was in meeting Gary Glitter, who had just relaunched a successful career playing the university circuit. Tim recorded the interview in the back of Gary's Rolls-Royce as they drove through the streets of Glasgow. That was true fame. 'He was exceptionally friendly,' said Tim. 'But, then, you never really know people, do you?'

That interview was not half as thrilling as going down to London to talk to Paul McCartney. McCartney was Tim's idol, of course: he had sung Beatles songs to his Auntie Jean and at the railway yard. He couldn't have been more excited as he flew south. On the flight, at eight in the morning, the very nervous Tim had a few little bottles of airline wine yet the Martini Kid arrived at Abbey Road Studios stone-cold sober. Adrenaline was rushing through his veins.

At the recording studios a buffet had been laid on for the media people, with alcohol, of course, and Tim had a few more drinks, just to calm the butterflies. Again, he was unaffected. But just before he took his turn to interview the ex-Beatle he heard over the speaker-system an American radio journalist ask Paul about a previously unmentioned song he had written. It was *the* question Tim had been saving, in order to make an impression.

'I almost cried when I heard him ask that,' said Tim. 'So I went back to the hospitality room and had another drink. By the time I was ushered in to meet Paul I thought I was going to faint with nerves and stress. But, amazingly, it all went fantastically. He was great. He made it so easy for me. And after an hour as I left the studio Paul drove by in a Porsche, banged on the window and waved. I could have floated back to Glasgow on a cloud of happiness.'

Soon afterwards his son, Darren, was born at Stobhill. Tim had reached back to the *Bewitched* series when choosing the name for his baby son—Darren Stevens was the name of the male lead.

But if the world had any hope that Tim's impish behaviour would abate now that he had two kids, they were dreaming. At Clyde he would spend half his spare time thinking up pranks. New boy Paul Coia often bore the brunt of it. 'Paul did the show after me,' said Tim. 'At that time he was relatively nervous, as was normal. Every Saturday night on his show he'd start with an LP track and I'd sneak up behind him and change the speed fom 33rpm to 45. Every week he'd fall for it, and every week he had to come on air and apologise. I really don't know why he didn't kill me.'

News and sports broadcaster Paul Cooney, now the managing director of Radio Clyde, wasn't quite so tolerant. 'Paul was on radio news at lunchtimes,' recalled Tim, 'and one day he was doing his usual slick, professional performance when I crawled into the studio behind his back. At the time the studio was full of big green metal bins for all the waste paper and I decided to pee into this bin while Paul was reading the news on air.'

The noise of water hitting metal sounded like a road drill. 'Paul, to give him credit, managed to keep going without missing a beat, but when he came off air to go over to an AA report he looked up, realised what had happened and whacked me with the back of his hand right in the groin. It was so sore I fell to the floor in agony. I couldn't even scream out loud because he'd opened the mike again and the world would have heard me yell. I kept away from Paul and the bin for a while.'

The New Year saw a more positive outlook from Tim. He decided to focus his energies on the good of others. He still did the usual charity work that had become a feature of his life but he now decided to try and come to the aid of his favourite football team, Partick Thistle, who were in financial difficulties. He wrote a song for the team with the imaginative title *We Are the Thistle*. The song may not have propelled the Jags back into the black but the club were thankful nonetheless.

At the same time Tim's own football career came to an end. He had been becoming more and more tired after gigs—he put it down to his hectic schedule—and reckoned at thirty-one it was time to hang up his boots. His last football match was for the Radio Clyde All-Stars. 'It was between Scotland's two greatest rivals,' said Tim, 'Radio Clyde and Radio Forth, and we played at Petershill Park in Springburn. It was a beautiful day and there was a huge crowd. But I think my main contribution to the entire game was to stop a handbags-at-dawn fight between Paul Cooney and Jay Crawford of Radio Forth.'

His football career may have ended there and then and Tim would never play sport of any kind after that day, but his career had another fantastic opportunity to rocket skywards. BBC Scotland wanted the jock to front a new kids' programme, *The Untied Shoelaces Show*, as part of their summer schedule. Tim had been desperate to make the break into television and this time he didn't have to resort to a quiz-show appearance. 'I saw an ad in a newspaper saying that BBC Scotland had tried out hundreds of presenters for a new kids' show and were still looking. So I called David Meehan, who wasn't optimistic. He said, "Did you read it properly? They're looking for *new* faces."'

Since Tim had already fronted *The Best Disco in Town*, he didn't qualify. Nevertheless, he persisted, finally landed an interview and got the job, a daily show that went out throughout the school holidays. He even wrote the theme song with his brother-in-law, Jim McGinlay.

'It was a live show and kids made up the audience. A lot of them were from Maryhill and some of them were a little rough and ready. I got a wee bit of abuse from some of them—in fact I had to speak to them off-camera and remind them I was from Easterhouse and that I'd do them outside. After that they were fine.'

The same couldn't be said about Tim's television reputation. It wasn't that he did anything particularly wrong, but when you consider this was his big break, his chance to show that he could operate in a different medium, it has to be said that once again the Tiger didn't kill 'em dead.

'He would work with all these people,' said David Meehan, 'who had had years of TV and production experience, and Tim would ignore that and always be coming up with ideas: "Wouldn't it be better if we did this . . .?" and sometimes they were nice ideas but they weren't feasible in terms of budget and technology. Yet Tim didn't grasp this. He had a huge problem accepting that you have to work within the confines of the studio and the script. Instead, Tim wanted to do the outrageous and was told no. As a result, he was always complaining about the producers and directors, arguing that if they'd done what he wanted them to do the show could have been a network hit.'

David Meehan was frustrated once again to see a golden opportunity slip away due to his client's recalcitrance. 'You can imagine if someone from the BBC network liked his work on screen the first thing they'd do is get him checked out and so they'd call BBC Scotland for a reference. I'm not saying he was being a bit difficult. He was just very difficult to work with because he could never really control what he was doing. But he won't consider that he blew it. He'll think, "Well, if they'd done it the way I wanted them to do it . . ."'

Tim's BBC network chance never came. 'He was mentioned once or twice in despatches by top people at BBC Scotland who reckoned *The Untied Shoelaces Show* was a huge success. And they talked about doing more with him. But he would have blown it. He didn't play the game. You have to be able to bend in television and Tim wouldn't. He was, to a lesser extent, an Oliver Reed type of character. You know he will attract a crowd and be interesting but you never know what will happen next. Producers often don't want to take a chance on someone who's problematic and unpredictable.'

David did manage the following year to land his client another television job, although Tim was to do his best to place the job in jeopardy.

Still, he could rejoice in the knowledge that his fans still loved him.

It was this popularity that saw him invited to perform at a special Royal Charity Gala at the King's Theatre with his backing band, The Dolphins.

'The highlight for me was not meeting Princess Diana but on hearing the reaction of a wee girl from Glasgow when talking to her,' Tim recalled. 'This little girl was only three and when she was presented to the Princess her mother had of course told her to refer to Diana as "Your Majesty". But the little kid kept calling her "Your Menace". Eventually, Princess Diana couldn't hold back the laughter any longer and said to her, "You look like a menace."'

Earlier that day, Tim and his band had been thrown out of the sartorially fastidious Centre Court pub in Glasgow because they were still wearing the denim outfits they'd worn on stage during rehearsals. He and his pals went back to the theatre where the Princess didn't seem to mind their clothes at all.

Still, Tim could see the funny side: that morning he'd received a call from David Meehan. Tim was to be paid a great deal of money to wear funny outfits. The DJ was to become a panto star. 'I'd never even been to a panto in my life before,' said Tim, 'but it seemed like a great idea. What I could never have predicted was the response I got from the kids. I had no idea they would go so mental. I suppose I was in my natural environment.'

David Meehan was certainly delighted Tim had landed the gig, appearing at the Pavilion Theatre alongside Christian in *Dick Whittington*. 'Panto time was a bit of a relief for me,' he said. 'Once Tim committed to a regular five or six nights a week, it was easier for us to handle. He only had to remember to go to one place.'

The panto deal did, however, bring its own set of problems. 'The worrying part was what he was getting up to on stage,' said David. 'You would get the phone calls from the choreographer or the director saying, "He did this, or he did that." Tim was the naughty schoolboy again. He'd start laughing during rehearsals or he'd deliberately try and trip people up on their lines—or even trip people up. He'd change the lines just before performance. He must have known that people who do regular panto are serious performers and they don't want to look like an arsehole.'

David Meehan found at this time his role was peace negotiator. 'What the directors would do is come back to me and say, "Look, Tim is absolutely fabulous. He's great with the kids and everyone loves him. But he's just got to do what he's told. Is there *any* way we can control him?" I'd have to say no.'

And, as happened with his television experience, Tim wanted to run the show. 'What Tim would do, for example, was say he wanted to do a big number with the band. You'd then say, "No, Tim, it's not a pop concert, it's a panto, it's fairly well scripted," and he'd say, "But what if I just do one song?" And you'd argue it out till he gave in.'

Eddie Tobin was both excited and frustrated by Tim's panto performance. 'The opportunity to get into theatre is fantastic, it's a door to lead you on to other things. It's well known in the business that it can take you on to STV, but Tim didn't see that at all. He wouldn't play the game.'

Colin Robertson pointed out that Tim was happy to act and look the clown in real life, but it had to be on his own terms. 'The panto character he used to play was actually Dim Tim. We would wind him up about it and he hated that. He felt the name was stigmatising and belittling. I'd say to him, "Look, it's showbiz, there are men wearing women's dresses in this, it's supposed to be a send-up." But he didn't like it at all. He felt that the characters he was playing were undermining his position as a top DJ. He had no intention of playing anything but The Star. He couldn't join the bottom rung.'

Tim disagreed: 'This was a whole new world for me. I'd have done anything to make the show work well.'

Back at Clyde, preparations were being made to move from Anderston to a new state-of-the art studio out at Clydebank. In the final week Tim would have had his Very Final Warning if Clyde bosses had known of his farewell address to Anderston.

One night presenter Iain Anderson brought in a media student, a very attractive woman in her early twenties, to see round the studio and gain some experience of live broadcasting. Tim was asked to show the student around the building. But he went a little bit too far in revealing all the nooks and crannies when he showed her the big stationery cupboard. She walked all the way inside, peeled off her ribbed polo-neck and offered to show Tim the easiest way to lick stamps.

'I thanked her for the offer,' said Tim, 'and told her I used to be a fully qualified GPO stamp-licker. It was all very tempting but I was a married man.' Not for too much longer, though.

13

Naked Video, Perfect Breasts and Andy Cameron

It seemed almost inevitable that when Tim and Clare moved into their heavenly temple in the Bearsden skyline, they were tempting fate. Life would never be quite the same again. The couple had grown further and further apart. 'I remember Clare asking me one time when I had a night off if we should go out or stay in,' remembered Tim. 'I stayed in because I was out so much. We had the usual meal and a bottle of wine, but I can remember looking at her and thinking we'd become strangers. I asked, "Do you still love me?" and she replied, "Yes, I love you, but I'm not in love with you." For me this was the beginning of the end.'

Tim was still hell-bent on pursuing success and working every hour he could. When he left Clyde most nights he would go off and do gigs. With the gigs came the attention of the hordes of girls who flocked around him. As time went on, he stopped saying no and it's not really that surprising.

Tim had married at the age of twenty and he was a very naïve twenty-year-old at that. The Christmas before his wedding he had been given *The Beano*, *The Dandy* and *The Beezer* annuals as presents—at his own request. Here was a man reading comic books and about to be married. Thirteen years later he was still reading the same comics. It's fair to say he didn't see the big adult picture in life. Nor did he view casual involvement with female fans as breaking his commitment to

Clare. Somehow he managed to separate the two concepts in his head. But every time he came home late or sometimes didn't come home at all, the structure of his marriage crumbled a little bit more.

Yet he didn't really see it. He saw Clare as the comfort blanket at home when life on the road became too much to cope with. His wife, on the other hand, had a very different lifestyle. She stayed home and looked after Melanie and Darren. She was the bedrock of the relationship. She made sure the bills were paid, that Tim's clothes were washed and the kids were looked after. Most of the family responsibility lay with her and Tim was very fortunate in that he could operate on very thin elastic. But Tim was to stretch that elastic to breaking point. There was an inevitability about the gradual break-up of the marriage. The relationship seemed to be precariously balanced.

David Meehan, meanwhile, was working hard to make sure his client had every career opportunity. He proposed Tim as the presenter of a new Grampian Television pop hits programme, *The Video Show*, for transmission across Scotland. It was a music format show playing chart hits, and perfect for Tim. But David, not surprisingly, was concerned his client might do something to endanger the opportunity. Past experience with the Clyde jock had taught him to be very wary. 'I hadn't been out with him once, I think, without his trousers coming down at some stage of the proceedings,' said David. 'Anyway, I arranged to meet the producer, Jim Brown, in Lautrec's in Glasgow's West End. And as a damage-limitation exercise I told Tim to come later. I even told him what to wear and what to say. To be fair, he did as I suggested and he was very well behaved, although he had a look on his face that worried me.'

David was right to be worried. 'Tim left—as planned—and I asked the producer what he thought. He said he figured Tim would have been a bit more bubbly but I said this was because he was playing it all a bit low key. But he seemed to be happy with Tim and we shook hands on the deal.

'So I left the restaurant and we both got into my car, as I was taking him down to Queen Street. But as we drove off from Woodside Crescent, there, at three o'clock in the afternoon, was Tim, waddling down the middle of the road with his trousers round his ankles. I rolled down the window and all he could say, smiling at me, was "I'm sorry, Davy. I just couldn't resist it." He got the gig in spite of himself.'

Tim's incredible predilection for exhibitionism continued right through the relationship with David Meehan. 'One night we went up to a meeting in Aberdeen to sort out details for *The Video Show*. We booked a table in a very plush restaurant and Tim sat there giggling for about fifteen minutes. We knew why. He had his trousers down again. Psychologists would have a field day with that sort of case. The sad thing is he's probably one of the most talented DJs ever, in terms of putting people at their ease. But over the years it's been so frustrating to see him spoil chances.'

Changes at Radio Clyde saw David Meehan leave behind Tim and the other presenters he had looked after. It had been a long eight years. 'It was fantastic fun and we had some real wild times,' said David, 'and Tim is one of nicest guys you will ever meet. But he made life very hard work.'

Towards the end of the year Tim was back in panto at the Pavilion. His popularity in the first season had been immense. Now he was a year older and wiser and would not repeat any of the mistakes he'd made the first time around.

Oh yes he would.

In *Jack and the Beanstalk*, he appeared alongside Andy Cameron, by this time a panto veteran. Tim was immediately to incur the wrath of the comedian. 'Andy had worked out this sketch with a great gag at the end,' recalled Tim, 'and I had to deliver the final line that let Andy come in with the punchline. But I was so unprofessional that I delivered the punchline and the whole thing fell flat. Andy just walked off the stage and wouldn't talk to me. Yet, I couldn't see what his problem was. I just figured it was a mistake and I reckoned Andy was being a bit too precious about all of it.

'Later on, I walked into the toilets and there was Mr Abie, who was one of the dames in the panto, standing there in a long dress having a pee but he wasn't laughing at the absurdity of our present situation. It was clear he was also in a huff with me. He told me in no uncertain terms I was in the wrong about spoiling Andy's gag and I should go to Andy and apologise. My first reaction was "Will I hell!" but Abie made the very valid point that there was a long run of the panto still to go and we all had to get on.

'Eventually it sunk in that Abie was right. I went up to Andy's dressing-room, knocked on the door and asked if I could come in. He nodded that it was okay to enter and I said, "Look, Andy, I'm really sorry. . ." and before I had to crawl any longer he came over, put his arms around me and gave me a big hug. I think he said something like "You're a blinking idiot" or words to that effect, and from that point on we became close. It was great. It made for a really good run.'

Tim would go on to complete the rest of the run all the way through till the end of January 1985 without incident.

Oh no he wouldn't.

As was the case with most panto performers Tim had a dresser. But in his case the young lady's title was something of a misnomer. The attractive young blonde turned out to be more of an undresser. 'One night she came in to get me ready for the show and get me into my costume,' said Tim. 'It all had to be done very quickly because I had been wee bit late arriving. Except that I didn't quite make it in time because we got to fooling around a little bit in the dressing-room and for every item she put on I seemed to take two off. Anyway, I missed the curtain call for the big entrance scene, where I was supposed to be on stage cracking a few jokes with all the cast and then breaking into a big ring-a-roses-type dance.

'God, I panicked when we heard the audience roar downstairs. I knew for sure everyone was on stage. My heart flipped and I pulled my Dim Tim outfit on as fast as I could, thanking God for Velcro in the process. I pulled up my tights and so did the young lady, then I ran down the stairs, jumping six at a time while pulling on my hat as I ran. When I got to the stage I didn't even stop, I just leapt right on, and as the big dance was already in progress with everyone in a circle holding hands I just grabbed someone's hands and joined in. I don't think any of the audience noticed my late arrival wasn't in the script.'

The next stage of Tim's life couldn't have been scripted. He had no idea that he would meet a stunning model and fall head over heels in love. He certainly had no idea the love story was to develop as a result of a craving for fish suppers.

One day in Clyde Tim was listening to a new record called *Like a Virgin* and commenting to a pal that he thought there was a chance it could make no.1. Talk then wandered to the news stories of the day, how Margaret Thatcher was destroying the country and so on, and then Tim's pal pointed out an article in that night's *Evening Times*. It was a story about Karen Flynn, a model on the Glasgow circuit who came from Balornock, just a couple of miles from Easterhouse, but who now lived in the south side of the city.

Karen was one of the famous Tennent's Lager can girls. She was an icon, a face that launched a thousand sips, the object of every lager-drinker's desires.

This feature story saw Karen tell the world about how her favourite food was chips. Apparently, she could eat sackloads and not put on weight. And the accompanying pictures of Karen proved her metabolism certainly had the ability to defy the effects of saturated fats. It appeared Karen's food intake had no adverse effects on her chest either. Karen was the Marks & Spencer's Lovable Bra ad model, chosen because she had the perfect size 34B.

The two pals at Clyde were looking at the newspaper and doing a little bit of drooling. Tim's pal then revealed a little secret: he had actually been seeing Karen. And just to get under the Tiger's skin, he played a little trick that night as Tim was about to go on-air. It was a gesture of one-upmanship that was to backfire. 'The receptionist rang through and said, "That's Karen Flynn on the phone," and I was more than surprised,' said Tim. 'I picked up the phone, said hello and Karen admitted straight off she'd been told to call to upset me. But I couldn't speak to her at this point so I said I'd call her back later for a wee chat.'

After Tim's show he did make the five-minute call which turned into an hour and a half. 'For some reason we were really hitting if off on the phone and at the end of the call she asked if she could come and meet me. I know at this time I should have said to Karen that I couldn't possibly put myself into a compromising position. I was a married man. And to add to it all this was a girl who was seeing my pal—albeit in a very casual way—but by this time I was thinking naughty thoughts about this wonderful body that's immune to the powers of Cookeen. So I agreed.'

David Meehan, incidentally, wasn't surprised when he heard Tim was prepared to put friendship on the line when an attractive woman came into view. 'If we were all out for the night and one of the guys happened to say, "Look, she's really attractive," Tim would go straight for her. He liked the spirit of competition.'

It was to be a few days before Tim and Karen met in the flesh. 'One night after I'd finished a show one of the crew came up to me and said there was a girl looking to talk to me. I was really tired so I said I'd give it a miss. But the roadie persisted: "You really should see this one," he urged. "She's something else."

'He brought the girl into the dressing-room where I was getting changed, and I was standing there in my underpants. Contrastingly, the girl had this huge fur coat on and looked like she had just stepped off the set of *Dr Zhivago*. She looked about nine foot seven. And she was stunning. It was Karen.

'She said, "Hi. Can I come in?" and then sat down on the couch and we had a drink. She was good fun and a real laugh, though different from the way I thought she would be, because I reckoned she'd be a bit of poseur being a Tennent's girl and all.

'At that point the roadie came and announced he was closing up and that meant I had to go as well, and I got my trousers on. But Karen had a little look of disappointment on her face. "Don't I even get a kiss?" she said. And I said, "Of course," and kissed her on the forehead, teasingly. She looked a wee bit huffy and said, "Is that it?" and I thought, "I'll show you," so I kissed her properly. That seemed to do the trick because she dragged me down on to the couch. Luckily, the roadie had gone at this point.'

An hour later the couple stepped out into the cold night air. Karen announced she was hungry. But since there was nowhere open by this time off they went, appropriately enough, to a chip shop where they sealed their union with chips and two pickled onions. 'I then offered to run Karen home but she said she didn't feel in the mood to go. She suggested we just pull over the car into a wee side street and talk for a while. It seemed a good idea, but we didn't really talk for very long. The excitement of this first meeting was still with us and it was clear the fur coat had to come off.'

The attempts at hot winter passion going on in Tim's Volvo were rapidly halted. 'Just as I managed to wrestle the fur skin to the floor there was a frightening bang on the window. A wee man was out walking his dog and had seen the shock absorbers on the car heaving and the windows were all steamed up. Thank heaven for Neighbourhood Watch citizens, protecting the world from having serious fun in the back of a Volvo estate.'

Clare wouldn't have thought the night was funny at all.

The next day Tim's thoughts were a swirling mass of confusion, a mixture of excitement and deep regret. 'When I met Karen at first it was all very strange and alluring, yet at the same time I was feeling low because things hadn't been right with Clare for some time,' he said. 'We'd just been drifting further and further apart and I didn't know how to reverse that process. I loved my job and loved the fun that came with it, and yet I was aware I had responsibilities at home. Believe me, I hadn't planned it. When Melanie was born I thought my life was complete and then when Darren came along I felt totally complete. I had a wee boy and a wee girl and a lovely wife and that was all I needed—so much so, in fact, that I had a vasectomy.'

But the dream of living life on Walton's Mountain didn't last. 'As far as Karen was concerned I really didn't know what to do. I was lost and confused. And I guess she walked into my life at the right time—or the wrong time, depending on which way you look at it.

'I didn't know where I was. I was a working-class boy from Easterhouse who was thrust into the glamour world of TV life and pop stars and models and I guess it opened my eyes. Karen represented part of that glamour. She was the unattainable and then suddenly she was within my grasp. Either way, things happened very quickly.'

Tim wanted to tell Clare about his involvement but he found it impossible. The Tiger had never really shown any signs up to now of being good at dealing with responsibility or confronting awkward predicaments, and this situation was impossible for him.

'The affair with Karen happened so fast,' he said. 'At first I thought I could handle it, that I was calling the shots and that I could make it all stop and nobody would be affected. But it didn't work out that way. It grew so quickly. Then I figured I could get her out of my system by spending enough time with her. So I had some time away with Karen but in fact it only pulled us closer together. I was hooked.'

He realised he was in love with Karen. 'The pressure, the intensity of the relationship was so great that I gave in to her. But of course I felt terrible about the kids, that was the main thing, but I still couldn't confess to Clare. One night I tried to talk to her about why I was so miserable but I simply couldn't put it into words. This may sound naff but coincidentally there was a can of Tennent's lager lying around with Karen's face on it and I picked it up and showed it to her. She knew immediately what it meant. She must have already heard the gossip. She ran upstairs and cried and I stayed down in the living-room and cried and it was awful. I couldn't cope with what I'd done to her. But at the same time I tried to console myself with the knowledge that we weren't the same two people we had been when we got married. We really had grown apart.'

Clare had been worn down. After a lot of tears and debate, Tim moved out to go and live with his Uncle William who had since moved from Partick to north Kelvinside.

He now had another issue to contend with. What would he do with Karen? Initially, she had still been seeing Tim's friend. 'I hadn't taken Karen seriously. After all, she was seeing someone else and she was a model. Models came with this tag of arrogance attached to them. But, then, the more I had talked to Karen the more I learned how down to earth she was. After all, she came from Balornock, just along the road.

'I called her up and she had just arrived back from holiday. I asked her out on the following night but she said she couldn't make it. She was seeing the other guy. Now I realised I was hurt and this made me even more determined. I put my foot down. I told her this guy was my pal and I wouldn't do anything (more) behind his back so it was make-your-mind-up time. I said she had to finish with him.'

The ultimatum worked. Karen, as it happens, had decided she wanted to see Tim.

Tim and his DJ pal didn't speak for a while. It was obvious the other guy felt betrayed by his mate but Tim eased his own conscience with the thought his friend had another girl on the go at the same time. 'All's fair in love and war,' he thought. And that's what the affair with Karen became: love and war.

Meantime, Clare and the kids moved into a new house in Bearsden. Tim moved out of Uncle William's house and into Karen's place on the south side.

'We were like Richard Burton and Elizabeth Taylor,' said Karen, 'only a bit more volatile. I think part of the problem was we were both jealous of the other getting attention from the opposite sex. And we were both flirts so there was never really a quiet time. But we did have great fun together.'

Karen was clearly a strong-minded character who was more than a match for the Tiger. 'She loved cats,' said Tim. 'She had six kittens—all strays—and two cats. When you woke up in the morning there would be cats climbing the curtains, all over the bed, all over you. When I first moved in I said to Karen, "Look, you've got to get rid of them." And she didn't. That should have told me a great deal.'

Karen put a slightly more truthful spin on the tale. 'What Tim said was "It's me or the cats," and I said, "Well, there's the door!" And he left. And about ten minutes later he came back.'

'It was a fiery, tempestuous relationship,' said Tim. 'We had great fun and great arguments. But I owed her a lot. At this time I wasn't making any real money—any money I had was going to Clare and the kids. Karen would feed me and do everything for me. I had nowhere to live and she said I could come and live with her. She'd take the bus to work in the morning, do her modelling shoot and come back and make the meals.'

Karen converted Tim to vegetarianism. She refused to cook him meat and Tim, too lazy to look after himself, agreed his body would be a meat-free zone. There's no doubt that Karen was always the dominant partner in the relationship.

Tim had a hard time coming to terms with a woman who would set the agenda, who didn't worship at his feet because he was well known. 'I remember one night we were driving up Hope Street,' said Karen, 'when we noticed a crowd of guys in a car waving to us. Tim smiled over and the guys kept waving. Tim said when we pulled up at the next traffic lights he'd better say a word to them because they were obviously fans. But when he rolled down the window one of the guys shouted out, "Hey, Karen!" and that really burst Tim's bubble. I think he liked the idea of going out with someone who was recognised but the reality of that could leave him a little jealous.'

She took no nonsense from Tim either. One night in Glasgow's Peking Inn restaurant Tim played a childish prank on his girlfriend, pulling her chair away as she went to sit down. 'Karen whacked me across the face and told me to grow up,' said Tim. 'I didn't try that trick again.'

The Burton–Taylor image Karen suggested was accurate. The couple would split up regularly. 'We'd fall out, I'd leave and I'd go back and she'd have cheese and toast ready for me. I suppose it was all a bit predictable and I guess we enjoyed the making-up part of it all.'

They enjoyed it enough to get engaged. 'Yes, I suppose we were,' said Karen, 'although I can't recall any official moment of proposal or anything. Maybe I never took things that seriously. I was only about twenty-one at the time, after all.'

She may have been twelve years younger but in most ways Karen was the determined half of the relationship. On holiday in Portugal, for example, it was Karen who fought to have their hotel changed when they were booked into a building site, taking no nonsense from the tour operators. And one weekend when the couple took a break at a cottage on Arran it was Karen who protected Tim from crazed sex beasts.

'We went over and on the way some guys there were winding Tim up about the rutting stags. They told Tim he had better beware because they liked nothing better than to have a go at virile young men. Tim bought it. When we arrived he refused to get out of the car in case the stags rutted him and I ended up carrying the luggage into the cottage.'

Tim laughed as he recalled the incident: 'I didn't know what "rutting" meant, then. I thought it meant they were demented or something.'

Tiger Tim was to have many exciting adventures with the new love of his life, some of them very painful. Karen, in sharp contrast to Clare, would accompany Tim to gigs and she loved the atmosphere of it all. It was just as well she went along that night to the Royal in Coatbridge.

'There was a record in the charts at the time called *Superman* by the truly awful Black Lace and there was a dance craze that came along with it,' said Karen. 'This dance involved people putting their arms out and suddenly marching forward. Well, Tim was playing this record while standing on a stool just in front of the DJ box. But as the crowd surged forward in time to the music, he was knocked off his stool and right through the plate-glass DJ box.'

The rest of the night was spent at Monklands Hospital where Tim had fourteen stitches in his right arm.

'Tim was always a wee boy,' said Karen. 'He needed looking after. He was always disaster-prone, always late and always, I remember, very tired. Sometimes we'd come back from gigs and Tim would be so drowsy he'd fall asleep in the car the second he switched the engine off. And rather than wake him up I'd sleep beside him. I don't know if this was an indication of future health problems but at the time he was always exhausted.'

14

Frank Carson, Biggins and
the Beauty Queen with the Horse

Tim wasn't concerned with his continual battle against tiredness. It was, he reckoned, the price you had to pay for working day and night. He was more concerned about his appearance. 'He was terrified he would go bald,' said Karen. 'As such, he was always doing something with his hair. It always had to be perfect. In fact, my brother picked up on this and when he came to our house he would break eggs on Tim's head to get him going. And, boy, did it work.'

Tim would agree he was obsessed about hair loss, particularly since he has a perfect head of hair and no one in his family ever suffered from premature baldness. 'It's true. When I was a teenager I remember buying different shampoos—in sachets—for every day of the week. I figured that if each of them did what they claimed, I'd have no worries with hair loss.'

He knew why he had this follicular fixation. 'My mammy,' he said. 'She was always on about my hair when I was young, fixing it up into a wavy shed. She has to take full responsibility.'

Karen Flynn could put up with Tim's little idiosyncrasies because in many ways they were perfectly matched. She may have been quite a bit younger but Tim had never really left his teens. And Karen, now twenty-two, was full of life and fun. 'Karen used to come up to Clyde a lot and she'd sit there while I did the night-time show,' said Tim.

'One night we got to kissing and cuddling and as I was playing records she began kissing my neck. She sat on my lap and all I can recall from that point was becoming lost in a haze of passion.'

The main studio at Radio Clyde had a glass window to an adjoining studio. Luckily, there was no one in it at the time—although Tiger Tim's little adventure was seen: his PA at the time, Ronnie Bergman, happened to walk by, catch an eyeful and discreetly disappear.

'The record I had on the turntable lasted two minutes and forty-five seconds,' said Tim. 'I remember glancing at the clock and thinking, "I wish I'd put on an album track." But then again, it was getting pretty hot in that studio so perhaps it was better I hadn't.'

Karen and Tim's little studio moments continued. One night while Iain Anderson was broadcasting, Tim and Karen were in the studio, sitting opposite. Iain decided to take advantage of Tim being around to capture some of the DJ's thoughts about holidays to Saltcoats for a series he was working on. Tim walked around to Iain's microphone and, standing beside the desk, listened to Iain say: 'Tiger Tim has been to Saltcoats on holiday—haven't you, Tim?' And just at that point he realised Karen had disappeared from her seat. A big grin appeared on Tim's face and he was clearly unable to speak. In a flash Iain glanced at the floor and realised Tim's trousers had been pulled down to his ankles. To his credit, Iain hardly missed a beat and simply announced: 'Well, listeners, I think the Tiger is rather indisposed at the moment so we'll get his views on the seaside town later.'

But although Karen and Tim were liberal in their attitudes to public displays of affection, that open-mindedness did not transfer to Tim's perception of what newspaper readers should see. 'We had some huge arguments about what she would or would not wear when she was doing fashion shoots,' said Tim. 'Sometimes I felt she went over the top and, to be honest, I didn't like it at all. We both agreed, though, that she wouldn't do topless modelling. That would have been going too far.'

The biggest source of friction was Tim's kids. He missed Darren and Melanie. They couldn't come to Karen's flat because it was so small, so Tim would go back to their house in Bearsden. It was a strange, confusing situation for Karen. Here was her partner going back to his wife at weekends. It didn't matter to her that Tim and Clare were no longer sleeping together. The important factor was he was with Clare and the kids at their home when he should have been with her. 'Things with Clare were amicable,' said Tim. 'It seemed to make sense to go home. And I was desperate to see the kids. They were of paramount importance.'

Karen and Tim settled back into their Burton–Taylor on-off kiss'n'make-up madness that was perfect for both of them.

It was at this time that one night Tim enjoyed a Radio Clyde boys night-out with Paul Cooney and Gerry McNee at The Granary pub in Shawlands. The trio took to discussing the attractions of the female staff, in particular a young waitress called Carol Smillie.

'The other two sort of dared me to chat her up,' said Tim. 'I didn't want to, at least not in front of everybody, but after a couple of dry Martinis I gave in to the pressure and decided to make my pitch. "Hi Carol," I said, "fancy going out some time?"

'She said, "No, I don't think so."

'And I said "Why?"

' "Because you've got a girlfriend."

'At this point I should have quit while I was losing because Carol knew Karen—she worked part-time as a model alongside her. But I didn't. "Karen and I have split up," I told her.

' "Since when?"

' "Since yesterday."

' "Yes, and tomorrow you'll be back together again," replied Carol.

'I couldn't argue with that sort of inescapable logic.'

Tim was to get another chance with the attractive young waitress many years later.

But now, for the first time ever, he had a problem with the media. Although most of the Scottish press saw the popular DJ as being virtually flameproof against attack—who would want to have a go at the cuddly Tiger?—that view wasn't shared by Irish comedian Frank Carson. Carson hated Tim. It seemed he had taken an absolute and immediate dislike of the DJ even though they had never met.

The situation developed after Tim had appeared on *Good Morning Britain*, ITV's flagship breakfast programme. He was booked to come on and discuss an item about the cold weather and he was asked, in the usual patronising manner, to give Londoners advice on how to keep warm. Tim was never one to pass up the opportunity for a bit of national publicity. True to form, he decided to dress up for the occasion and have a bit of a laugh with the London-based TV pro-ducers. And so he appeared on national television—at the age of thirty-three—sitting in a deckchair, under a parasol, dressed in a tigerskin leotard and tiger boots.

Frank Carson was clearly not impressed with Tim's mini-perfor-mance. Speaking the following day on BBC Scotland's *The Art Sutter Show*, he described Tim as being as 'entertaining as a burning orphan-age'. The conversation on the show had wandered onto the fertile ground of the merits of Scottish performers when the normally jovial Irishman launched his attack. He said Tim was the worst possible ambassador Scotland could ever have. And he told Art Sutter—and thousands of listeners—that he recommended Tim 'not to give up the day job'.

Carson, who was appearing in a panto at the Ayr Gaiety at the time even continued his attack after the show. He declared: 'To me, Tiger Tim has nothing. It's a mystery how he ever got an Equity Card. I was embarrassed for him and for Scotland when he appeared on ITV's breakfast show.'

The Tiger was saddened to hear the criticism. 'I'm amazed at why Frank Carson should be slagging me,' he exclaimed in the papers the next day. 'But I'm not going to lose any sleep over it. And I should point out I was quite pleased with my TV performance. And on a point of detail, I actually gave up my day job fourteen years ago when I left British Rail to go and work as a DJ in the Electric Gardens. Having said that, it's a pity Frank thinks I'm rotten. I quite like him.'

BBC Scotland refused to fuel the flames any more and played down the incident. 'We have nothing but friendship and respect for Tiger Tim,' they said. 'There's nothing we can do about off-the-cuff comments.'

Tim's magnanimous comments, considering he had been slated, went down well with the media the following day. It wasn't difficult to work out why Carson had hit out at the Glasgow favourite. Frank Carson was performing at a struggling panto in Ayr. Tim was a sell-out in the city centre.

Meanwhile, back in pantoland with *Jack and the Beanstalk*, the Tiger tried to put his personal problems to one side, doing what he did best—mischief.

'At the end of the last week Christopher Biggins came in for Andy Cameron and he was nice bloke and a complete luvvy. We got on very well and we'd have chats in his dressing-room, so I figured he could take a laugh.

'On the last night, when it is customary for people to have a little joke, I decided I couldn't miss out on the opportunity. The scene came when Biggins—who was playing Jack's mother—throws the beans through the open window of Jack's house and the beans then grow overnight into a beanstalk.

'But, unknown to Biggins and to the audience, I was behind the fake window set with pots and pans in both hands, so that as the beans came flying through the window I caught them and threw them right back. I thought it was hilarious. The more beans he threw the more came right back at him. And then I began throwing the pots and pans.

'Biggins managed to finish his wee scene and kept a straight face but then he stormed off stage yelling, "I've ever seen such unprofessionalism in all my life!" The crowd were fine with it. They sort of expect things to go wrong in the last night, don't they? But Biggins didn't see it that way. In fact, I was scared to go up and apologise to him. So I didn't. I kept right out of his way and I've never seen him since.'

There was more mischief at Clyde. This time it was Tim's mouth which once again got him into deep trouble. 'A new girl had started at the station and her name was Jackie McPherson [who later became Jackie Bird] and one day all the guys in the canteen were talking about how gorgeous she was. Just to attract attention and shut them up at the same time, I butted in and said, "Whit? Jackie? Och, I had her ages ago." And, sure enough, the boys all fell silent.

'It wasn't until a couple of days later that Jackie marched up to me in the corridor like she was marching on Poland and said, "Right, I want a word with you! What's this you've been telling people you had sex with me?" I could have died. I wanted to be in the bottom of the canal. I wanted never to have been born. I muttered something about it being a little joke but she would have none of it. I apologised, of course, but that wouldn't do either. She said to me, "You and I are going to go into every single office in this building and you are going to tell everyone there that you did not have sex with me. Do you understand? And you are going to do it now." And we did. And I felt small. I was now tiny Tim.'

In some ways Karen was perfect for tiny Tim, always the mischievous little boy who had to be kept on a rein. Karen could pull on the reins when she had to but she could also be equally, if not more, outrageous. When they were out together there was always a chance of an incident that would become the talk of the steamie for days to come. One example was a ski fashion night at the Hospitality Inn, which saw all of Scotland's top models assembled in one room as they prepared to get their salopettes out for the watching world. Karen was one of the models that night, and Tim spent some time with her and her colleagues as they got dressed for the occasion. Well, he was harmless, wasn't he? He was Karen's boyfriend, after all.

Tim had a problem that night, however. He couldn't take his eyes off one of the models, Georgina Kearney. It wasn't that he fancied Georgina exactly, though as a former Miss Scotland, the blonde was certainly attractive. What grabbed Tim's attention was the sheer size of the young lady's breasts. The cotton top she was wearing served only to accentuate the curves and Tim found himself like a little boy in a fairground. He had an uncontrollable urge to explore all the delights on display.

His moment suddenly arrived just before the girls went on the catwalk. Georgina took the opportunity to nip to the toilets round the back of the hallway but just as she turned to close the door she realised a little Tiger had crept in behind her. She told Tim to get lost. He shrugged. And then began pleading: 'I only want to get a look at them, please.'

'Get lost, Tim. Your girlfriend's in the room, for goodness sake.'

'Look, I'll leave. But just let me have a look. If I can have just one wee look, I'll leave straight away.'

'Tim, get lost. You're a sad degenerate of a man. Go away.'

'Yes, I know I am, but just let me have a wee look.'

And to ensure the Tiger would purr contentedly, the model formerly known as Miss Scotland lifted her top and revealed to the little boy the secrets of her treasure chest.

Tim didn't stop there. 'I could see that I was on a roll so I said, "What's the chance of a wee squeeze? Look, I'll never ask again, honest," and she shrugged and said, "Oh, go on, then. Hurry up. I'm dying for a pee."'

Tim performed his strip squeeze and returned to the main room where Karen and the other girls were dressing. 'I've seen them,' he announced to Karen, in the same proud way that a nineteenth-century African explorer would announce his latest discovery to the National Geographical Society.

And on this occasion Karen didn't perform the role of the jealous girlfriend. 'Well, Georgina was her pal,' Tim explained. 'Karen knew it was just me playing the fool.'

As the summer approached, Tim and Karen were to find themselves yet again in the company of a group of lovelies. Tim was asked to be the compère for the Ayrshire heats of the Miss Scotland competition. It proved to be a night of confusion and madness. He had been invited to Ayr by Ricky Fillingham, an agent, and Bryce Curdy, a West Sound DJ and television presenter. Bryce's wife Margaret was the event organiser.

The night got off to the worst of starts. 'I went up on stage and announced, "Welcome to Miss Scotland," and then my job was to bring on the girls individually and introduce them so that the judges could weigh up their communication skills,' said Tim. 'But in my mind I had a mission to stop them saying all the usual vacuous things beauty contestants come out with—like they want to work with handicapped kids, love their grannies and plan single-handedly to end Third World poverty.

'The first girl came up and I asked her what she did in her spare time. She said, "I breed horses," and I said I was stunned and muttered something about that being the last thing I expected a beauty queen to do. I should have moved on from there but I was intrigued. My mind was caught up it in the mechanics of it all and I had visions of a beauty queen with a sash and tiara crawling under a big horse and trying to guide it into the right position. I was laughing in my head as I came out with the next question: "Is it hard to get them together?" And she looked dumfounded. Like a clown I pursued this daft line of enquiry. And then I asked her how she managed to find the right two horses who fancied each other, and did they get a chance to be together for a while on a sort of date before they got down to it. I could hear groans coming from the audience and I don't think I'd even had one Martini that day. There was no excuse for the nonsense. Meanwhile, I could see the judges looking at me and wondering what I was going to say next.'

The rest of the interviews, about fourteen more, passed off more smoothly. But there was real trauma ahead. 'I went upstairs for a break and to see Karen and I saw her chatting over at the other end of the hall with a couple of other models. So I went back downstairs and got to blethering at the reception with the organiser, Margaret. As we were chatting, suddenly the lift doors opened and out came Karen with her two pals. She came over cheerily and I introduced her to Margaret as my girlfriend.'

From this point events turned ugly. 'Margaret Curdy looked at her and said, "*This* is your girlfriend? What happened to your beautiful wife?" I explained we were divorced, or we had split up, and she said, "Oh, so *this* is it?" looking over at Karen.'

Karen, not being subtle, and certainly not the type to turn the other cheek, sought immediate retribution for the injustice committed against her by a perfect stranger. 'She cracked Margaret right across the jaw,' said Tim, 'and then followed it up with a "Fuck off, you old bastard." There was hair everywhere. I grabbed Karen away from Margaret, then went back outside to the main function hall just as Ricky arrived. He grabbed me and asked what the hell was going on. I tried to explain the little skirmish but he told me I wasn't doing the second half, "Because your girlfriend has slugged the chairman's wife."

'Bryce Curdy had to do the second half himself and I had to leave the hall discreetly and head for home. Karen and I had a big fight in the car and I asked why she hadn't shown some self-restraint, and she argued, "No one will talk to me like that." In retrospect, she was absolutely right. She'd done nothing to deserve the insult.'

They got over the events of that night but there was the ongoing dilemma between the two: Tim's children. Karen agreed the situation was pulling the couple apart. 'They were nice kids but I was young. It wasn't what I wanted. Gradually, I found myself doing more and more work in London and this added to the strain on the relationship.'

Tim found himself torn. 'One night, after an argument, Karen announced the kids wouldn't be allowed back into her house under any circumstances. And, as you can imagine, the relationship deteriorated from there.

'But we didn't walk out of each other's lives—we had been too close. We couldn't be together, but we couldn't be apart either. We had no idea what to do.'

By the end of the year Tim had the feeling his life would never be quite the same again.

15

Life's a Beach

'THE TIGER LEAVES CLYDE' ran the headline in the *Evening Times* in February 1986. No one could believe it. Clyde's most famous DJ had announced he was leaving the station. The newspaper revealed that Tim had been 'lured doon the watter' for £30,000 a year to join West Sound, a radio station in Ayr. None other than Sydney Devine, who had once been a Clyde presenter, was the middleman in bringing Tim to the coast.

Speaking to the *Evening Times*, Tim joked about why he'd gone with the singer. 'I'm a good friend of Sydney—his only one, I think. And I liked what he showed me of the station. I got the old buzz back again. It was like being back in the early days of Clyde when there was bags of enthusiasm all around.'

That wasn't the reason for Tim's departure to the coast. His deteriorating relationship with Karen was a pivotal factor. He felt deeply unhappy that life wasn't going the way he wanted it to. Tim was also unhappy with his position at Clyde. He was enjoying working on his 7–10 p.m. show and relationships with the other jocks were great but he occasionally felt he was on stony ground with boss Alex Dickson.

'Tim was going through a very difficult time,' said David Meehan. 'After the attempts to break into television he again returned to the pop star thing and that didn't work out. Tim again figured he was more than a DJ. To cap it all, there was a major change at Clyde when Andy

Park left and Alex Dickson came in. Alex certainly didn't give Tim the same leeway that Andy had. I imagine that Tim had reached the stage where he no longer enjoyed working at Clyde. It was really the end of an era. A lot of faces had moved on. Clyde had become much more of a business at this time. It certainly wasn't the fun palace any more.'

Matters had come to a head when Tim was signed to do the panto with Andy Cameron at the Pavilion. The pantomime was a co-production between Radio Clyde and the Pavilion Theatre. As a result, Tim, for the first time, negotiated his fee through Clyde. 'I was talking to Alex Dickson about the cash,' recalled Tim, 'and I made the point that I was pulling in as many punters as anyone. And since I was a Clyde jock I expected to be looked after. Alex assured me I'd be paid as much as Andy Cameron. But I reckoned that wasn't the case. Someone told me they'd seen a list of salaries on a desk at Clyde which said Andy was being paid much more than me—more than double—and it just seemed so unfair.

'Alex argued these figures weren't the reality but it left a bad feeling between us at the time. We had some words and I said, "Look, if I don't get the same as Andy, I'm leaving." Alex said, "Well, go then, if that's what you want to do." It was a Mexican stand-off. I didn't really want to go but it was about pride and self-respect. I had no choice.'

Tim, in several minds, prepared to leave Glasgow behind. Fortunately Karen got him organised. 'He had just bought a new house in Prestwick and I said to him, "Here's £1,000, use that to get a new washing-machine and other things." He said to me, "I don't want your money, Karen. I can't take it." And I said, "Tim, it's not my money, it's yours." He was useless with money. He used to leave cheques lying around all over the house and I'd find them and bank them. He had no idea until I gave him the bank book with the money in it.'

It was a strange experience for Tim to be in Ayrshire. The Glasgow boy felt like a fish out of water. He bought a house in Links Road in Prestwick that looked out over Arran. There was a fabulous view— unless you glanced to the left, where you could see a public toilet. But Tim chose to accentuate the positive.

However, his friends and family were concerned about Tim's personal and professional future. At the time Clyde had 1.2 million listeners. West Sound picked up 176,000. 'I'll be after all the ears I can get,' said Tim of his new show.

Dora was particularly concerned. 'He had a lovely house in Prestwick and I'd take the train down and do his washing,' she said. 'But he was very unhappy. He liked the quiet but he had an awful time. I remember going down in the first week and he was sitting in a corner, all hunched up and unshaven, and he was going right down the hill. I felt West Sound was a dead end for him and with the break-up of the marriage and with Karen Flynn . . . oh, goodness.'

Tim was a lost boy. 'I was pretty sad,' he admitted. 'In the first couple of weeks there I even arranged to go and see a psychologist about my behaviour and try and find out why I was so miserable. After talking to me for a couple of hours, she told me there were several theories to explain my unhappiness. She said perhaps it could be a constant need for approval on my part that left me driven. She suggested it may even be an attempt at covering up a natural shyness or perhaps my wild behaviour was a reflection of how I can't deal with any kind of loss in my life.

'And at the end of the session she paused for a moment, looked me in the eye and explained she'd rejected all the textbook theories. She had her own theory. She said, "You're nuts, Tim. That's the best explanation I can offer you." I had to laugh. It's just as well she didn't charge me.'

Radio presenter Terry McGeadie had become friendly with Tim just before he left for the coast. Out for a drive one day with his wife

Caroline he decided to drop in on his pal. 'He came to the door looking like a strange apparition,' said Terry. 'He was wearing a pink dressing-gown—at two in the afternoon. He had pinkish hair and he was wearing a pair of tigerskin slippers with huge claws. I took one look at the tiger feet and said, "Oops, erm, I think we'll come back later," and we got in the car and drove off. But as we pulled out of his driveway Caroline let out a shriek. She had turned around to wave goodbye and there was Tim's bare arse on view. She reckoned he was as mad as a hatter.'

There was little happening at the time to rouse the Tiger from his morose mood. Not even a surprise visit.

'My marriage had ended and my relationship with Karen had ended, although she did come down to see me a couple of times,' said Tim. 'I remember she turned up once unannounced. It was raining heavily, she was soaking wet and she looked fabulous. But my mammy had also come to visit that weekend. It was a nightmare situation, having your mother and your ex-girlfriend under the same roof. The atmosphere was as heavy as a Black Sabbath concert.'

Tim, even at the age of thirty-five, didn't want to be seen sleeping with a girl while his mother was around. And Dora wasn't too pleased about her boy spending the night with a strange woman. Tim could understand Dora's point of view. 'It doesn't matter how old you are. In your mother's eyes you're always ten years old. But even without my mother there, it wasn't going to work out with Karen. We agreed not to see each other again. I was sad about the situation but we just couldn't get over the barrier that was the kids.

'And, at the risk of sounding melodramatic, I had the feeling I never wanted to be in a serious relationship with a woman again. The feeling was that the game's a bogey.'

Tim did see Karen again, although the next time it had nothing to do with the lure of a 'can't live with him, can't live without him' relationship. 'I was ill,' said Tim. 'I was really ill. I think I got some bug and I was sick all the time. And when Karen called I told her. She was working in London at the time and she took the first flight up. She stayed with me for a week until I got better. That meant a huge amount to me.'

In the weeks ahead, Tim resolved to make the best of his situation. But first of all he had to get over what was to be a frightening glimpse into his own future. 'I remember walking up the street in Prestwick with a friend from West Sound and I saw this girl come towards me using a zimmer frame to walk with. I was astonished to discover it was my cousin Elizabeth, my Uncle Jackie's daughter on my dad's side, who'd moved down to live there with her husband. We stood and spoke for a while and then I remember she waited until I had walked off before she began to move. It was obvious she didn't want me to see her in such a bad condition.' Elizabeth had multiple sclerosis.

Tim tried not to dwell too long on Elizabeth's condition because he was still something of a lost soul in Prestwick and trying to come to terms with life in a strange town and living on his own for the first time in his life. He also found his first day at West Sound very strange. It wasn't the huge state-of-the-art-studio he'd enjoyed at Clyde. There was no indoor swimming-pool here or patio or custom-built canteen. West Sound was a converted house and it was tiny in comparison. But the people were nice. Tim knew Bryce Curdy, of course, particularly since Karen had socked his wife, although that incident was never mentioned again. And Sydney was a pal. Fate was kind to Tim, however, and he quickly discovered the coastal town had its attractions. One attraction was so powerful Tim's commitment to celibacy lasted only a matter of days.

'When I had started at West Sound John MacAulay, the programme boss, had a secretary named Anne McNaught. I'd heard she was a really lovely girl. But John took me to one side and told me he didn't want me to go anywhere near her. He also added that her father was the vice-chairman of the company.

'When I met her, I thought, "Wow!" She was lovely—and really posh. John had also told me, laughing, that I wouldn't have any chance with her because I was a scruff from Easterhouse. It turned out she did look at me twice. We became an item, but then I blew it big time. I have to admit my immaturity really showed me up. The morning after Anne and I had consummated our relationship I told John what had happened. It was all so childish. It was as if I was getting my own back at him for suggesting I wasn't good enough for his secretary. And just at that point Anne walked into the building.'

Tim, incredibly, managed to make such an awkward situation even worse. 'I said cheekily to Anne, "I've just been telling John that I slept with you last night." She glared at me and said angrily, "Don't be so stupid." John just laughed and said, "Told you. No chance."

'But later on she got me on the stairs and really ripped into me. She yelled, "How dare you tell people what happened between us!" I tried to argue that no one believed me anyway.

Anne was more forgiving than she should have been and she and Tim went on to become boyfriend and girlfriend. Things seemed to run smoothly for a few months—well, as smoothly as they can run when half of the partnership is an immigrant DJ from Easterhouse who refuses to grow up.

Sadly, the relationship collapsed thanks to another surprise visit. 'We got all dressed up for the West Sound dance one night,' said Tim. 'I had been at the station for about ten months by this time and we were really looking forward to the big do. But just as the music kicked off, I turned around and there was Karen, standing there dressed to kill and clearly out to make a statement. I was both shocked and delighted at the same time. And if Karen had a plan, it worked. I went off with her and that, of course, was the end of the relationship with Anne.'

Tim was a two-time loser. 'I never saw Karen again after that night and in retrospect it was a crazy thing to do, but I loved the craziness, the madness about Karen. She was a siren—she pulled you onto the rocks and you couldn't help yourself. And Anne? She never spoke to me again.'

Tim was now a single man. By this time he had become very close friends with his dentist, Blair Anderson, and they did what single men do: they went to the pub to mingle and check out the talent. One night in a bar in Prestwick, Blair pointed out that a girl behind the bar was looking at Tim. Tim looked over and the young lady smiled. After a few Martinis, Tim approached her. Her name was Gillian Eaglesham. 'It was totally crass, but the first thing I said to her was "Why don't you come back to my place tonight?" And she said, "Pardon?" in a completely disbelieving way.'

Tim's famous mouth had once again engaged before his brain was in gear. 'I got nowhere with her and I tried to speak to her for a few nights. Each time I approached her, though, I was pretty drunk and this didn't go unnoticed.

'Anyway, one night, sober, I went into the pub, leapt up on the bar and began to sing—very loudly—*Arrivederci Roma*. I don't know why. She told me to get down but I insisted that I'd get down only if she agreed to go out with me. She said nothing and I took that as a positive sign. So I asked her if she was free the following night but she told me she was working at the Modern Homes Exhibition in Glasgow. Surprised, I asked what she was doing there. Was she a builder? A chippy? Did she work in a chippy? And when I heard the reply my heart sank. "I'm a model," she said. And I thought, "Oh, no. Not another model.

That's the last thing I need."

'I agreed to pick her up the following night in Glasgow and bring her back home and from that point, life changed. I had fallen in love. I guess I never learn. It was like the situation with Karen—it was all fast and furious. But again there was an age gap. Gillian was just celebrating her twenty-first birthday. I was thirty-five.'

In spite of this, the pair figured they had a future together. 'I bought Gillian a birthday cake and put an engagement ring in the middle of it. She thought it was wonderful. And it was. Sheer bliss. The relationship ran like a dream.' For a few months at least.

But, for now, he was enjoying life on the beach. He had a gorgeous girlfriend, he was popular at West Sound, Darren and Melanie would come down and stay at weekends and his mammy would come one day a week to put his life and socks in order. What more could a man want? Of course, just as things were going well, Tim would repeat the regular pattern and bring about some angst in his life. Again, he managed to combine showing off and self-destruction in one sweet move.

One day in West Sound in the summer of '87 it was a very hot day and the air-conditioning system was going full-out. Tim shook his head as he recalled the stunt he pulled. 'Someone called Elliot Davis had sent me a cassette with songs on it by a new Glasgow band. They were called Wet Wet Wet and I thought the songs were okay, but what really struck me was the power behind the singer's voice. I thought he'd do well.'

After listening to a very young Marti Pellow, Tim had a little thought to himself. He reckoned he'd do his radio show in the nude. 'I've never had so many visitors to my studio in my life,' he said, laughing at the recollection. 'There were girls coming in from all over the building, coincidentally. And I announced over the air I was naked but I guess the listeners all thought it was a gag.'

It wasn't. Radio Clyde presenter Suzie McGuire was working at West Sound at the time, answering the phones. 'I walked into the studio and there was Tim sitting stark naked,' she recalled. 'The programme controller John MacAulay [now a Clyde Two presenter] stormed in and really wiped the floor with him. He told Tim he'd be taken off the air, and in fact he'd be taken to the police station. Yes, I've seen Tim in all his glory. And most of the other girls at West Sound have too.'

His colleagues reckoned Tim had left all his common sense back at the Lanarkshire border. But that was to do him a great mis-service— he'd never had any in the first place. Still, they appreciated he had a sense of humour.

It has to be pointed out that not everybody at West Sound was a Tiger fan. Certainly not DJ and country singer Tommy Truesdale. 'Tommy did the show just before mine and at the changeover I'd always make a little comment, something along the lines of "And there goes Tommy riding off into the sunset, pardners . . ."—something corny like that, but apparently Tommy didn't think it humorous. And one day as I sat down in the studio chair he stormed in and shouted out, "You bastard, Stevens! You've been talking about me on air! Step outside and strip to the waist!" Now, I have no problem taking my clothes off, but not outside when I'm supposed to be broadcasting.

'I later learned that Tommy had an album out at the time and someone had put it back in the music library in bits. He probably figured I was the likely suspect, but in actual fact I quite liked his music.' He laughed. 'My money's on Sydney Devine.'

The Tommy Truesdale Affair apart, it seems the Easterhouse boy was born to bare all. And there were many young women keen to indulge his willingness to roam as nature intended. 'One girl from a local newspaper came to interview me at the radio station in Ayr. She was a lovely-looking girl with long blond hair, and after we'd finished the chat she asked if I had any good photographs from older times to illustrate the article and I said I did but that they were back at my house. She suggested we go back to my house and pick them up. And, to be honest, I never thought anything of it, but she obviously did. Back at the house we had a cup of tea and a chocolate biscuit and a chat and before you could say "Suggestive digestive" we were shaking the crumbs out of the bedsheets.

'I saw her a few times after that and I really liked her. She had a sense of fun about her. Well, I suppose that was lucky because one night at my home she had an idea. She said, "Do you know what I've always wanted to do? I've always fancied a midnight swim." So that's what we did. My house was right on the beach—but, remember, this wasn't Benidorm, it was Ayrshire.

'So we went down onto the sand and she whipped off her little dress and dived in. It was all too cold for me, and although I come from Easterhouse I wasn't that tough. So I did what any fine gentleman would do under the circumstances: I picked up her clothes and ran off with them.

'About a quarter of an hour later she appeared at the door. She looked great, dripping wet, her hair clapped into her head all very Deborah Kerr, and she said, "You bastard!" And I burst out laughing. Luckily, she came in, had a shower and we made up in the nicest possible way.'

The relationship didn't last. 'I discovered I wasn't the only man in her life,' said Tim. 'It seems I was unknowingly one corner of an eternal triangle. It's sad because I was really keen. I guess it was pretty bad timing. Maybe if she hadn't been involved it could have become really serious. I think it would have.'

And maybe if Tim himself hadn't been engaged at the time? 'The engagement idea had faded by this time,' he claimed. 'And I guess at twenty-one Gillian was ready to tackle the world. She was very ambitious.'

There was another familiar problem in the relationship. 'Gillian couldn't handle the kids when I had them at weekends. She was fine at first but later she figured they were taking up too much space in her life.

'With the kids aged three and four at the time they would come to see me and it was like a wee holiday for them, because my house was right by the seaside. I loved it. In the car on the way down I'd play a Superman tape for Darren and he loved the theme music. He'd put his arms out the back window and pretend he was flying. I had to play that tape about ten times between Glasgow and Prestwick.'

About nine months into the West Sound job, a new girl joined the station. She was fresh-faced and stood out not only for her English accent but for her natural talent behind the microphone. Her name was Jackie Brambles. Tim and Jackie, who was later to go on to become a star name at Radio One and is today GMTV's Hollywood reporter, quickly became real friends. 'We had a great relationship,' said Tim. 'She worked night-times and she came on air after my *Drive Time* show, so we both had afternoons off. We'd go for long walks on the beach and have ice-creams and just generally hang out together.'

Almost inevitably, a little *frisson* gradually developed between the two. One afternoon they were having tea in Tim's house and things reached the point where Tim figured the couple might get around to that very first kiss. Neither of them had planned the moment. It was just something that looked like it might happen. But before Tim could take time to thank his lucky stars at having the chance to snog the attractive young blonde with the sexy voice, fate intervened. The telephone rang downstairs in the hall.

'I didn't know whether to laugh or cry,' said Tim. 'It was Karen on the phone. I hadn't heard from her for months and she picked this day of all days to call and see how I was doing. As was always the case with Karen, she was an Olympic-level talker and I couldn't get her off the phone. And as I was trying to make my excuses and say I'd ring her back later I turned and saw Jackie coming down the stairs with her coat on. She walked past me, slammed the door and left.

'As soon as I got Karen off the phone I jumped in the car and drove up to the station. The train to Troon was pulling away when I got there and I could see Jackie through the window. I shrugged at her in disbelief and she stared back at me. About twenty minutes later I called her at her flat and asked her why she'd run off. She asked why she should she sit waiting for me while I was on the phone to my girl-friend. That sort of logic makes perfect sense to me now, but at the time I couldn't comprehend it. As far as I was concerned, Karen was an ex-girlfriend.'

Tim and Jackie continued to be good friends. If there was ever to have been a moment between them, it had passed.

But Tim was to get other opportunities at West Sound. It wasn't only the ladies at the radio station who thought the Tiger was quite cuddly. 'There was one young guy who worked in the record library, a very clever boy, who was obsessed by Tim in a nice sort of way,' said Suzie McGuire. 'He would follow Tim around like a little puppy. It's not to say the boy was gay, but he certainly thought Tim was a god.'

The god, however, was to prove to be mortal.

16

MS

The day arrived that was to change Tim's life forever. "I'll never forget the moment,' he recalled. 'I was running up the Links Road in Prestwick on a lovely summer's day when suddenly my legs went askew. I was with Gillian at the time and she said, "Your legs look a bit funny when you run. What's wrong?" I said, "My legs always look a bit odd when I run." But I knew there was a real problem. So did Gillian. She said, "Tim, you'd better go the doctor and get checked out."

'I didn't have a doctor so I went to Gillian's doctor in Troon. He was very nice and told me there could be a chance it was MS. But he said not to worry because there was only a one-in-a-thousand chance that it would be.

'The fear didn't register with me at first because I'd always run a bit awkwardly. My Uncle William had even told me that when I was eleven. But I suppose I knew something was wrong, although I was in denial for a while.

'Later, I had a lumbar puncture at a local hospital and nothing was found, so I was sent to the Southern General for a series of tests. It was there that the specialist confirmed the original diagnosis. It was multiple sclerosis. I felt like someone had hit me in the face with a cricket bat. I was stunned. I couldn't speak. I had to drive back to Prestwick and I could hardly see for tears running down my face. All I could think was "I'm going to die. I'm going to be in a wheelchair." I kept thinking of Stuart Henry—he was a disc jockey like me, he had MS and he died.'

Henry, the first Scots DJ on Radio One, had suffered from MS, so badly in fact that he had spent the last ten years of his life trapped in a wheelchair and requiring constant attention. He died of MS related-illnesses in 1986.

Tim couldn't cope with the news. His mind was hit by an avalanche of sheer terror. 'That drive back to Prestwick took forever,' he said. 'To compound matters, I had no wife, no long-standing relationship because the situation with Gillian had broken up, and I couldn't even call Karen. It wouldn't have been fair to burden her with this when we'd agreed to move on.'

Arriving in Prestwick, Tim tried to think about what the doctors had told him about the disease. He read an information booklet someone had given him.

'Multiple sclerosis (MS) is the most common disease of the central nervous system. The disease attacks the myelin covering of the central nervous system, causing inflammation and often destroying the myelin in patches. This process interrupts and distorts the natural flow of nerve impulses. The result may be vision problems, numbness, loss of balance, extreme fatigue, tremors and even paralysis.'

The more Tim learned of the illness the more he cried.

'Spontaneous recovery from symptoms can occur and last for several months or years. But multiple sclerosis is often progressive and characterised by unpredictable attacks causing further disability. As yet, the cause and cure are unknown, but recently drugs to reduce the frequency and severity of MS attacks have become available. In addition, many MS symptoms can be helped by medication and therapy.'

Drugs? Medication? Therapy? None of that had helped Stuart

Henry. And he was a DJ just like Tim.

'I drove down to the seafront and sat on a bench, looking out at the waves for what seemed like forever. I never felt I would throw myself in the sea—I had too many responsibilities—but I remember looking at an old couple walking by, holding hands, and thinking I'd never get the chance to be like them.'

Tim began to realise he'd had warning signs: the chronic fatigue, sleeping in the car with Karen. There were a couple of times he'd felt wobbly, but he'd put it down to tiredness and stress.

None of that mattered now. He had to speak to someone. He called Gillian. 'When I told her about the MS she was okay about it. She was supportive. But we weren't a couple any more and I couldn't expect too much from her. She had to get on with her own life.' Shortly afterwards Gillian went off to Dubai to become an air stewardess.

The Tiger had to get on with his own life and show some Easterhouse toughness. To get him through the days he would take comfort in the knowledge that there are several very different forms of MS. And that at thirty-five it was likely his was the least debilitating form. God willing, he may not even have another attack of the wobbly legs for years to come.

'In the beginning you think that something awful is going to happen every minute of every day but then when nothing does happen you put it to the back of your mind. It's not something you can allow to dominate your life. If you worried about it you'd be depressed the entire time and that would affect the nervous system even more.

'So I put it to the back of my mind and got on with my life. Some sufferers panic when they feel a twinge or a spasm. I never felt like that. I tried to be positive. And I think that's because I kept seeing people who were so much worse than me. And I kept hearing all these horror stories of people who are *really* badly off.'

There was also the recent memory of his cousin Elizabeth to contend with. 'That did make me think,' he said. 'But I tried to push her condition to the back of my mind. I just had to try and move on.'

17

Humble Pie and Bad Headlines

Tim's spirits were revived one morning in September when he turned up for work on his new breakfast show. A young woman had phoned programme boss John MacAulay and asked if she could come in to the station for work experience. Rashly, he assigned the girl, who was still at school, to the Tiger's show, as his assistant.

'She would come in every morning really smartly dressed,' said Tim, 'and of course the rest of the guys started having little fantasies about her. She was gorgeous, she was seventeen—almost eighteen, as it happens—and she was a dead ringer for Jennifer Lopez. And they'd tease me about getting her to come in wearing her school uniform. You know what perverts some men can be.

'Anyway, just to humour the other guys, one day I asked her why she wore such trendy clothes to school. She told me she dressed like that for work experience and then nipped home to get changed into her school uniform. Now, I was thinking that this was really inconvenient for the girl. So, for her sake—and I suppose for the rest of the guys— I suggested she wore the uniform when she came in to do the programme. She said, entirely innocently, "Would that be okay?" and me being magnanimous to the hilt said, "Oh, sure, I think that would be fine." My eyes must have been a dead copy for the Big Bad Wolf's at that point. Anyway, she agreed it was a sensible idea. And I told the rest of the guys that she'd be wearing the blazer and tie the next morning.

'At seven thirty the next day the station was packed with men I'd hardly ever seen before. They'd all come in to see her in the uniform.' The story with the schoolgirl ended there. For the moment.

In the meantime Tim was becoming more and more unsettled at West Sound. After a couple of years the novelty of life at the seaside had worn off. To make the situation even worse, his pal Jackie Brambles phoned one day to tell him she'd been offered a job with Capital Radio in London. Former Radio Clyde presenter Richard Park, now Capital's station boss, had heard Jackie's programme when driving in the area. 'She called me up to say she'd been offered a job as a weather girl or something,' said Tim, 'but I told her to ask for her own show. She stuck to her guns and got it. It was a fantastic opportunity for her but it was really sad to see her go.'

Tim was also aware that Radio Clyde in 1988 were growing all the time. Ratings continued to improve at his old station while West Sound's audience seemed to be static.

'I felt everything was so localised and that I'd come to a dead end,' said Tim. 'I thought I needed to get back to Clyde. I really missed Glasgow. So I bit the bullet, called Alex Dickson and said I'd like to come back. He didn't exactly bite my hand off with jubilation—perhaps understandably, since we'd left on less than great terms.

'He told me they had Ross King and Gary Marshall—the Sunshine Boys—who were doing very well with the night-time slot that had been mine. But he didn't slam the door in my face. He said to leave it with him and he'd call me back. And he did. But it wasn't great news. He rang to say the best he could offer me was one or two shows a week and a wee bit of filling in for other jocks on holiday. I was pretty disappointed but I think I managed to hide it. I said, "Thanks, but no thanks," and that was that. I wouldn't have been able to afford to live on the kind of money that would pay. But not long after Alex called back to offer me my old show, the 7–10 p.m. slot. I was delighted. I was going home. I could kickstart my life again.'

Unknown to him, he had a secret ally. A few weeks before, Tim had met up with Paul Cooney and Ross King down in Ayr where Clyde were staging a summer roadshow. 'Tim came up on stage to say hello to the crowd,' recalled Paul Cooney, 'and the response he got from them was fantastic. That night we went out to dinner and I got the feeling he wasn't all that happy at West Sound. And when I got back to Glasgow I spoke to Alex Dickson and said, "Look, we really have to get the Tiger back on Clyde. The fans love him." And that's what happened.'

Dora was also delighted for her son. 'He was very lucky to get back into Clyde. It was very good of Alex Dickson to take him back.'

Tim put his house on the market and had no problems finding a buyer. To celebrate, he went out that night for a drink in his local. 'I walked into the same pub where I'd met Gillian,' he recalled, 'and who should be there but the schoolgirl who had worked on my show. She had left school by this time and was celebrating her eighteenth birthday. We got talking. In fact, we got talking a lot. We talked right through to the next morning.'

The day before Tim moved back to Glasgow, there was a letter on the mat from Joe Campbell, the station boss at West Sound. 'It was a lovely letter. He thanked me for the time I'd spent there and said he didn't think I would have stayed too long because the station wasn't big enough for me. It was really nice of him to make me feel appreciated.'

Tim moved back to Glasgow, to buy a house in Hogganfield on the north side of the city next to the famous loch. Actor Tony Roper and his wife Isabel lived along the road. Life was a great deal happier. He was still in touch with Gillian, although romance was not at the top of the agenda, and she'd come to visit her ex in his new house. Except that the house wasn't Tim's. He only thought he'd bought it. Once again confusion had followed the Tiger trail and caught up with him. He even had extensive work and other developments carried out but it turned out he didn't actually own the place. There was a problem with the title deeds. The people Tim had bought it from didn't own the deeds and lawyers hadn't picked up on the discrepancy. Tim had to leave. This time he decided to move back to the northern leafy suburb of Bearsden.

He didn't make the move on his own, though. Journalist Lorraine Davidson, who was then a TV reporter with Scottish Television, was an old friend. She helped him move to Bearsden, to a terraced house in Ilay Court. It was a cosy situation. DJ pal Ross King lived two doors along. And although there was no permanent woman in Tim's life he had no shortage of offers to help him choose borders for his new wallpaper.

At Clyde, he had settled in straight away. It was as if he had never been away. He was once again excited about work. At Christmas he even got together with his old pal Rikki Brown, now a comedy writer at BBC Scotland, to write the radio panto *Tiger Tim's Christmas Adventure*. Rikki used the opportunity to embarrass his friend whenever he could by including brief segments of *Star Girl*. The story of the panto was fundamentally nonsense but Rikki had managed to incorporate most of the characters who'd played a key role in Tim's life. 'Someone actually played the part of Jet Mayfair,' said Rikki. 'Well, you couldn't ask a legend to play himself, could you?'

Tim was very much his old self at the start of 1989. He was enjoying life in Bearsden and being near the kids and for the moment the demons of ambition were resting. Perhaps it had something to do with making the most of every day life had to offer. He hadn't had any MS attacks, for which he was thankful. On occasion he felt very tired, but then that had always been the case. He worked in a high-adrenaline business. But, overall, there was more self-awareness about the boy who refused to grow up. Perhaps that's why he agreed to play along with an idea for a feature in the *Sunday Mail*. The plan was Tim would be hypnotised in an attempt to take him back to his childhood—it was an idea that caused most people who knew him to smile, realising the journey wouldn't take very long.

'It worked,' said Tim. 'I had never been hypnotised before and I reckoned it just wouldn't work on me which shows how much I know.

'I went under straight away and I revealed all sorts of details about my past lives. It turns out I was once a fourteenth-century schoolboy who lived in Paris and I had an affair with my schoolteacher. I liked the sound of that French adventure. Then, in another life, I was a farm boy in the north of Scotland. I actually described my full outfit, and I was wearing flannel trousers or something. Luckily, I didn't seem to be a mass murderer or anything in any of my previous lives. But it was all a very strange experience and quite frightening. In fact, it was so disconcerting that I haven't been hypnotised since.'

By the autumn of 1989, however, Tim found himself in a trance-like condition again—as he weighed up the talent at what had become Glasgow's in-place, the Cotton Club in Scott Street. Wednesday nights were popular with the good-looking girls, the models and trolley dollies who arrived by the planeload. It was also very popular with the cream of Glasgow's footballing talent, who went along for the midweek beer, the chat and a wee bit of attention from the posing females and fly girls.

It was at the Cotton Club that Tim developed a friendship with the likes of Ally McCoist. 'Ally was great to hang out with,' said Tim. 'As you can imagine, the girls would flock around him at the bar and there would be too many for him to chat to so I'd get the overspill. Although

I wasn't getting the attention at first hand, that didn't matter at all.'

Tim did get first-hand attention from one of the models on display. Alison Dragoonis was a dark-haired beauty from Rutherglen who had all the boys at the bar drooling. And the fact that there was unanimous approval of Alison made Tim determined that he would win her over. He caught her eye and asked her to dance. And, for the first few seconds at least, he was making all the right moves. 'Then I lost the plot,' he said, smiling. 'For some reason unknown to me or anyone else, I began dancing really stupidly. There were arms and legs going everywhere. If you can imagine John Travolta meets Donald O'Connor meets Michael Flatley, you'll have some idea of what went into my performance.'

The boys at the bar thought it was hilarious, but Tim's partner didn't take it well at all. 'She yelled, "How dare you! I've never been so embarrassed in all my life!" I couldn't do anything but laugh and walk away. She really, really hated me at that point.'

One girl at the Cotton Club clearly didn't hate Tim. 'I never did find out this girl's name but as I was leaving the club one night she grabbed my car keys and jumped in my car. I said, "What are you doing?" And she said, "I'm coming home with you." I said, "I don't think so."

'Now, don't get me wrong: the girl was stunningly attractive. But she went on to tell me that she'd fallen out with her boyfriend and this was her way of getting back at him. As we were talking she yelled out, "Look, there he is!" and this big black Mercedes drove past and I slid down in the seat, half expecting the side window to go in or something. I'd had enough. After a great deal of persuasion, she left the car.'

The public at this time had no idea Tim had MS. He hadn't had any real problems with the condition and didn't see any reason to let it be known. He certainly didn't want sympathy, nor did he want to be constantly reminded that he had what could become a fatal disease. As a result, he told only those closest to him. Even Karen Flynn, who was now living permanently in London, was unaware of Tim's illness. 'I was shocked when one of the family told me,' she said. 'Tim had such life about him and I felt it was tragic. I suppose it did explain his tiredness and health problems.'

In Glasgow, where it's always been difficult to keep a secret, the rumour factory was working overtime. Tim had been seen out a few times when he'd lost his balance, and there were the odd occasions when his voice sounded heavy and slightly slurred. It didn't take too long before word was going round, first of all, that Tim had a drink problem—which the Martini Kid thought was a real irony—and then that he had AIDS. At this time the world was in the grip of AIDS terror and just about every celebrity who couldn't complete a triathlon was supposedly dying from the dreaded virus.

Just to make matters worse, Tim actually fuelled the flames of hot gossip. In an interview where he attempted to fudge questions about his health, he gave a newspaper the chance to sensationalise a throwaway remark. 'In one silly line in an interview at the end of 1989 I told a reporter that when I'd been speaking to my doctor about feeling rough, I casually suggested, "See while I'm here, you might as well give me an AIDS test." I went on to tell the journalist that the doctor laughed and said, "What's the point? You don't have AIDS." And then I told the journalist I'd persisted, just to pass the time, sort of thing.

'I didn't tell the journalist this, but I suppose what I was really doing with the AIDS test was giving myself some platform where I could be proved negative and then say to myself, "Well, Tim, son, at least you don't have AIDS, you don't have the worst disease imaginable." I suppose I thought after AIDS that just about everything else was negotiable.

'Anyway, the reporter picked up on this AIDS–doctor line and the next day the billboards outside every newsagent's in the city screamed "TIGER TIM IN AIDS SCARE".'

Tim was horrified when he saw it. 'It was irresponsible journalism but I guess I was irresponsible in mentioning that I had once had an AIDS test. Of course my mammy was walking down Byres Road that day and she saw it and nearly died.'

Dora admitted that was the case. 'When I saw the posters in the street saying he had AIDS I almost had a heart attack. I couldn't go outside the door. I knew people would say to me, "Well, of course, that's the type of life people have in showbiz."'

Tim's mother recalled it was a hugely difficult time for the immediate family; and she knew that trying to keep secrets in Glasgow is next to impossible. 'My sister told me she saw him in Argyle Street,' said Dora, 'and she thought he was drunk. That's how difficult it was.'

In the Clyde studio, Tim never showed any signs of MS. His speech was always clear, perhaps due to the adrenaline rush he still experienced before each show.

Gavin Docherty, a writer, interviewed Tim for the *Evening Times* during this period and painted a colourful picture of the DJ's working life. 'Tim is preparing for his Thursday-night '70s show, holding court while being joined briefly in the sound studio by DJ Gary Marshall. The show is rude, crude and hysterically funny, featuring heavy *double entendre*. With age the energy is less. But with the exception of the giveaway eyes which have the permanently tired look of someone whose sleep-wake cycles are mixed up, the boyish looks remain intact. He plays to his own legend. "I'm really hyper," he says. "People think I'm gassed or on accelerants, but honestly, I don't booze much any more and I've never done drugs, not ever."'

'He spoke about his health. Two years ago while doing a gig at a disco he felt his left leg go from under him as he had begun to walk towards the stage. Stevens crashed into a table and bounced off the deck, before picking himself up and going on with the show. He has since endured painful exploratory tests, during which a hypodermic needle of the kind they use to fell a bull was inserted into the base of his spine and fluid withdrawn. Stevens has been tested for the muscle-wasting disease MS, and ME.'

Tim clearly wasn't being honest with Gavin Docherty. The writer continued: 'Stevens was the subject of a grotesque and humiliating newspaper article insinuating he had AIDS (he was merely blood-tested for it, a commonplace thing with suspected viral cases). He pushed thoughts of illness out of his mind but he was tired at the gig at the Tin Pan Alley club the following night. The first thing he did on arrival was to head to the bar and down a glass of Coke, a chaser for pills prescribed by a homoeopathic specialist for the recurring waves of fatigue that seize him. Someone suggested there was nothing wrong with him that one early night in bed wouldn't cure. Tim laughed contemptuously. "ME? MS? I've had all sorts of things thrown at me," he said. Tim figured his own personal physiotherapist Bobby Preston [the same Bobby who'd worked security at the David Cassidy concert] had got nearest the mark. He told Tim it was nothing more than a bad dose of LB. "Whit's that?" Tim asked. Preston's smile widened. "Ye're just a lazy b . . ."'

It was clear Tim was having problems living the lie. The tiredness had to be explained somehow.

But not straight away. It would be another year before he was ready to tell the world. In any case, he felt fine most of the time. And in spite of the feelings of exhaustion that would sometimes engulf him, he signed up for the panto once again at the Pavilion. He was back appearing with old friend Andy Cameron, this time in *Robinson*

Crusoe. There was a little condition drawn up in his contract with the producers which ran: 'Mindful of the state of his health, Tim will ask to be excluded from overly physical dance routines on stage.' There would be no more late dressing sessions and leaping onto the stage while tucking his tights into his underpants.

That's not to say, however, that Tim planned to lead a life of celibacy. Far from it.

18

TV Blondes and Marti

In the New Year Tim continued to make his Wednesday-night trips to the Cotton Club and the attention from the attractive girls who gathered around him kept him more than entertained. He didn't have a serious girlfriend, but he had lots of serious offers. There was one which surprised him. It came from the girl who really, really hated him, Alison Dragoonis. 'She hated me quite a few late nights,' said Tim. 'She hated me with a passion.' There were other girls Tim was to become exceptionally friendly with over the months, such as another Glasgow model, Susan McKechnie.

But with the arrival of the new decade Tim's energies were again focused on his career. 'I'll have to break out and diversify,' he said at the time. 'I'd love to get into TV again. And perhaps a business venture ought to be on the cards. Maybe a pub or something.'

Andy Park, who had once hired Tim at Clyde, agreed that the DJ had to move on. 'I said to him within the first couple of years of him being at Clyde, "When are you going to stop calling yourself Tiger?" I think the root of his dilemma lies in that fact.'

Tim was reluctant to let the Tiger loose. 'Andy was my mentor. But dropping the nickname will be easier said than done,' he said then. 'I've always regarded "Tiger" as a term of endearment and people regularly use it. But I guess this is my first attempt at growing up. I've really got to concentrate on my career.'

Tim's fleeting moment of career concentration was disturbed one day while working at Radio Clyde. As you would imagine, the disturbance came in female form. 'I had given up all thoughts romance when Linda Baker, who worked in advertising, came down to see me. She said she had a wee surprise for me. She said, "My friend who works at the BBC and reads the news wants to come in and have a look at you doing the programme. I think you'll like her. She's got lovely long blond hair," she added, mischievously. So Linda brought this girl in and true enough, she was lovely. Linda introduced her: "Tim, this is Kirsty, Kirsty Young."

'To be honest, I thought she was really posh. And I thought she was pretty but also a bit off-hand. She asked a couple of questions about what I was working on and acted interested, but I felt she was going through the motions.

'The pair left and then about ten minutes later Linda stuck her head back around the door and asked me what I thought of her. "Good-looking girl," I said, "but too posh for me." Linda said, "Oh, don't say that." And I said, "Why not?" And Linda said, "Well, because she likes you. In fact, she was going to ask you out." I said, "Yeah, you're winding me up." Really, at that point, I didn't care too much because the blonde hadn't made that much of an impact as far as personality goes, but Linda insisted I call this Kirsty girl up. So I did. And that deep voice answered. So, in my own inimitable, subtle style, I played around the edges of intriguing conversation and teased her with anticipation.'

No he didn't.

'No, I didn't. I hit her between the eyes with the schoolboy opening line: "Linda says you really like me". And she said yes.

'I thought, "Oh, God, what do I say now?" So I said, "Well, do you want to go out some time?" immediately realising I sounded remarkably like a thirteen-year-old boy who fancies the girl in the newsagent's.

'It turned out she was reading the news at nights on the radio so I suggested that since I worked till ten we'd meet afterwards and go for a late-night curry. And that's what happened. Off we went to a place in Jamaica Street and we had a chat. She came across as a lovely girl with a great personality, and the relationship grew from there.'

Tim waited for the right moment to tell Kirsty that he suffered from MS. But that moment always seemed to be in the distant horizon. 'I never told her,' he said. 'I just didn't. It never came up in the conversation. No, that's not true. I guess I wanted the relationship to be stable before I told her. At what point when you meet someone do you tell them you have an illness like MS? Yes, ideally you should be honest from the start, but what if you only have one date—or three dates? Do you tell them at that point? Do you announce to the world that you have an incurable illness?'

At this time Tim had told Gillian, of course, his mum, Bobby Preston Snr and his pal Ian Donaldson but they were the only people who knew. 'I guess I never told Kirsty because I didn't want to jeopardise the relationship. And I guess I felt embarrassed. But at this time the MS didn't show. There were no real signs. My balance was a wee bit dodgy at times, but it was fairly unnoticeable.'

Tim discovered that Kirsty wasn't at all stuck up and she could be every bit as earthy as he was. 'We had lots of fun together and she had a really good sense of humour. One night, for example, we were in the studio at Clyde and she was helping me make jingles. I really thought I would put that deep, dark sexy voice of hers to good use. In one of the jingles she had to say "I really love Tiger Tim" and after she said the line I came in with the wee ad lib "Great. Any chance of a shag?" But she just laughed and said, "You really are disgusting," but in that "Ooh, you are awful" Dick Emery sort of way. There was very little that could shock Kirsty. Although believe me, I tried.'

And vice versa. 'Kirsty could be very wild,' said the Tiger. 'She's not at all as she appears to be on television.'

The more Tim saw of her the more he became smitten. 'We had a great time together and she was great with the kids. I remember her down at the beach on Prestwick with Darren on her shoulders. And we went on holiday together to York for a few days. We found this lovely little hotel after the long drive and fell on the bed, shattered. But not too shattered. Then we went for a walk to see York and I tried to look interested in the local architecture, knowing she really liked the area. I remember I pointed up at one church and said, "That's a nice wee building, isn't it." But Kirsty put me right: "Tim, that nice wee building is York Minster." But we had a nice time.'

They had a great night out at the Rangers Edmiston Club at Ibrox one night when Tim and Marti Pellow teamed up on the panel of judges to pick Miss Rangers News. 'Marti was called up by the MC, Terry McGeddie and he came along with Eileen Catterson, his girl-friend.

'Now, early in the evening, Eileen had predicted how the night would go. She told me that at some point in the proceedings the band would ask Marti to sing but Marti had already said he wouldn't get up on stage, no matter what. But she said he'd shrug and he'd say, "What the hell," and get up. And that's exactly what happened. He got up and sang four songs and he was absolutely fantastic—he's undoubtedly one of the best singers Britain has ever produced.

'But the point of the story is that because Marti was up there I wanted to get up and do my bit. I didn't want to be outdone by a mere pop star so I offered my services and took Marti's place on the stage. Not surprisingly, I sang *Roll Over Beethoven*—in D—and in the middle of the song, where there's a little quiet instrumental bit, I shouted out, "Listen, Marti, this is how a song should be sung!"

'Marti wasn't to be outdone, however. He called back, "You carry on, Tiger. Just remember I'm back here with your burd."'

Kirsty liked to sing, too. One night at the Jaguar Club in Govan, Tim was invited along to judge a karaoke competition. 'The committee got both of us up to sing and Kirsty chose *Islands in the Stream*, the Kenny Rogers and Dolly Parton song. And I have to say she was a very good singer.'

The couple may have been in harmony on stage, but away from the limelight there were problems which came to a head after three months. By this time Tim was in love with the lady with the sexy voice but he had concerns about the relationship. He sensed Kirsty wasn't as serious about it as he was.

'One night we sat in my car outside her flat in Glasgow's south side and I asked her where we were going. She was pretty blunt. She said that if a job came up in London she'd have to go for it. She added the sweetener that she'd still have weekends off and we could get to see each other. But in my mind I was thinking that she'd move on and meet new people and all of the things that do happen in life. She maintained she was only being honest with me. And I appreciated that. So I wished her well in life, all the time hoping she'd suddenly stop me and say something like "Don't be crazy, I'll never leave you, we'll work it out somehow" but she didn't. She said goodbye. She got out of the car and walked up the stairs to her flat.

'I just sat there in the car and I remember thinking, "Oh no, here's another gorgeous girl I've lost." But what could I do? I couldn't beg her to continue a relationship with me. So I drove off. But I didn't head for home. I drove round the block and thought to myself I was a real idiot. I really liked the girl. I was in love with her for God's sake. So I pulled up in front of her flat again. I would go back and talk sense into her. And I sat there thinking this for about fifteen minutes. But I figured it out. I figured that it wasn't meant to be. Kirsty had other plans in her head and I wasn't included in them. It was very hard but I drove away.'

It was to be another three years before Kirsty actually left for London. And, after the initial hurt from rejection, Tim decided he wanted to see her again. 'I reckoned if we were going to split up it had to be in a special way. That sounds a bit gushy, I know, and I suppose I was being a bit melodramatic but I didn't want it all to be over so thoughtlessly. I guess you could say I wanted to bring about a sense of closure. So I called Kirsty and we agreed to meet in a Glasgow restaurant, Café Gandolfi, in Candleriggs. And, just to gild the lily, I phoned young Bobby Preston, the musician, to arrange a wee surprise.'

What Tim was suggesting was certainly a surprise to Bobby Preston. 'I said to him, "I want you to come into a restaurant and sing for me." He didn't hesitate with his reply: "Get to fuck, Tim." But I said "No, Bobby, it's better than that. I want you to wear a tigerskin shirt and carry a rose for me." Amazingly, after some lengthy debate, he agreed.

'So there we were, Kirsty and I, in posh Café Gandolfi having our coffee, and in bursts Bobby wearing the tiger outfit, carrying a rose and playing a guitar. He began to sing *You've Lost That Tiger Feeling* in front of a packed restaurant and everybody in the place loved it. They burst into loud applause and it was like a scene from a Hollywood romantic comedy with people all round standing up and cheering and smiling. Except Kirsty. She didn't know where to look.'

If Tim had hoped deep inside that the restaurant stunt would somehow see Kirsty turn somersaults, he was wrong. Anyway, she had a new man in her life. But Tim and Kirsty had one last rendezvous which had been arranged some months before the split, the Rangers FC dance at Peebles Hydro. Kirsty still wanted to go and pushed aside the fact that the couple had since gone their separate ways. And Kirsty again took great delight in meeting Wet Wet Wet singer Marti Pellow.

'We were again sitting at a table with Marti and Eileen when suddenly the band announced, "Can we have Marti Pellow up for a song, please?" And Marti looked a little unsure, so I said jokingly that I'd go up and take his place. Obviously he realised, quite rightly, that the crowd wouldn't be too excited at that prospect, so he suggested a compromise: that we both get up and sing *Da Doo Ron Ron*, with me doing the lead vocal, and Marti, Kirsty and Eileen doing the backing vocals. Of course that was a stupid idea—Marti Pellow backing me? So I argued a bit and Marti ended up singing the lead.'

The night out with the pop star and his girlfriend went well. By this time Tim and Marti had come to know each other fairly well. 'We got to chatting about whether or not he would ever go it alone. There had been a lot of talk in the papers about Marti being offered films and West End shows but he was unequivocal. He said he'd never go solo. The band were all mates and he wouldn't leave them.'

As for Kirsty, it would be another three years before Tim saw her again.

19

Cool Blondes, Crimpers and Excess Baggage

After the Kirsty affair, Tim convinced himself he really was destined to remain single. The romantic in him hoped that he'd find a permanent partner in life but, being realistic, he reckoned the chances weren't good. Part of the problem was his choice of woman: Karen Flynn, Gillian Eaglesham and Kirsty Young were, well, young and ambitious and all looking to further their own careers. They would come to realise that being the Tiger's girlfriend was something of a full-time job. And, it had to be said, it would take a very special type of woman to be able to cope with Tim's foibles. 'Tim never really grew up and I did,' said Karen Flynn. 'He's a great person but anyone who enters into a relationship with him has to be prepared to take on Peter Pan.'

Tim, understandably, was feeling at little lost at the beginning of 1990. Ideally, he would have liked to have kicked off the New Year with one special woman. At this time, the only person in his life matching that description was Dora. But one morning in February that was all to change. 'I was sitting in the house one morning when the phone rang. It was my ex-girlfriend Gillian who had just returned from Dubai. She asked if I fancied going to lunch and I thought, "Why not?" And so we met at Princes Square in Glasgow and had a nice chat about old times.

'After lunch was over I suggested we go and see Rikki Brown from Easterhouse who, in his pre-newspaper days, worked in Fraser's in the menswear department. Gillian agreed and off we went across the road. But as we walked into the store I saw this girl working there, a real stunner with long blond hair, who had on a very sexy blue dress. Not being slow to miss an opportunity, I sent Gillian off to look at clothes so that I could find an excuse to chat to the blonde. I strolled over and asked her how I could find Rikki. It turned out he was in the cupboard on the second floor, his usual hideaway, scribbling away little ideas for TV scripts, and so I had a quick chat with the blonde. I discovered her name was Moira Townsley, she came from Balornock and had a fantastic smile.

'Just then, Rikki came into sight and she disappeared. I asked him about her—did she have a boyfriend and so on—and he was brutally frank. He said, "Forget it, Tim. She's well out of your league. You have no chance." But that was like a red rag to a bull.'

Moira recalled her first impressions of Tim. 'That day in Fraser's was the first time I met Tim but I knew he was a cheeky bugger. When I was younger I'd listened to him on the radio. In fact, one night I was at my friend's house, Helen McGill, who also lived in Balornock, while she was on the show winning a competition. But I had no idea what he looked like until the day he walked into the store.'

Bearing in mind she worked in a fashion department, Moira couldn't have been less impressed with her first perceptions of the Tiger. 'He was a tramp,' she said. 'He was wearing old Physique joggers that were full of holes in the backside, he had on an old T-shirt and his hair was all over the place. But there was something about him that told me he was more than interested. And as he walked out of the store I can remember thinking to myself, "He'll be back."'

Moira was right. Tim was intrigued by her and no doubt spurred on by his pal's determined opinion that he was wasting his time. 'The next day I was really curious about Moira and I called Rikki for her number.

He wouldn't give me it, saying rightly that it was against company policy and he could be sacked for passing it on. But, eventually, after a lot of haranguing, threats and promises, he surrendered the number and I called her.

'I said, "Hello, it's Tim Stevens," all bright and hopeful, and she said, "Who?" I thought, "Oh, oh. Problems." And then she said indignantly, "How did you get my number?"

'When I told her Rikki had given me it after a great deal of persuasion, which was true, she put the phone down. I called her back and she put the phone down again.

'I tried again and said, "Look, I'm just trying to explain—and about this hanging-up business, gonnae no' dae that," or words to that effect. Click. She must have hung up on me about ten times.

'Eventually, I tried again and said, "Please, don't put the phone down. Can we go out sometime and have a talk?" I was desperate for something to say. Luckily, she finally said, "Look, if I agree to go out with you, will you stop phoning this number?" And I said, "Yes. Now, where would you like to go?" I was testing her a little here so I suggested we go to the Wimpy on Byres Road. Without batting an eyelid, I guess, because I couldn't see her face, she agreed.'

Tim had won a great victory. He was living proof that persistence and the ability to lower yourself to the level of a snake's belly would win over a reluctant female. Although it has to be said that Moira couldn't have been that reluctant or she wouldn't have kept picking up the phone.

'We met at Provand's Lordship on the High Street,' said Tim. 'She turned up wearing a black leather suit with skin-tight trousers and a tight top. I looked at her and thought, "Wow!" I was speechless. She even asked if there was something wrong.'

The couple headed off to dinner—but not to the Wimpy. 'I had booked a table at a nice Italian restaurant on the south side but, of course, me being me, I got lost after crossing the Kingston Bridge. We turned up over an hour late and luckily the waitress was very nice about it. And so we sat and chatted and the more we talked the more I liked her.'

The evening, in spite of the directional problems, had gone well. Tim, however, had never been one for quitting while he was ahead. 'During the pudding I took the bull by the horns and said, "Look, I think I've got to kiss you." And she said, "What, here? Now?" Being an optimist I took this as a positive reaction and said, "Yes. Here. Now."

'Moira said, "No chance," and that just fired me up even more. I laughed and said "Look, if you don't let me kiss you, I'm going to climb right up on top of this table and take the kiss." She said, "Yeah, right."'

Obviously she didn't know Tim that well. 'I climbed up on top of the table and leaned down towards her and kissed her. The restaurant was mobbed and the looks I got were more than strange. Meanwhile, Moira just sat there in total disbelief.

'The night went really well, so well that I eventually talked her into coming back to my house in Bearsden—my line was that we would play a new video game—but it worked. We had a nice kiss'n'cuddle. And I knew I really liked her.'

Tim liked Moira so much he never called her the next day. Or the next. In fact, he didn't call for over a week. 'I was scared,' he said. 'It didn't feel right.'

That wasn't to suggest Tim was frightened of the emotional en-tanglement, terrified of commitment or of being hurt. It had nothing to do with the fact Moira was only twenty-four. No, it was more straightforward than that. He was scared of being discovered as a several ladies' man. He was clearly taken with Moira, but he hadn't quite got round to clearing out the debris that was his personal life. The process of dumping ex-girlfriends and female acquaintances was a slow one, as Moira was to discover. Tim, as it happens, hadn't taken the Cliff Richard route to contentment after the trauma of the break up with Kirsty. Instead, he chose the other option and threw himself into the arms of comfort.

One comfort zone came in the form of the woman who cut his hair. They had an unusual relationship. What would happen was she'd cut Tim's hair and then they'd have sex. It was a fairly straightforward transaction that seemed to suit both parties. The attractive hairdresser at first cut Tim's precious locks in her city-centre salon but as the relationship progressed, she would come to Tim's house and administer the trim there. It seemed, given the circumstances, almost improper for Tim to pay money for her services.

But one morning soon after he'd met Moira, Tim felt in desperate need for a cut and blow dry. It was to create ructions when Moira discovered what was going on.

Tim explained the backdrop to the delicate situation. 'I met the girl through a female friend a few years back. This girl would go to my friend's house and cut her hair. She was pretty good. And I guess I thought it might be quite handy if she cut my hair, too. There developed an unwritten arrangement that she wouldn't take any money from me, but we'd somehow seal the arrangement with a physical bonding at the end of the haircut. This was a regular once-a-month occurrence. We didn't have a relationship beyond this and I'm not even sure what her personal status was. I never thought to ask.'

However, one day the post-haircut situation developed and thanks to a couple of bottles of wine, the hairdresser ending up working overtime at Tim's house. Tim by this time had phoned Moira, made his excuses for not contacting her after their first date and they'd gone out a few times. The relationship was simmering nicely until that night when Moira called Tim.

'The hairdresser was upstairs at the time, just out of the shower, and I ran downstairs, all out of breath, to pick up the phone in the hall. But just then in the background I could hear this loud whirring noise. The problem was, Moira heard it too. She said, "What's up with you?" I just shrugged and said something feeble about rushing to the phone. '

Moira can smile now about the situation, but she wasn't laughing at the time. 'I was still staying at my mum's house and one day I called, knowing Tim was getting a haircut at home. But he answered the phone all huffing and puffing. I asked him what was wrong and he said he was tired from running up the stairs. I thought this was odd and asked him why he hadn't picked up the one at the bottom of the stairs and he got all edgy. Then the phone went a bit muffled, the way it does when someone puts their hand over the receiver. I asked him if there was anyone there and he said, "Oh, no, no." So I knew there was. Just at that point I heard a hairdryer in the background. Tim made his apologies and hung up.

'About an hour later he called me back and said all was fine. I said, "Were you still getting your hair cut when I called?" but he said of course that was nonsense, that the girl was long gone.'

But the next day Moira discovered all. 'I stayed at Tim's house the following night, and the phone rang. I picked it up and a female voice said: "Who's that?" obviously surprised to hear my voice. And I replied, "Who are you? You called my number." She said, "I didn't, I called Tim Stevens' house," and I said, "Well, you've got it right. I'm Tim's fiancée," adding a little white lie for emphasis.

'But she didn't accept this. Or rather she wasn't happy about the situation. She said, "Oh, don't be silly. Anyway, you called last night and I guess you were asking why Tim was all out of breath. Well, I'll tell you.

It's because he and I were in bed and we'd been having sex all day.'

At this point the cuddly Tiger disappeared from the house. Moira can't recall which hole he climbed into.

'The next day this girl called me at work—goodness knows how she got my number,' she said. 'The point of her call was to inform me that she'd already seen Kirsty Young off and I was likely to be far less of a challenge. She was convinced she was going to get married to Tim. So I said to her, "Look, go away—you're nothing but a Fatal Attraction." And she said, "You'd better hope I'm not. I know where you work."

'What I later discovered, when I finally trapped the Tiger, was that Tim had planned to open a hairdressing salon with her, or at least he would bankroll it. So, obviously, she wasn't sleeping with him just for the exercise.

'But he wouldn't admit to doing the deed. He just kept denying he'd had sex with her. It wasn't until about six months later he admitted the error of his ways, and even then he said he'd only had sex with her once. But she'd told me she'd had sex with him every time she cut his hair.'

The hairdresser didn't disappear totally. She would still turn up at different events around town. Understandably, it all got a bit awkward. 'I had to realise early on there was a bit of left luggage in his locker and simply make sure it was thrown out,' said Moira. 'I could have got upset but it wasn't worth it. The best way to deal with it was throw it away.'

There were to be regular examples of Moira's clear-outs. 'We were lying in bed early one Saturday morning when the door opened downstairs. I heard this female voice shout out, "You don't need to get up. I'll put the tea on." And I looked at Tim, shook my head and said, "Oh, come on, this is a bit much. Your ex-girlfriends are walking into the house?" It turned out it was Alison Dragoonis. And I couldn't go downstairs. I wasn't going to face a glam female first thing in the morning for a confrontation. Tim went down, told her I was upstairs and, you know, she hadn't even the decency to disappear right away. She hung around and made a cup of tea.'

Tim defended his position at the time. 'She was just a friend,' he said. 'Really, that's all there was to it.'

But there was more baggage in Tim's life than an airport carousel. One day Moira was sitting at the phone in the hallway and through the glass door she could see a female figure approach the house. But as the girl got closer she obviously saw Moira's silhouette through the door— and bolted. 'I was about to open the door and I called out, "Are you looking for Tim?" It turned out she was a girl he'd met at the Jaguar Club in Govan.'

There were other moments which trapped the wild Tiger. One day at home Moira was drying her hair and flicking though a box of music tapes, looking for something relaxing to listen to. She popped in a tape but instead of hearing Steve Wonder, Moira sat in wonder at the strange noises emanating from the C90. 'It was two people enjoying each other's company,' said Moira. 'And they weren't playing Trivial Pursuit. One of them was Tim and I later learned the other was the girl from the Jaguar Club.'

Of course Tim had an alibi for the audio evidence. The tape was made during a little fun session a long, long time before he and Moira had even met. It was all very plausible.

But even he couldn't deny hard video evidence—although he had a damned good try.

'I was in the Jaguar Club with Tim one night, while he was doing a gig there,' said Moira, 'and to pass the time I popped into the manager's office for a chat. While I was blethering away I happened to look up at a security camera which linked into the hall and there was the bold Tiger snogging a blonde. Her name was Marie. I actually knew the girl. And when I quizzed him about it later he took the Fifth Amendment. He wouldn't even admit it.'

Of course, Moira was hurt and angry and felt let down. This was a crunch moment in their relationship. After having thought she'd cleared away all of the extras in Tim's life, here she was confronted by yet more hard evidence of his sad need for attention. She even had to witness him kiss a girl before her very eyes. And then he had the bare-faced cheek to deny it. It was frustrating and humiliating. There was only one thing to do. She agreed to marry him.

'He had asked me to move in with him after a few months,' said Moira. 'And I think that was to show how sincere he was about me and somehow to convince me all the other girls were merely incidentals.'

Tim smiled as he recalled the circumstances of his proposal. 'I think I was blackmailed. Moira had moved in and we'd gotten along great, once she'd tidied up the remnants from my previous life, but one day she said she was moving out. She said she didn't think I loved her. I protested, saying I did, but then she came out with the real cruncher: "If you loved me that much, you would ask me to marry you."

'I said, "I do love you that much." But at the same time I was thinking about the fact that I already had one failed marriage behind me. Yet, I did love her and my back was against the wall so I said, "Right, let's get married." And, you know, I've never regretted it. We're devoted to each other.'

Moira brought a level-headedness to the relationship. 'I've been a scattercash, with money going out all over the place,' said Tim. 'When I met Moira I was working really hard but I had nothing to show for it. Moira organised me and she also began doing some promotion work. Things began to work out fine for us.'

The relationship with Moira also had a lovely surprise. She had a daughter, four-year-old Carissa, from a relationship that had broken up a few years before. 'I remember seeing them together for the first time and thinking how great Moira was with her daughter,' said Tim. 'Luckily, Carissa liked me. I'd call up and she'd answer the phone. I'd say, "Hello, is your mummy there?" and she'd say, "Who's calling?" And rather than say "It's Tim", I'd say, "Tell her it's the cuddly Tiger." Boy, was she in for a shock when she met me.'

Tim's MS condition wasn't an issue in the relationship. 'He told me about it that first night we went out,' said Moria. 'Of course, it wasn't as bad then. It was nothing like it is now. But, to be honest, it didn't overly concern me. He looked fine and I guess I didn't understand what it was. And when we discussed it Tim said the doctor claimed it wasn't progressive. On those terms it wasn't that much of a big deal.'

But Tim did have a medical problem which was to create real problems for the engaged couple. He'd had a vasectomy. 'That really shocked me because I only had one kid,' said Moira, 'and I figured that if things went well with Tim I'd want to have another baby. Being honest, if I didn't already have Carissa I wouldn't have stayed with Tim. I'd have wanted a baby.'

Moira and Tim discussed their options. 'I suggested he have a vasectomy reversal but the big cry-baby said he'd heard they were really painful. He said the original vasectomy was sore enough without going through something even more difficult. But he did go to the doctor and was told there was only a very slight chance of the reversal being successful. I guess that knowledge, plus the thought of impending pain, was enough to crush the idea in his head.

'We did talk about the possibility of adopting kids but the fact that we already had three between us made that all very unlikely. And when the adoption people learned Tim had MS, it made the issue a non-starter.'

With Tim's personal life back on track, his pal Terry McGeddie suggested a way in which his career could be given a boost. Terry figured Tim needed a new manager and arranged a meeting between Tim and Bill McMurdo. The agent was more regularly associated with footballers than radio presenters but it seemed an interesting marriage.

'Terry reckoned that Bill could bring some work my way,' said Tim, 'and radio was the sort of area he'd like to step into. I decided on a meeting at Fraser's in Buchanan Street, upstairs in the coffee lounge. I had an ulterior motive for picking that place because, of course, Moira worked there and it gave me an excuse to pop in and see her. Anyway I turned up to meet Bill and had a few friends in tow that day.'

For some inexplicable reason, one person in the entourage who hadn't been invited somehow had just appeared on the day: Jet Mayfair.

It took Moira some time to adjust to the legend that was Jet and to some of Tim's other friends: 'Tim had a DJ friend from East Kilbride, and the way I learned of him was when I took a call one afternoon from a woman saying, "Hello, I'm Joe The Bear's wife, Oonagh, and I'm looking for Tiger Tim." I laughed and I thought to myself, "Jings, my life is now a zoo."'

But there was a more immediate concern for the couple. Loose talk in Glasgow about Tim's mystery illness had increased. Many people simply thought the Martini Kid had taken too much of a liking to drink.

Tim and Moira reckoned it was time to come clean, and so in October Tim spilled the beans to the *Sunday Mail*. He talked about his MS for the first time and the newspaper revealed that the DJ, on hearing the diagnosis at first, assumed he was going to die. The article stressed that Tim had faced up to the debilitating illness. 'Tim has kept his illness secret for almost a year,' wrote Lorna Frame. (In fact it had been four years.) 'But now he wants to encourage and reassure other sufferers.'

'There's no point being dramatic. It's there. it's something I've got to live with,' said Tim in the article. And the writer went on to say that Tim wanted to be open about his problem because he reckoned people who saw him stagger at times thought he was blind drunk. 'I would fall over things and find it difficult to walk in a straight line. One night I was at a gig and fell over a table. I guess that looked bad.'

Tim said that his doctor had reassured him that his MS was fairly mild and he was optimistically defiant. 'It's really not as bad as some people think, although some cases can be very severe. And it's much easier to handle when I'm working. The adrenaline starts pumping and I stop feeling sorry for myself. There's no way it's going to get me down but I'm aware it's there. The end of the world is not nearly as nigh as I first thought.'

With a new fiancée and life at Clyde ticking over nicely (he moved to a 7–10 p.m. slot on weekdays and 2–4 p.m. on Sundays), Tim was excited about the future. Moira, however, was to discover she still had to fight to protect the Tiger from himself.

20

Carol Smillie, Wedding Bells and Bluenoses

Moira had tried her best to put a stop to the phone calls that came to the house from Tim's model friends, hairdressers and old nightclub girls. And she was largely successful. 'Once I had a word they gave up the ghost,' said Moira.

But there were several instances when young ladies were still attracted to the twinkle in the Tiger's brown eyes, despite the fact Moira was now very much in the picture. One such example came about in August 1990. Former model-turned-TV presenter Carol Smillie was the woman who incurred Moira's wrath.

'I was invited to do a charity fashion show in the Hamilton Palace nightclub,' recalled Tim, 'and I went along with Moira and Bobby Preston. And although the day got off to a bad start—I made a point of telling Moira she was wearing an awful dress and upsetting her—things got better. The idea was that I would be auctioning off the items and Carol Smillie would be doing the promotion work, walking around the audience, looking glam and letting people see what they could bid for.

'Anyway, we did the gig and it all went fine. There was a huge amount of money raised and Moira and Bobby Preston busied themselves helping out as well.

'At the end of the night, Carol came over to the back of the hall and we chatted. She asked what was I up to and asked where I was going off to for dinner and I said I was going to take my girlfriend home. But she looked puzzled. She said, "Why?" And I said, "Well, because she's my girlfriend." And Carol replied, "Why don't you get rid of your wee girlfriend and you and I will go off somewhere for dinner."'

To make things worse, the indelicate offer was made while Moira was standing just a few feet away.

Tim being Tim said nothing, of course. It was a moment he couldn't face up to. And that enraged Moira far more than the fact Carol had made her fiancé the offer of a late dinner. 'I couldn't believe my ears at what she'd just said, that someone could be so nasty right to your face,' said Moira. 'But worse than that, I couldn't believe he took it. He didn't even say, "Excuse me, Carol, my girlfriend is in fact standing right next to me." I was so angry I just cried out to Tim, "You and I are going home—now!" And we did.'

The Carol Smillie incident wasn't over. Moira, after spending so much time keeping women away from Tim's home—and phone line—simply couldn't cope with the continued overtures, particularly when she was on the spot. 'Tim and I didn't speak for weeks after that,' said Moira. 'And he spent the time in between crawling and buying me chocolates and flowers.'

Tim and Carol parted on the night of the charity show with a peck on the cheek, and he said he'd call her some time and they stayed on friendly terms. In fact, Tim played a part in Carol's developing media career. The model was keen to become a radio presenter and Tim arranged for her to spend time at Clyde. It was a fruitful period for her and she landed her own show.

Although Carol never asked Tim out again, Moira still had other female admirers to contend with. Susan McKechnie, a model, had landed a secretarial job at Radio Clyde. Like Carol Smillie, she had hopes of a career in the media. Tim got her gigs as he had done for

Carol, at the Jaguar Club in Govan, doing his little bit for the aspirational model community. Susan took a shine to Tim, so much so that she reckoned they should in fact move in together at Ilay Court. Moira found her attention a little hard to take: 'She phoned the house a few times one night to speak to Tim. It got to the point where I had to take the call and say, "Look, Susan, please don't call again. Tim and I are engaged and you're just embarrassing yourself." To be fair to her, she didn't.'

Another young lady who continued to hover on the periphery of Tim's life was Alison Dragoonis, the model with whom Tim had danced so badly at the Cotton Club and who liked to make him morning tea. Coincidentally, Alison was Susan's best friend, but Tim didn't think that fact should get in the way of a fun relationship. 'Someone came out with a nice quote recently,' said Tim, 'which said: "Anything before I Love You doesn't count". And that's the defence I'm offering up to the public. Alison and I went out a few times although I never danced with her again. All I would say is that she didn't want to move in with me and I was very happy about that. In fact, I think she had another option. But that's sometimes what happens in less-than-serious relationships.'

Given Tim's not inconsiderable experience with the opposite sex, it made perfect sense that he should be chosen to front a new health campaign. Bill McMurdo had lined up his first job for his new client and the theme was Safe Sex. Tim's task was to preach the virtues of using condoms on holiday.

His former manager, David Meehan, told a story which highlights just how appropriate a choice Tim was for that particular promotion. 'He used to borrow my flat at Queensgate Lane and go back there with girls. At the time I had a regular girlfriend but one day we had a huge argument and fell out and I didn't know why. It was only years later when we were having a chat about old times that she said to me: "I knew you were seeing someone back then because I found a condom packet under your bed."'

Moira laughed as she recalled the Safe Sex campaign. 'We were given hundreds of condoms as part of the promotion and we came home one day to find the kids had blown them all up like balloons and they were bouncing them all over the house.'

In the New Year of 1991 Tim's children were to present their own set of problems to their father's relationship with Moira. The couple planned to marry in February but Melanie and Darren were not happy about it at all. Aged nine and eight, they had their own plans for the future. 'The kids had always hoped their mum and dad would get back together,' said Moira. 'When Tim and I announced we were going to be married it was the final nail in the coffin for that dream.'

Tim admitted he didn't handle the situation too well. 'If I have one regret it's that I should have told the kids what was going on much sooner.'

The wedding went ahead at Eastbank registry office. It was a quiet affair. The couple didn't want the papers to know. Tim and Moira didn't even take pictures. 'I'd been married before,' said Tim, 'and I didn't think it was a good idea to publicise the occasion. It was a case of being sensitive.'

Tim was also more than considerate when it came to making arrangements for the wedding reception. Two weeks before the big day Tim's uncle William had had a heart attack and undergone a triple bypass.

Tim knew there was a way to cheer his uncle up. William was Celtic daft and Tim decided to hold his wedding reception at Celtic Park. 'I had a white Mercedes pull up at the hospital to collect William and take him to Parkhead,' said Tim. 'And as he arrived at the football ground the first person we met was Paul McStay, the team captain at the time. I then took William down the tunnel that led onto the pitch and you would have thought by the look in his face he was in heaven. His face was a dream. And that smile had made it all worth while.'

The honeymoon was a week in Los Cristianos in Tenerife. And the Tiger, once again, confirmed he wasn't programmed to travel without incident. 'Radio Clyde presenter George Bowie's dad had a flat on the island and we borrowed it,' said Tim. 'George had described it to us and it all seemed perfect. But the honeymoon got off to a very bad start. When we arrived at the flat at three in the morning it was all locked up. So we had to knock on the door of the guy next door and eventually a wee caretaker arrived in his long johns. Moira went into his flat, onto his balcony and climbed over from there into George's dad's flat.' Once again Tim's chivalry knew all bounds.

Back home, Celtic were to come to play a fairly significant part in Tim's professional life. Ironically, the connection came about via his manager, Bill McMurdo, a self-confessed fanatical supporter of the opposition. 'Bill Smith, my fellow Clyde DJ, was working with Rangers at the time doing the half-time music spot, and I'd always figured it would be nice to do something like that. But I really wanted to do it with Partick Thistle. It was all about history, really, since my uncles had taken me to see them as a kid. Although I'd grown up in the East End most of my weekends had been spent in Partick. And, of course, when you identify with a club like Thistle you don't risk alienating one half of the Old Firm.'

Tim, to his credit, had always successfully managed to cut across the religious and football gulf in Glasgow. He didn't see any merit in moving from his position, sitting comfortably as he was on the fence of the sectarianism issue.

'When I let Bill know I was interested in doing something for

Thistle he laughed at the idea. But I was pretty determined and, to be fair to him, he called John Lambie, the Thistle manager. As a result I went to see John and we had a chat and it was agreed I would go there.

'But somehow Celtic got wind of all this and before I knew what was happening, Tom Grant, the Celtic director, asked me to come and talk to him. I'm not sure how Celtic heard of the Thistle arrangement, but to be courteous I went up to Parkhead—alone—to have a chat. Bill McMurdo couldn't come with me because he was banned, thanks to the notorious Maurice Johnston quick-change incident. When I met Tom Grant I was impressed with his logic. He said to remember this was Glasgow Celtic and not to even compare them with Partick Thistle. I then called Bill to let him know the details and he was adamant I should take up the Celtic offer. He said, "Look, there's only one other team in Scotland, so you have to go with Celtic on this one." He had my interests at heart.'

It wasn't that Tim's manager had the 10 per cent at heart. The money was insignificant.

And so Tim was now a Celtic man. Thistle understood Tim's reasoning and the DJ looked forward to broadcasting in front of fifty thousand fans.

But Tim's first Parkhead adventure saw the DJ score an immediate own-goal: he turned up at the stadium wearing a *blue-and-white* tracksuit. He was approached by an irate Tom Grant. 'He called out to me, "What do you think you're doing?" And I said, "I'm just getting ready to go on the park." And then he said to me, in a very serious voice, "There's no way you can go onto that park in that tracksuit." And he called over to the Celtic shop to get me a Celtic tracksuit, which I put on very quickly. I just hadn't realised when I got dressed that morning. I felt an idiot.'

The excitement for the day wasn't over. 'The match was Celtic against St Mirren and I was in the DJ box when Gerry Cullin, one of the assistants, suggested I go down onto the park while the teams were warming up and he would then introduce me over the PA system. So I strolled down to the park and Gerry called out, "Here he is, Celtic's latest signing—Tiger Tim!" and the crowd went wild. It was a fabulous moment. Paul McStay, the captain, came over and shook hands with me and said, "Good luck, Tim" and it was a really nice gesture.

'But then a huge moment of panic hit me. Striker Tommy Coyne was over at the other end of the park and he yelled out, "Tiger!" and then hit the ball way up in the air towards me. I was terrified that I'd make a total arse of myself in front of fifty thousand fans. As the ball flew into the sky for what seemed like a year, I just concentrated so hard and somehow managed to trap it under my foot and even kick it back. I felt so relieved.'

Although Tim's illness didn't trouble him often and he could walk around unaided, there were days when his legs were a little wobbly. The problem was that he was never sure when his legs would give way. Fortunately, that day wasn't one of them and he was able to keep face with the Celtic faithful.

Six months later, however, that relationship with the fans was to be tested. It was yet another example of words coming out of Tim's mouth which indicated his brain had never been introduced to the concept of cause and effect. 'The Celtic PA system was about the worst in the world and I was always complaining about it,' he recalled. 'I asked for a new radio mike and unfortunately on the day I got it Celtic were playing Rangers. As usual I walked down on the pitch where I intended to entertain the fans and make a few announcements, and as I got there I waved up to Gerry in the DJ box, which was the signal for him to switch me on. But for some unknown reason, instead of testing the mike with the usual "One-two, one-two", I said, "Hello, hello," and no sooner had the words come out than thousands of Rangers fans immediately roared back with "We are the Billy boys!".

'Cringing with stupidity, I made my way back up the steps to the DJ box and no sooner had I sat down than the back door of the box was kicked open. Tom Grant was standing there, yelling, "What the hell do you think you're doing?" '

The Tiger tried to look innocent 'I didn't know,' he said. 'I guess I was just plain stupid because everyone in Scotland who knows anything about football has heard Rangers fans sing that song.'

Tim's Parkhead exploits weren't all negative. Overall, he had a great three years at the stadium. One afternoon, for example, he got huge laughs at the expense of the visiting Aberdeen fans. 'I got a tractor—I think I borrowed it from workmen on a site—and drove through the stadium over to the Aberdeen fans and called out, "I got this to make you feel at home—but sorry, I couldn't find any sheep." '

The Celtic fans certainly took to Tim and appreciated his efforts to entertain them. One fan, perhaps remembering the 'Hello, hello' saga, was confused about where Tim's loyalties lay, though. 'Before one match I walked over to the Jungle as usual and heard a voice call out, "Hey, Tiger Tim, you dirty bluenose bastard!" And I called back, "Are you colour-blind or something?" because I had the Celtic tracksuit on. The Celtic supporters laughed at my reply but the fan who'd made the comment was thrown out by the stewards, which I thought at the time was all a wee bit unnecessary.'

Life at Parkhead continued without incident for a couple of years at least, but meantime at Radio Clyde Tim was to renew an acquaintance with Marti Pellow. The singer came into the radio station with the band's drummer Tommy Cunningham. The pair were doing some promotion work for their new single, *Goodnight Girl*. Tim happened to mention that his new bride Moira was a big fan and Marti's famous grin appeared. 'He said, "Give me the phone and I'll call her," ' recalled Tim. 'And he did. Moira picked up the phone at home to hear someone say he was Marti Pellow and that he was just calling to say hello.' She hung up.

Marti's gestures of friendship were to continue over the years. One day Tim and Darren were driving to an Indian takeaway in Dalmuir. Just as Tim got out of the car, a BMW pulled up with Marti and his girlfriend Eileen inside. There were a lot of kids running around and Marti was recognised. But just at that point, Marti spotted Tim.

'Marti asked who I was with and I told him this was my son. He then made a point of forgetting about his curry and went off to talk to Darren. But because Darren knew Marti was a pop star he was more than a wee bit nervous. All the other kids were quite envious, though. It was nice of Marti to take the time.'

At this point Darren lived with his mum and sister in Bearsden while Tim, Moira and Carissa lived just a mile away. The following summer Tim and Moira decided they would have their first entire family holiday. Not surprisingly, it had its moments of madness.

'I took Moira and all the kids to Florida,' said Tim. 'And at the airport we picked up a hire car and headed for the hotel, which was fifteen minutes away. Two and a half hours later we arrived. I didn't stop to ask directions because I figured that we'd find the place at any minute. But that of course wasn't the case. I'm just hopeless with directions and the longer it all went on the more the kids became grumpy. We didn't even stop for drinks, thinking arrival was imminent, and the poor wee things must have been dehydrated.

'The funny thing is we went through the same toll bridge about five times and after the third time the girl there looked at me as if I was daft. Moira was raging. But I guess by this time she knew what I was like.'

The holiday turned out fine and during the following year the couple settled down to enjoy married life. In the summer of 1993 Tim reckoned it would no longer be upsetting for other people or tempting fate if he told the world about his new(ish) relationship. The *Evening Times* revealed the story of Tim's 'secret wedding' after a 'whirlwind romance', which it most certainly had been. The couple had only known each other a year before they were married and Moira had spent the first few months of the relationship whirling around clearing up Tim's old relationship leftovers. In the article, Tim was nothing but appreciative. 'Moira and the children are the most important things in my life and it's time to make that known,' he said.

He acknowledged that his physical condition, at this point showing few signs of worsening, was a burden for any woman to cope with. 'My main concern was in saddling her with a big problem,' he said. 'Still, it hasn't got too bad. I think I'm going to be able to live with it. But please don't call it an illness. I prefer to use the word "condition".'

At the time writer Gavin Docherty described Tim as 'looking tired, like a prize-fighter slumped in his corner after the final bell'. Tim admitted he was having a little difficulty with his balance and was prone to dropping off instantly into deep sleep.

He also spoke for the first time in public about why he split up with Clare, although he wasn't being entirely honest. 'I was working too hard all the time,' he said. 'My drive was pure ambition. Looking back, I don't know what possessed me. I had a relationship with my work— at my family's expense.'

But he felt with Moira by his side, his life was on track. 'Moira saved me from going nuts,' he said. 'God knows where I'd be now if she hadn't been around. I'm proud of her. And proud of the fact I've proved to myself that I can make a relationship work.'

Tim had worked hard at the relationship, and he'd learned a lesson from the Carol Smillie incident. Whenever the Devil popped up to tempt him, he'd make sure she knew he had a wife he was very much in love with.

For the first time, too, he admitted he was becoming more religious, looking for answers beyond the material world. Tim may have been brought up a Catholic but he had not been a practising Catholic for a long time. 'I pray to God,' he said. 'I questioned my faith when I had terrible fears of what MS was going to do to me. Now, I often pray when I'm driving. People see it and probably think I'm gibbering to myself.'

But while he may have been looking to the heavens for answers to his physical state, there were signs his emotional condition was worsening. The Tiger's confidence, which had been so much a part of his personality, seemed to be waning. His moments of self-doubt were increasing. 'He sometimes thinks he is only working at the station because he once was somebody,' Moira said in a rare unguarded moment.

Tim needed a confidence-booster. Perhaps someone was looking over him because it came in the form of a call from Scottish Television.

21

Green Jungle Juice, Faith-healing and Noddy

In the late summer of 1993 Tim received a job offer that was to raise his spirits: he was asked to join Scottish Television as a reporter. He wasn't being taken on to cover serious issues, but to report on the light and the wacky. The plan was to let the Tiger loose on the streets to question the unsuspecting public. Tim brought his unique personality into his work. There is no way he could ever have been accused of being boring and bland.

The story he covered one day in June was a spin-off from the tale of a man who'd been in the papers at the time for being a desert-island castaway. Tim set off to ask people if they would give up everything and do the same. He realised the report needed the right atmosphere and so, with a camera crew in tow, he headed for Paisley swimming-pool at the Lagoon Centre with its own tropical temperatures and foliage. And, true to form, he took off his clothes to do the report. A few stories in the can later, Tim spoke of his new daytime job with Scottish. 'I've been working on the *Scotland Today* show for three days now, and I've taken my trousers off every day.'

Nevertheless, *Scotland Today* producer Jeff Beattie reckoned the Tiger was one of the best. 'He has a terrific rapport with the people he interviews. He manages to get the best out of everyone.'

The stint at Scottish saw Tim meet his old flame, Kirsty Young, who by this time had moved from the BBC and now had her own chat show at Cowcaddens. 'She was at the reception one day when I walked in and we said hello to each other. There was a bit of trepidation on both our parts, understandably I guess, but we arranged to have lunch in the canteen. When it was time to go she leaned over and gave me a kiss and said it was nice to see me. That was the last time I saw her.'

That same week, Tim became a model. It seemed a natural progression since he'd been out with so many. But it was all in a good cause. He teamed up with TV presenters Cathy MacDonald, Liz Kristiansen and Shereen Nanjiani to model 'an exclusive collection of evening and cocktail wear'. The designs came from Glasgow's own Lex McFadyen and Tim paraded himself on the catwalk of the Moat House International Hotel alongside members of the band Hue and Cry and actor Forbes Masson. The clothes show was organised to raise funds for the Scottish Aids Monitor.

Back at Celtic Park Tim was lamenting the news that a section of the stadium was to be removed as part of a modernisation scheme. Little did he know that it wasn't only the Jungle that would be going for ever. 'My DJ box where I do my broadcasts on a Saturday afternoon faces right into the Jungle,' said a saddened Tiger when he heard the news that the famous terracing was to be replaced with seats. 'The atmosphere the place generates is incredible, and the fans there set the mood for the rest of the ground. For me, the Jungle is what makes Parkhead really come alive. It will be a sad moment when the fans make their last stand. That's where the real characters emerged. I remember once going round the park on a float and as I came to the Jungle, a lot of the fans started shouting jokey abuse at me. To get back at them I lifted my jumper to bare my chest. Instantly, hundreds of fans yelled together, "Tiger Tim's a baldy!" It's a magical place and the fans in that area are incredible.'

At the time of reconstruction Tim worked hard for the club promoting the image it hoped to develop. He was even pictured in newspapers drinking green Jungle Juice, a new soft drink created by the Celtic FC marketing team. But a couple of months later, at the end of September, Tim was choking at the very thought of having given so much to the club. It was the day he was sacked.

Tim's remit at Parkhead was to make the punters smile. Celtic had been having a miserable time of it in recent years and one night Tom Grant instructed Tim to try and do a bit more to lift the supporters' spirits.

Celtic were playing in a UEFA Cup tie against Young Boys of Berne while Rangers were also in action in Europe, away to the Bulgarian side Levski Sofia. News came through at half-time that Rangers were being beaten. 'Being a smart arse, I thought I'd say something funny, so I announced solemnly: "We will now have a minute's silence for Rangers because they have just been put out of the European Cup."

'I was pretty pleased with myself because the reaction from the fans was tremendous. But I had no idea of the furore that would result. After all, I was preaching to the converted. Or so I thought.

'Tom Grant came running up and demanded to know why I'd said what I did. I looked at him quizzically. "Said what?" I asked, because at this time I was genuinely confused. Here was a man who'd once said to me, "I don't care who we beat as long as we beat Rangers," and here I was having a bit of fun at their expense. And now it looked as though I was being reprimanded for that. It didn't add up.'

It did, in the mind of Tom Grant. It turned out that in the stand with the Celtic directors that night were a troupe of FIFA dignitaries. Tom Grant clearly didn't want his employees echoing his private sentiments in public. At least, not when European top dogs were within earshot. Despite the duplicity of it all, Tom Grant was enraged. Here he was questioning an act of Tim's which seemed to reflect his own feelings and that of the Celtic fans.

Tim was bewildered. 'He came up to me and yelled "Don't speak again. Say nothing!" and about ten minutes into the second half I thought, "To hell with this," and got up and left. But as I was going down the stairs I was met by one of the security men who announced he'd been sent to escort me from the premises. I was dumfounded. I felt like a subversive. The bloke was sympathetic and apologised for having to eject me. But as we were making for the back door a call came through on his walkie-talkie from the head security man and I could hear it clearly. It said, "Can you just confirm that Tiger Tim has now left the premises?" And this bloke with me looked very apologetic. "Just say aye," I told him, and he did. The indignity of it was awful.'

The awfulness of the night wasn't over. 'I got to the car park and found that someone had slashed one of my tyres. And needless to say I didn't know how to change a wheel. But a bloke was walking by, a Rangers supporter as it happens, and he stopped and helped me change it. As he finished he smiled and said, "Should you no' be in there?"'

Tim was never officially sacked from his job at Parkhead. Celtic dramatically held a press conference about the Tiger incident and told reporters Tim had been sacked but the DJ himself was never contacted by the club. Instead, he learned of his fate from the newspaper reporters who turned up on his doorstep that night. The press in the following days were more than sympathetic to Tim. Sure, most of them knew him well enough to know he suffered from occasional foot-in-mouth disease, but on this occasion he was pronounced the innocent party.

The following Sunday Gerry McNee, writing in the *Sunday Mail*, posed the question 'How do you cover up the inadequacies of the Celtic board? Sack the DJ!'

'I did allow myself a little smile when I read that,' said Tim.

He could also take heart from the support that came from all over

Scotland, particularly from Rangers fans. His friend at Radio Clyde, Bill Smith, who was the club DJ at Ibrox, summed up the sentiments at Ibrox. 'No one at Rangers took any offence,' said Bill. 'Most fans took it as a good laugh. You know, I've had wee digs at Celtic in the past and no one got upset.'

Tim never heard from Tom Grant officially after that eventful night, but he did bump into him a few months later. 'We were in Pavarotti's restaurant in Glasgow,' recalled Moira, 'when Tom Grant walked in with his wife. He asked if we could forget about all that had happened and said he wasn't responsible for sacking Tim, that it was the rest of the Celtic board. Tim said something about there being no point in crying over spilt milk. We met him again a couple of months later and he reiterated the point that it was others who had made the decision, not him.'

Rangers, meanwhile, were not slow to see the window of opportunity open to them and the chance to take advantage of the Celtic Park debacle. Tim could have followed in the footsteps of his McMurdo stablemate Maurice Johnston and moved from Parkhead to Ibrox. 'The day after Celtic fired Tim, Rangers called and asked him if he wanted to record some jingles,' said Moira. 'They maintained they had no problem with the comments he had made about Rangers and about the minute's silence gag. They said they knew it was all a bit of fun and acknowledged they would never have sacked their jock for saying that.

'But there was no way Tim could take up their offer. He wouldn't go that direction. After all, since Tim had joined Celtic, he and I got hassle from some very bitter Rangers fans who'd shout obscenities, that sort of thing. If only they'd known Rangers FC were looking to employ Tim. But he was all too aware of what that sort of move would have meant to the Celtic supporters. He doesn't like to upset anyone.' She paused for a moment. 'It's just that sometimes words come out of his mouth that have that effect.'

The following year Tim was to utter meaningless words that would result in a life-lasting sadness. Early in 1994 Steely Dan had called Tim when he was on air at Radio Clyde and asked his nephew to play a request on the show for his new wife, Esther. Tim refused and let his Uncle Danny know his mother didn't like Esther. 'She maintained she wasn't right for Danny and I sort of took all of this in. I shouldn't have and I shouldn't have let this interfere with my relationship with him. But Danny took the huff over the fact I wouldn't play this daft record and didn't speak to me again.'

Shortly afterwards, Steely Dan died. 'It's become one of the greatest regrets of my life,' said Tim. 'He collapsed at home with a heart attack and I never got the chance to make my peace with him. This was the guy who built my record box for me and humphed it all over Scotland. This was the guy who protected me against the world. He was a great guy and I loved him a lot.'

Dora said Danny's death had a devastating the effect on her son. 'He was grief-stricken,' she said. 'Danny thought the world of him. It was one of those silly family things that should never have been allowed to develop. It still comes back to haunt him.' Tim's loss hit him badly. It was not a coincidence that his health suffered. The attacks of paralysis became more frequent. He tired more easily.

His work didn't suffer, however. His Radio Clyde evening show had higher listening figures than most shows in Britain. On air, Tim Stevens could raise a smile from a man whose lips had been stapled shut.

And the fact he was winning Top DJ awards in national magazines every year strongly suggested he was as popular as he was when he first joined Radio Clyde. But the quality of life he had once enjoyed was no longer there. Away from Clyde he often became weary and lethargic. For a man who had spent his life working and playing hard, it was clearly getting him down.

Tim admitted at the time that he was thinking more and more about Stuart Henry, the DJ who had spent the last ten years of his life as a sad, incoherent figure. 'I feel tired at times,' Tim conceded. 'When Dr Thomas from the Southern General treated me she said there was a good chance the illness wouldn't get any worse and that's been the case. But some days I just don't have any energy. And that's why I feel I've got to do something to improve things.'

Tim's quest had already begun for a cure, to discover something— anything—that might help to ease the symptoms and give him back some of the spark he once took for granted. The search for a better life saw him delve into faith-healing. The DJ sought out a celebrated Irish healer, Finbar Nolan, who came to Glasgow on one of his periodic visits. Nolan had been a faith-healer for as long as he could remember. As the seventh son of a seventh son, he was said to be able to harness a special power that can cure. Tim turned up at Nolan's surgery at Glasgow's Pond Hotel (there was no payment for a consultation, only donations) where a queue had formed already for the afternoon session. There were no strict appointment times, just lines of desperate people.

Tim later explained to the *Evening Times* why he felt it worth while trying for a miracle cure, which most doctors would dismiss as a complete waste of time. 'A friend of mine recently came to see Finbar with a tumour the size of a grapefruit. But after several sessions with the faith healer, the tumour had gone. Doctors confirmed it. I figured if Finbar can do that, anything is possible.'

Over the years Finbar Nolan was reputed to have cured thousands of people. But he was aware of the scepticism which surrounded his work. Just prior to him laying hands on Tim, he handed over the name and address of a woman he had treated the week before. Doris McKenzie, he said, had had an incurable eye disease. Now it had gone.

As Tim sat in the chair his face revealed the mixed emotions that were running through his mind. Hope and doubt seemed to flicker alternately.

When asked if he could cure Tim, Finbar shrugged his shoulders. 'I really don't know the answer to that question,' he said. 'It's a hit-and-miss thing, really. I don't feel power or energy, I don't know when something is happening. With Tim, I just don't know.'

Tim didn't know either. 'You've got to be hopeful,' he said, producing a grin. 'But I've tried everything. I've tried homoeopathic medicine and Chinese medicine. I've tried visiting the Jan de Vries clinic. I've even been on special diets . . .' He broke into a laugh, 'Although I soon got sick of them.'

Finbar laid his healing hands on the radio presenter's neck. He touched his head, his back, his knees. The process took about twenty seconds. Tim didn't react. 'That's it,' said Finbar. 'We'll try it again later on.'

After two sessions with Finbar, Tim felt more or less the same. 'You have to go three times, though,' said the DJ, as if encouraging himself to think positively.

After the third visit, Tim still felt sluggish. 'Nothing seems to have happened,' he said, his voice sounding dull, and he was obviously feeling down. 'But I'm not despondent. You have to keep on trying.'

A few moments later, the Tiger's face resorted to a more familiar grin and the twinkle in his eyes reappeared.

'You know, I've been talking to an Indian friend of mine and he suggested something different. Apparently, there is this fakir in India who has a huge success rate in curing people with MS. My mate even has a video he can show me of the man himself in action.' His face produced a wide smile. 'How much do you think it costs to fly to India?'

He reiterated how important Moira was in his bid to stay healthy. 'She turned my world around and smartened up my act. It sounds weepy, but she does everything for me. My diet was awful—in fact, I was eating absolute garbage, the kind of stuff which gave burgers and junk-food a bad name. She is very supportive and gives me a kick up the backside whenever I feel sorry for myself. If I hadn't met her, I'd probably be rolling around in the gutter somewhere.'

Tim went on to try a variety of hopeful cures. At one time, he took a course of natural remedies amounting to sixty tablets a day. But nothing seemed to work.

It was time to forget about cures. It was time for a holiday. Tim, Moira, Darren, Melanie and Carissa all set off once again for Florida. You would have thought Moira would have learned her lesson but, no, she let Tim drive. 'Not only did he get us lost, he almost got us killed,' she said. 'We ended up taking a turning on a highway and facing oncoming traffic. We had to swerve into a ditch to avoid certain death.'

That short trip from the airport to the hotel wasn't without injury: Tim ran over his son. 'Darren was standing behind the car,' said Moira, 'and Tim decided to take it upon himself to reverse—right over Darren's foot. The wee soul didn't know what had hit him and after it happened you could see the tyre mark on his training shoe. Luckily, the angle of impact didn't break the foot. But Darren was sobbing, and Tim was shouting at Darren for being behind the car, which of course was nonsense.'

Tim leapt to his own defence over the Florida foot-crushing incident. 'I was upset as well,' he said.

'Not as upset as the rest of us,' said Moira. 'It was a rotten start to a rotten holiday.'

Tim took another trip that summer, this time to Los Angeles for the opening of the Disney theme park, Toontown. With him was Radio Clyde producer David Tanner, now a sports presenter at Scottish Television. 'It was a good experience to broadcast from Los Angeles,' said Tim, 'but it confirmed to me how bizarre life in America is. When I arrived I went into the hotel toilet, lifted the lid and suddenly Whitney Houston started singing. The toilet seat was connected to a stereo system. I was knocked out. I called David in to hear this and he was amazed as well. We laughed for ages. Now, whenever I hear *I Will Always Love You* I immediately want to go to the bathroom.'

Back home, Tim's life had become a much more confused place. On the one hand he was entirely happy living with Moira and Carissa, particularly since they'd all moved into a new house in Old Kilpatrick, just a mile along the road from Radio Clyde. On the other hand, though, he was becoming more concerned about his condition. On alternate days he'd sway between facing the illness head on and pretending, when possible, it simply didn't exist.

In December Tim was faced with a difficult decision when he was asked to confront his worst fears. He got a call from the PR people representing the MS centre in Maryhill. It was a live-in centre for severe MS cases. Tim hadn't been to the centre before, in spite of having the illness, partly because he didn't feel bad enough to have to go, and partly because he didn't want to confront the reality of MS. Tim preferred to take life as it came. But he made the decision to go because he felt guilty at perhaps passing up the chance to help others.

Sadly, when he arrived at the centre, all his worst fears were realised. 'It affected me quite badly,' he said. 'Everyone there was worse off than I was. There were people in wheelchairs, people who even couldn't walk or talk. And I couldn't cope. I wanted to go to help the centre raise money but it was sheer hell. They put me in the hyperbaric chamber, which was supposed to help MS cases, but it did me no good. And although I felt sorry for myself I was also so depressed and sorry for the poor souls who were clearly struggling. Psychologically, it knocked me way back.

'You find that people in places like this talk to you in a very quiet voice and that's because it's tinged with sympathy. But that's not what you want to hear when you have a problem. You want people to speak to you normally. That's why Moira is so important to me. She doesn't treat me as though I have a condition.'

The month wasn't all depressing, although it seemed bad luck would continue. Tim was standing in the Clyde hallway one day chatting to a pop band called Ten Years After when he was interrupted by the receptionist. 'It's David Essex,' she said. Tim was due to interview the singer the following day. Without turning round, Tim called out, 'Oh, tell the diddy I'll call him back.' But the receptionist interrupted Tim once again and whispered, 'No, you don't understand, he's not on the phone, he's here,' and she pointed a sly finger and there of course was David Essex standing next to the trophy cabinet, all white teeth and perfect smile. 'That was the interview stone dead,' said Tim, 'or so I thought. To my amazement he laughed the whole thing off and he turned out to be a dead nice guy. Which is just as well, 'cause if he'd thumped me I'd have deserved it.'

Tim got a far more pleasant surprise one day at Clyde when Noddy Holder arrived to do some promotion work. It had been twenty-five years since they last met all those years ago in the Electric Gardens when Tim had been up on stage with the Slade singer. He was stunned—and delighted—when Noddy walked into the station and his face told Tim his old pal remembered him. But he was even more surprised at the first words to come out of the charismatic singer's mouth. 'How's Jet?' asked a grinning Noddy.

22

Diet Coke Cures and Married Eight-year-olds

Perhaps it was the memory of Jet Mayfair standing there in all his naked glory at the Electric Gardens which resulted in Tim's mind wandering to subjects of an anatomical nature. Or perhaps thoughts of displaying reproductive organs are never too far from Tim's vivid imagination. Whatever the reason, psychologists would have a hard time trying to work out why he chose to expose himself to a new Radio Clyde DJ, Dougie Jackson (now with QFM in Paisley), one afternoon early in 1996. Admittedly, it wasn't at all out of character, bearing in mind Tim's predilection for sharing the geography of his nether regions with just about anyone who was prepared to open their eyes.

Looking back at the incident, he laughed and cringed at the same time about how he managed to frighten the wits out of the new kid on the Clydebank block. 'Dougie Jackson had joined Clyde a few days before and I hadn't met him officially. Unfortunately, the first time we were actually in the same place was in the toilets, at the urinal.

'Of course, I didn't want to say hello—it's not the place for shaking hands, is it?—but as I was standing there having a pee a nagging thought came into my mind. I'd been wondering for some time if I had been circumcised, but no one could ever tell me. Without going into too much detail, I reckoned I had a bit less on top than I should have. I couldn't ask my mammy—that's not the sort of question she'd answer—and I'd never asked a Jewish person, who I thought would have known for sure. So I asked Dougie Jackson, since he happened to be on hand, so to speak.

'He must have been mortified when the first words out of my mouth in his direction were "Excuse me, do you think I've been circumcised?" and then I proceeded to show him the evidence. With a very odd glint in his eye he looked at me, completely dumbfounded, and said cautiously, "Erm, I don't think so."'

Tim conceded that this is more than odd behaviour. 'The thought of circumcision had just flashed into my head at that precise moment,' he said, 'and I guess it was my way of breaking the ice. Not surprisingly, Dougie kept out of my way for a few weeks, probably until someone told him I don't make a habit of turning a pee into a public demonstration.'

When the Clyde management heard of the incident in the toilets, there was not much anyone could do but laugh. But MD Alex Dickson wouldn't have been laughing if he realised how close Tim had come to ruining his book programme.

'After Gary Marshall's show was Alex Dickson's *Bookcase*, a programme was which was pre-recorded on tape, and Gary had to run this tape after his own show. But one night he and I got to teasing each other a bit as he was setting up Alex's show, and he pushed me. Because I wasn't all that steady on my feet I went right over the top of the tape deck and the whole machine went flying. There were reels of tape everywhere. Gary opened up the mike and apologised to the listeners, saying, "We are very sorry but we seem to have encountered a slight technical problem here and we'll be back in a moment after this commercial."

'During the ad break we scrambled around like lunatics trying to unfankle the bits of tape that made up the boss's show. Thankfully, we put it back together again just in time.'

Timing played a big part in Tim agreeing to return to Parkhead in March 1996. Not surprisingly, the DJ was initially stunned to get a call from Celtic FC, asking him to appear at a club fundraiser. 'At first I said no, because I couldn't get rid of the bad taste Celtic had left in my mouth—and it wasn't caused by the Jungle Juice,' he recalled. 'But the club's PR office pointed out that the benefit night was for other people, homeless people of all denominations. Yet, it was also the night of my anniversary, so it was a hard call. I agreed to do it, though. It was hard to say no to such a worthwhile cause and I had a lot of time for the Celtic manager, Tommy Burns. Moira recognised it was important to do something for charity and she nudged me to do it. I was glad in the end that I did it because I managed to help raise a lot of money for the homeless. One guy, who happened to be a lottery-winner, paid seven grand for Ronaldo's football shirt.'

Tim had quite a few friends who were footballers, but he was probably closest to the former Partick Thistle player, Albert Craig. That summer he, Moira and Dora took off on holiday to Santa Ponsa in Majorca with Albert and his wife Norma. But, once again, Tim's lack of attention to detail caused problems.

'I screwed up the arrangements,' he said, candidly. 'During the last few days of the holiday I had agreed to front a gig at the SECC for *The Clothes Show*. I couldn't be in two places at the one time and I didn't want to let the organisers down, so it meant I had to fly back early to do the show. Moira stayed on, the company were good enough to pay for the flight and I got a pair of Easy jeans into the bargain.'

But Tim missed the highlight of the holiday. While walking down the main street in Santa Ponsa, Dora happened to glance through the window of one of the town's busiest tourist bars. Her eyes popped with delight at what she saw inside. A Spanish version of the Chippendales were performing their set and Dora was captivated by their performance. 'Her wee face was stuck right up against the window,' said Moira, 'and her palms were held high and pressed right up against the glass.'

And that was to be Dora's downfall. 'It turned out these windows were the tilt'n'turn type, and because she was pushing so hard, almost willing herself to be on the other side of the glass, before we knew what was happening, Dora had flipped right through the revolving window and landed in a manner that could only be described in less polite circles as arse over tit.

'When she arrived inside the bar it created an uproar and the big Spanish Chippendales all ran over to pick her up. Dora, I have to say, loved every moment of it. She's a natural performer. It's easy to see where Tim gets it from.'

Tim probably got a great deal of his natural concern from Dora as well. He found it hard to turn down charity requests and he had in the past found it hard to turn down models, so when the call came from a model asking Tim to front a charity night, it was generally no contest. But even though the hostess at the Moat House Hotel gig in Glasgow was Tim's old pal Carol Smillie and the pair had long forgotten the dinner invitation incident, he certainly had cause for careful consideration: it was a benefit night to raise funds for MS research. The newspaper picture captions next day read: 'Tim, who suffers from MS himself, was really delighted to lend a hand.'

The reality was very different. As Tim's illness progressed, the last thing he wanted was to be reminded of his own condition. He couldn't refuse the charity, however. Nor could he refuse the nurse who asked him to come along to Canniesburn Hospital, which had a special MS centre, but he most certainly wished he had.

'It was even more depressing than the centre at Maryhill,' he said. 'These people were terminally ill, with some very extreme cases, and I deeply regretted going. It gave me the shock of my life. I spoke to some patients and I don't even think they knew I was there. It was that bad. It was almost as if I was looking through a window into the hell that my life could become. I think I stayed about an hour but that was enough. These people had the same disease I had and I couldn't continue because it left me feeling so down. How do you be positive and talk to someone in a wheelchair who can hardly speak? What do you say to them?'

Tim acknowledged he simply can't cope with the understandable requests for him to become involved with MS sufferers. 'On the one hand I feel I should go to places like this and perhaps talk to people and say hello, but at the same time it's hell.'

Moira was with her husband that day. 'It was so sad watching Tim looking hard at these people with symptoms he could develop.'

With each passing month, Tim would consider a possible new cure for the illness. He refused to accept there was no treatment that could help. He even tried the Diet Coke 'cure'. 'I saw a documentary programme on TV one night about Cari Lauder, a woman from London who had been "cured" of MS by drinking Diet Coke and taking B12 injections. I thought, "Wow," and the next day I called her up for a chat. She was fairly dismissive, though. She said she had a book coming out so she wouldn't spill the beans prematurely.

'I found out through other people about the recipe. And I tried it. I drank Diet Coke for about six months. And I had to get these prescription injections from the doctor, which were horrendously painful. But it didn't work. I didn't feel in the least bit better. The only consequence was that I didn't drink Diet Coke for a long time afterwards. I couldn't face the sight of it. It still brings back memories of a sore backside.'

Tim's condition may have worsened but his skill as a broadcaster was unaffected. Early in 1997 he won yet another award for his evening show. 'Not only has Tim Stevens managed to survive in the business, but two and a half decades on he is still cheeky, still winding people up and still flirting with every female from the age of five to fifty who features on his show,' said one newspaper. 'His multiple sclerosis makes ordinary life difficult, but put him in a sound studio and the problems are temporarily brushed aside.'

The newspaper went on to talk about how the personality presenter in British radio had become an endangered species. Except, of course, for the Tiger. 'While he bemoans the death of the personality DJ, Tim admits there would be no place for a Tiger in today's radio jungle. "It seems the people in charge think punters want to hear music more than people talking," he explained. "But I don't agree with this thinking. I think there is a place for both. Because the focus is on music, it doesn't allow for personalities to develop. The people in charge aren't looking for loonies. They want straight guys. If I went to Clyde now I wouldn't get the job. I'm not what people in radio are looking for."

Luckily, the listeners didn't agree with the radio bosses and Tim was able to celebrate his success—which in reality was survival. It was becoming all too easy to see why Tim stood out from the rest in the radio world: too many DJs sounded exactly the same, too many had never been through the apprenticeship Tim had—his days as a mobile DJ, working as a club jock at the Electric Gardens and even toiling away thanklessly behind the scenes in hospital radio. All of Tim's efforts meant that he had developed into a fantastic communicator. For all that reason and more, Tim Stevens remained one of the few jocks on radio who could open a microphone and make a stranger feel like his best friend. He could make little girls speak to him like he was a favourite uncle. He could make their mothers feel that there was a man in their lives they could talk to.

One night, Tim took a call from a little girl. 'Tell me,' said Tim, 'are you married?'

'I'm only eight,' was the reply.

'Yes, but are you married?' continued the Tiger. And the little girl squeaked with delight.

Another night Tim revealed to the listeners that he'd heard an old friend was dying. This is normally a taboo subject with radio presenters. They don't share problems with the world. Except that in this instance Tim did. And the listeners could hear the tears well up in his voice. Perhaps they realised the death had focused Tim's fears for his own mortality. The switchboard lit up with people trying to talk to the Tiger. Few DJs have ever had that sort of empathy with an audience.

'The last thing you want to hear on the radio is people bleating in self-pity,' acknowledged Tim. 'But I spoke about my friend because you don't want people to think you go through life having one big party. That would make you unreal. If something affects you that badly, you know people will share in it. They appreciate honesty. The amount of calls I get after sharing something is incredible.'

It seemed ironic that now he had finally reached a point in his professional life where he was reasonably content but in his private life Tim faced the continued torment of not knowing to what degree his condition would worsen.

On holiday in Florida in the summer of 1998, the worst situation possible occurred. The couple were lying by the pool enjoying the sunshine when Tim suddenly called out. He couldn't move. He was paralysed. 'He couldn't get off his lounger,' said Moira, 'and we had to call the security guys to carry him back to the bedroom. I would say that was the start of a major dip in Tim's health. The humidity in America certainly doesn't agree with him.'

The sheer ignominy he suffered worsened. Moira had to hire a wheelchair and for the next two weeks he was pushed around Disneyland. She could make light of the situation, in a way that only someone coping on a daily basis with the effects of illness can. 'My torso was brown—but my legs were white from standing behind a wheelchair for two weeks,' she said, in mock horror.

Tim, however, acknowledged the reality. 'I was terrified my legs wouldn't come back,' he said. 'It frightened the life out of me. I had this terrifying insight into what it would be like to be in a wheelchair for the rest of my life.'

That summer saw Tim face a catalogue of such incidents that are enough to bring a boulder to your throat. He was in a Glasgow restaurant with Moira and when he got up to leave his legs gave way and he collapsed across the table. The dishes flew skywards and he fell to earth. One of the other diners picked him up. 'Then, as I was leaving, I fell down the stairs. I couldn't get up—and again someone came from the restaurant to help me,' he recalled. 'Everything goes through your mind. It's sheer hell, lying on your back in a public place. And then your mind flashes back to the time when you were healthy, when you could walk normally.'

The wobbliness and falling down had become all too common. 'I remember being in Partick, and I was crossing the road on my own because I was secretly buying a birthday card for Moira. But I staggered across Dumbarton Road and cars were pumping their horns, and the more I panicked the less my feet would move. I sound like a wee boy but now I don't cross roads on my own any more.'

Tim thought for a moment about his limitations. 'It's so depressing to have to rely on someone.'

By the end of 1998 he had to take extensive measures simply to cope with everyday life. He had a gym installed in his home to build up his wasting muscles but he also had a chair-lift fitted. He couldn't get down the stairs on his own. Simple things became problematic. Tim learned never to lock the bathroom door.

'There are times when you get very depressed,' he said, with understatement. 'You just feel you can't make the best of it.'

As well as having to suffer the public humiliation, he also had to put up with physical and verbal abuse. 'Sometimes when you stumble, perhaps in a club, you bump into people. Basically, I can just about move in a straight line. But if I have to dodge past someone, I can't cope. It's horrible. And then you get the threats: "Whit the hell do you think you're doin'?" All you can do is try and apologise quickly enough before you get hit.'

Tim wasn't the only person to take abuse over the MS. His son Darren, now seventeen and living with Tim, Moira and Carissa, explained how he had to cope as well. 'When I started secondary school there were times when people learned I was Tiger Tim's son and things got difficult. One guy said to me that my dad was always drunk and that he was an old jakey. I tried to tell him my dad had a disease and that was why he couldn't walk properly and his speech was slurred at times. But you couldn't tell some people and it would invariably end in a fight.'

His daughter Melanie also had to battle for her dad. 'I was bullied at school because of who he was,' she said. 'Boys would pick on me. But that's not to say I blame my dad. And all the fun he's given us over the years makes up for the hassle.

'I can remember the delight I had in seeing him up on stage in a panto when I was about four, in amongst all these scary people with made-up faces. But while he's funny he also loves to act daft. Not long ago we went to Burger King and he walked out with one of those paper hats on his head that kids wear. He said it was to keep the rain off his hair. I argued the hat had a hole on the top, but he just laughed.

Sometimes I think he has a hole in his head where his brain should be.'

Carissa echoed the comments of Darren and Melanie. 'He'll give me a lift to school and when we get there he'll roll down the car window as people are passing by, turn on the radio and then start to sing along with whatever song is playing—really loudly. If there is any way Tim can embarrass you, he'll do it. Sometimes he'll even drive up to the playground and start doing that fake Tarzan-yell thing he does on the radio. You just want to curl up and die.'

She smiled. 'But I guess most of the time he's great, although he does tell me to tidy the house an awful lot.'

Melanie found it difficult to get used to the adulation her dad enjoyed. 'The number 44 bus goes past my house here in Newton Mearns and I see his huge face on the back of it. I look up at it and think, "Gosh, that's my dad."'

Tim realised how difficult his condition was for others to deal with, especially for those pals who didn't want to exclude him. 'Well, I don't play football for Radio Clyde any more, that's for sure,' he said, breaking into a laugh. 'The game's a bogey. The team asked me to blow the whistle and start games, but I couldn't even do that. As well as it being tokenist, I doubt if I could walk onto the park and walk off again. I wouldn't want to let people down.'

But that's not to say he spends all his time reflecting on what once was. When he becomes aware he is staring into dark spaces he'll turn the headlights on again. 'I can do my job,' he said, stoically. 'When I'm sitting down I'm fine. For three hours I'm just like everybody else. And they're all great at Clyde. When I bounce off the walls they just ignore me.'

He looked up and saw his throwaway comments had failed to force a laugh. 'Look, I'm all right. I'm from Easterhouse. I'm tough. And I'm aware there is always someone much worse off than me, someone, for example, who's had a child abducted or lost a son in a car crash. And life is not without its pleasures.' He grinned the widest of grins. "When I'm lying down I'm fine. And I'm great at horizontal dancing. That's one of the things you can still be as good at as anyone else.'

At the end 1998 Tim had a chat with one of the physios at Gartnavel during one of his check-ups. She suggested that if he was having problems walking he could try a small zimmer. He thought about it and decided yes, he would use any back-up if it would aid his mobility.

Of course he was more than aware of the stigma—zimmers were used by old people, after all. But Tim decided to turn a negative into a positive. He took the new zimmer down to Arnold Clark's garage and asked one of the panel beaters if they could do anything with it to jazz it up a bit. And they did. Tim was supplied with the first customised zimmer, complete with Tiger Tim aluminium panelling, a horn and flashing lights. There was even a special basket attached where Tim could keep a little furry Tiger and his car keys. 'I thought it was fantastic,' said Tim. 'It just looked so cheeky and it gave me a kick to ring the bell and flash the lights. But Moira hated it. She thought it attracted too much attention. As a compromise I agreed to take off the side panels.'

It has been hard to crush the indomitable spirit Tim Stevens possesses. He refuses to succumb to the illness.

In 1999 one newspaper reported that the Tiger was prepared to sell his house to buy a new MS wonder drug. He considered the idea after he fell and broke his arm. The new drug was Interferon. Beta Interferon has been used extensively in the States by MS sufferers and is said to slow the loss of brain tissue associated with many MS symptoms, including memory loss and slurred speech. The tissue loss can occur before symptoms even appear and continue while patients are in remission.

The American Academy of Neurology says Beta Interferon can reduce tissue loss by 55 per cent and patients who took it had fewer relapses and a lower risk of becoming progressively more disabled. But Tim had been told he couldn't get the drug on the NHS. It costs £10,000 a year. Incredibly, though, it is available to people with MS in some London health authority areas.

'I'm luckier than most MS sufferers in that I can still work,' said Tim. 'And I know there are a lot of people much worse off than me. If this drug was going to help I would go for it—even if it meant financing it myself. I'd even sell my house. At the moment, though, I'm not sure as to whether there is proof of it working.'

Greater Glasgow Health Board said they had funded a trial of Beta Interferon. 'It is a highly expensive drug and the benefits to patients are debatable and sometimes quite limited,' they claimed.

Tim received similar reports from a consultant at the Southern General and decided against buying the drug himself—for the moment.

Friends suggested he try cannabis. Apart from those two isolated experiments with his friend Alex Robertson's back-garden ganja, Tim had steered clear of all drugs. 'I've never really thought about trying cannabis. It's a drug, after all, and I know it sounds old-fashioned, but I've never really taken drugs and I hate the thought of being seen as an old hippy. I know also cannabis is not a cure. I want something that's going to end this.'

But that's not to say he would reject the cannabis idea out of hand. When he became aware that the British Medical Association are currently growing fields of marijuana with a view to carrying out trials of cannabinoids in a bid to find a cure for MS, Tim's eyebrows lifted. 'If it was legalised I'd be interested,' he said. 'I suppose you have to consider all the options.'

23

Blood, Sweat and Bacteria

In 1999 Tim was sitting in the studio about to go on air when he was told that he had a call from Marti Pellow, who was in the States. The singer had heard Tim's condition was worsening. 'Are you no' well,' said the long-distance voice. Tim replied he hadn't been feeling too great. 'Well, don't get any more no' well because there'll be no one there to play ma records.' It was a nice touch from the singer and it gave Tim a lift when he needed it.

In March 2000 he took a call from his old friend Jackie Brambles. 'She came on the line from Los Angeles,' he recalled. 'She was driving down Sunset Boulevard and had just been interviewing Bruce Willis. I had to smile when I thought about our walks along Prestwick beach. Somehow I figured she'd made the right move. I'm really proud of her.'

Tim's support came at the right time. A few days before he'd fallen outside a supermarket and fractured his skull. 'I got a real fright,' he said. 'There was blood everywhere. I spent a couple of days in hospital but I got over it.'

He continued to remain philosophical about his condition. 'I sometime wonder, "Why me?" But one night I spoke about my MS to a bloke called Henry, a steward at Hamilton Palace nightclub and he said something that made me stop and think. "Why not you?" he said. And I thought about it. It's an illness that just happens to people and that's it. There's no reason for it and I have to accept that.'

As part of Tim's positive outlook he spent a year learning about MS on the internet and reading about possible breakthroughs. He learned that he was just one of ten thousand Scots who were battling against multiple sclerosis. He learned that Scotland has a higher percentage of sufferers than anywhere else in Britain. He found out that, for some unknown reason, the closer you live to the Poles, the more chance you have of developing MS. The disease is virtually unheard of in countries close to the Equator.

Tim reckoned the more people know about the disease, the quicker they will find a cure. And he had some room for optimism. Scots doctor Ian Duncan, now based in Wisconsin in the USA, recorded some remarkable results through research on animals using the revolutionary drug Lorenzo's Oil. The treatment was discovered by the parents of a young boy called Lorenzo who suffered from a nerve-destroying illness similar to MS.

Tim is currently taking bacteria pills, after seeing a TV documentary about an Italian scientist who achieved immense results with MS patients after injecting them with bacteria. Apparently, the bacteria reminds the immune system what it's supposed to be doing.

He is also involved in several other treatments. One involves mixing Gale's honey into oil that was blessed and having it rubbed it onto his back, as suggested by a Pakistani guru who assured Tim he could cure his MS. 'I know it sounds completely wacky,' said Tim, 'but this guy seemed so convincing.'

What helps him cope with MS is the realisation there are others in a worse situation. He was doing a gig at the Braehead Centre, for example, and he'd been feeling really bad the week before and was having problems moving around. All his body movements were slow. But what he saw at Braehead helped him put things into perspective.

'It was a Clyde Roadshow and hundreds of people turned out,' he recalled. 'It went well and I had a lot of people up singing. But as I was getting the karaoke going, one wee boy in a wheelchair kept looking at me. I shouted to him to come up for a song. And, to my utter astonishment, the boy got out of the wheelchair and walked towards me. I thought to myself "Jeez, what have I done?" He came over to me and he had obvious speech troubles but he could communicate, and as the music began and the Spice Girls gave it laldy he actually sang along.

'I looked over at his mum and she was crying. The wee boy was thirteen and here he was, hardly able to walk and just able about speak, and he was up here for the karaoke.

'And as the tears were running down his mother's face, I felt them well up in my own eyes and I was embarrassed. So I bent down to tie my shoelaces. But then I realised I was wearing slip-ons. "Shit," I thought, "what do I do?" So I kept my head down, all the time pretending I was looking for something. And the wee boy finished his song and of course there was a tremendous applause, as you would imagine, for this terrific little character and he struggled back to his chair.

'A few minutes later his mum came up to me. She thanked me for encouraging him to get up and told me her boy—his name was Lee Cosgrove—had had meningitis and almost died. She said this experience had obviously done wonders to help him along. I think it put my own problem in its place.'

The first Saturday in June 2000 saw Tim appearing at Hutchesons' Grammar School, where an open day was held on behalf of the Girl Guides and children with disabilities. He launched into his show and the kids were loving it, particularly when the DJ invited them up on stage to talk about themselves.

He invited up one little girl who was about thirteen years old and had learning difficulties. When he spoke to her she shouted back at him, very loudly. It was an awkward situation, or at least it would have been for anyone but the Tiger. When the little girl shouted at Tim, he immediately shouted back and told her to be quiet. The girl laughed. She spoke in a normal voice for a couple of minutes then failed to realise how loud she had become and began shouting again. Tim shouted back. The girl laughed as she realised what she'd been doing. The 1,600 Girl Guides and their parents laughed—not at the little girl but at what had become a double act between Tim and the young co-star.

As usual, he had pitched the gig at exactly the right level. He has never been patronising towards people with learning difficulties, whether adults or children. Sure, his own condition has made him more aware of how difficult life can be for people with problems, but that's not the full story. For some reason he has not only always been able to connect, but to make people happy in the most adverse of circumstances.

Another hugely important agent in Tim's dealing with MS is the influence of his wife. Their life is never dull and they have their arguments like any other couple. But there is an underlying devotion. 'Moira is a woman with great integrity,' said Tim. 'She believes in working for anything she has. She works part-time in a shop and bought a car which she pays for. She also does everything for me. She goes to work, she comes back and looks after me. The house is always perfect. Even when we go on holiday together she doesn't get a rest. She has to look out for me all the time. She makes me eat properly. She's the perfect wife, the perfect lover. And the more this illness affects me, the more she does for me. If this was a battle I'd have lost it a long, long time ago if Moira hadn't been around.'

Tim took a moment and predictably all serious thoughts left his head. 'The only thing I can remember really falling out with her about was when she said she was going to have a tattoo. I hate tattoos, but I had to smile when she said she was going to have a tiger tattoo circling around her belly button. And I really laughed when she came back with her new imprint and admitted it was the most excruciating pain ever.'

Working life at Clyde has changed, too. Tim had moved to Clyde Two as part of a station revamp but when new station boss Paul Cooney took over, one of his first moves was to return Tim to his evening show on Clyde One and give him a Sunday lunchtime show on Clyde Two.

'Tim is the best DJ Clyde has ever had,' said Paul. 'We've had some real talent here over the years with the likes of Steve Jones and Richard Park and Dougie Donnelly, but I reckon the Tiger wins out. He has such an uncanny knack of knowing how to speak to people that makes his programmes so special. His longevity is testimony to his talent. And now he is on Clyde One and Two where everyone can hear him.'

'It was great news for me,' said Tim. 'I always felt I'd left home when I moved from Clyde One. Paul came round to my house to tell me about his proposal and we had toast and beans at lunchtime and to celebrate his appointment I bought a bottle of champagne.'

There was no doubt that Tim still had a very special rapport with his listeners and Paul Cooney recognised this.

Eddie Tobin felt Tim's popularity had everything to do with the fact he connected with people. 'The measure of greatness is your performance and Tim is the best. It's a fact that Tim's act hasn't changed substantially since the first day, even on the radio. And perhaps there have been times when some have thought it had become tiresome. But he's loved. People love him and that's why he's still around. He should be saying he's had a career that's lasted way beyond predictions. He's done things that 99 per cent of people will never do.'

Colin Robertson agreed with the sentiment. 'I had a fantastic time in the 1970s alongside Tim and I'd like to think that the Tiger could look back on his career without any regrets. He came very close to crossing the divide into the really big time but it wasn't to be. Who knows—perhaps he didn't really want it. But it doesn't matter because Tim Stevens has still been a massive success story. Seldom do you find someone with such incredible appeal that crosses not only the gender gap, the generation gap and the religious divide. Everybody loves the Tiger.

'I popped in to see him recently and saw his physical condition and feel it's so unfair. Tim Stevens has never committed an act of badness towards anyone that would merit what he has to put up with right now. For someone who was as vibrant as Tim and had as much energy, it says a lot that he has the character to maintain such a degree of fun about him.'

The Tiger has never stopped having fun. The public have been continually entertained by the DJ on air and at gigs although his family and close friends often hope that the infantile behaviour will slow down at little.

'He's never lost his innocence,' said Darren. 'He's younger than me—in fact, when I'm out with him socially, I'm the dad. I'm the one who has to tell him to behave when I introduce him to a new girlfriend. I'm the one who has to tell him to stop putting the spaghetti up his nose when we go to an Italian restaurant. He likes to be the centre of attention and you just have to accept that. But having said that he can talk to anybody and make them feel good—and that's a gift few people have.'

Darren's earliest recollections of his dad are of playing pitch'n'putt at Prestwick. 'He wouldn't pay during the day because it cost a pound,' said Darren, laughing. 'We'd go on at night instead and play with my little bag of plastic golf clubs. And there was the football we'd play with his Uncle William, while my dad was always in goal. I suppose I thought it odd that he couldn't play football with me, but he made up for it in other ways.

'And I remember he would read me stories he had written and it really was the Adventures of Tiger Tim, where he would be a Superman character. He had me convinced he could fly.'

The five-year-old who'd tried to fly off the verandah at Banton Place never really gave up the notion that anything was possible.

'He's great fun,' said Darren. 'He has a magical air about him. Sometimes I want to talk to him and he falls asleep and I get annoyed and he gets annoyed when he can't stay awake. But most of the time we have a laugh.'

Tim's mum worries about her son every day. 'I wish I could take it off him,' she said of the MS. 'When I see him with that zimmer it really breaks my heart. But I'm not hopeful. You never even see people out with charity boxes collecting for MS research. I think that's strange because surely it means there's nothing being done if there are no charities out there. But he seems to deal with it really well.'

Dora paused for a moment. It was a moment of realisation. 'You know, here's something I've just remembered. When he was a wee boy whenever he'd pass someone in a wheelchair, he'd say, "That'll be me." He always had that thought in his head. Perhaps somehow it was all planned for him.'

Dora's thoughts drifted onto a more positive plane and she smiled. 'I just thank God he has Moira. She doesn't treat him like an invalid. But she has a huge concern. She's one of the best. You know, they fight like cat and dog, but she'd do anything for him. And with her help the bold boy will get through this. As he keeps telling everybody, he's from Easterhouse. And he's a fighter.'

Tim maintains there has been a positive aspect to come out of his illness. 'I now appreciate all that I have so much more,' he said over lunch in a swish Glasgow restaurant, all smartly dressed in a suit and looking relaxed as he completed the series of interviews for this book.

'I appreciate my job—I still love broadcasting—I appreciate my wife and my family and, you know something? Contrary to the opinions of others, I really think the condition has made me that little bit more mature. I'm now far less likely to open my mouth at the wrong time or to do something in public that people would perhaps find distasteful.'

Tim said his goodbyes and made his way out of the restaurant. But just as he reached the doorway, he stopped, turned around, smiled and waved. There was a huge grin on his face, so wide you immediately thought of the wee boy in Banton Place who got the blue Dansette for his seventh birthday.

And his good suit trousers were down at his ankles.